THE TYRANNY OF GOOD INTENTIONS

THE
TYRANNY
OF GOOD
INTENTIONS

How Prosecutors
and Bureaucrats Are
Trampling the Constitution
in the Name of Justice

PAUL CRAIG ROBERTS

LAWRENCE M. STRATTON

FORUM
An Imprint of Prima Publishing

347.73
R646

FORUM
An Imprint of Prima Publishing
3000 Lava Ridge Court
Roseville, California 95661

PRIMA PUBLISHING, FORUM, and colophons are
registered trademarks of Prima Communications, Inc.

Library of Congress Cataloging-in-Publication Data

Roberts, Paul Craig.
The tyranny of good intentions: how prosecutors and bureaucrats are trampling the Constitution in the name of justice / by Paul Craig Roberts and Lawrence M. Stratton.
p. cm.
Includes bibliographical references and index.
ISBN 0-7615-2553-X
1. Law reform—United States.   2. Justice, Administration of—United States.
3. Political corruption—United States.   I. Stratton, Lawrence M.   II. Title.
KF384.R62 2000
347.73—dc21   99-054459
                                                                                  CIP
00 01 02 03 04 HH 10 9 8 7 6 5 4 3 2 1
Printed in the United States of America

FORUM books are available at special discount for bulk purchases
for educational, business, or sales promotion use.
For detals, contact Special Sales
Prima Publishing
1-800-632-8676 ext. 4444

Visit us online at www.primalifestyles.com

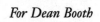
For Dean Booth

CONTENTS

ACKNOWLEDGMENTS

AUTHORS HAVE MANY people to whom they owe thanks: families, friends, colleagues, teachers, editors, and copyeditors. We owe thanks to all of these. We also owe thanks to the trustees, donors, and advisors of the Institute for Political Economy, a nonprofit research institute that made this book possible.

We wish to express our appreciation to the Independent Institute for its help in bringing this book to the attention of jurists and legal scholars. The Independent Institute (www.independent.org), located at 100 Swan Way, Oakland, CA 94621 (510-632-1366), is a nonprofit research and educational organization that supports independent research. With 130 affililiated research fellows, books, conferences, and a quarterly journal, the Independent Institute clarifies public issues and advances the frontiers of knowledge.

P.C.R.
L.M.S.

PREFACE

AMERICA'S REPUTATION AS "the land of the free" is rooted in its Anglo-Saxon legal and political tradition. As the twenty-first century begins, there is evidence that much of this tradition has been lost. Americans are losing the law that protects them from tyranny, and they are losing the accountability of law, which ensures that government is the servant rather than the master of the people. These erosions of liberty and constitutional order are not the work of organized interest groups or the result of the influence of money on the political process. We Americans are losing the protection and accountability of law because we have forgotten why these safeguards are important. We have become emotionally and intellectually disconnected from the long struggle to establish the people's sovereignty over the law.

Because Americans are losing the protection of law, our liberty is endangered. As a former British colony, Americans inherited the English legal system, in which law developed as a means of pursuing justice by finding truth. The U.S. legal system was based on English precedent. The U.S. Constitution begins with the words "We the People"; this founding document embodies the "Rights of Englishmen," which ensure that law protects people from arbitrary government power and serves the cause of justice.

The character of this legal system ensured that it would be revered. In recent times, however, reverence for our legal system is being replaced by fear, distrust, and dissatisfaction. For example, inner-city juries routinely refuse to convict criminal defendants on the basis of prosecutorial and police evidence alone. In 1993, twenty prosecutors resigned from the U.S. Department of Justice to avoid being investigated for improper conduct. Americans of all stripes increasingly feel that getting in trouble with the law is a random phenomenon, bearing little apparent relationship to guilt or justice.

As we debate the economic feasibility of Social Security and Medicare, the question arises of what one generation owes the next. Old-age financial security is important, but the primary obligation of each generation is to pass on, undiminished, the institutions of liberty along with the Rights of Englishmen— the legal principles that prevent law from being used as a weapon against the people. These legal principles and rights are human achievements—the product of a thousand-year struggle. Their preservation is an enormous responsibility for each generation, one that in our time has been neglected.

"That which thy fathers bequeathed thee, earn it anew if thou would'st possess it." The admonition of this Anglo-Saxon maxim applies to our responsibility to preserve the Rights of Englishmen. Our freedom in America is based on the restraint of government power by law that is accountable to the people. Earning our freedom anew requires that we believe in the accountability of law. In twentieth-century America, this belief was eroded by the view that government power is a force for good and must be less and less restrained. Consequently, we have experienced the transformation of our political order from a legislative to an administrative state. The Constitution's prohibition against the delegation of lawmaking power to executive branch agencies has not been in force since the 1930s. Today, law is made by bureaucrats who are largely unaccountable to anyone. There is some oversight by Congress, but the bureaucracy's lawmaking power has been buttressed by federal judicial rulings that the regulatory authorities' interpretations are "entitled to great deference."

It takes more than a generation for democracy to become hollowed out by the erosion of the separation of powers. But the executive branch cannot indefinitely function as a delegated lawmaker without becoming lawmaker in name as well as fact. We in America are gradually undergoing a transformation into an administrative state similar to that achieved overnight in Germany in 1933 with the passage by the German Reichstag of the Enabling Act, which transferred lawmaking power from the legislative to the executive branch of the National Socialist government.

The Enabling Act gave dictatorial power to Adolf Hitler. According to the editors of a compendium of documents of National Socialism, the English legal system reflects "a tradition of the defense of individual rights against the state," whereas "German law reflected the tradition of a strong state as the embodiment of the community by which individuals would be granted such rights as were considered compatible with its interests."[1] In this system, sovereignty rested with the state, not in "We the People," and law was a manifestation of the will of the state. This concept of jurisprudence enabled "the Civil Service to rationalize almost any action, however immoral, provided it took the form of a law or decree" and "greatly facilitated the Nazi takeover of power."

Self-rule ceases to exist when elected representatives don't make the law. Eventually, power that is unrestrained becomes, in Lenin's words, "unlimited power, resting directly on force. Nothing else but that." Throughout the ages government rested on power. After centuries of struggle, culminating in 1688 with

---

[1] Jeremy Noakes and Geoffrey Pridham, eds., *Documents on Nazism, 1919–1945* (New York: Viking Press, 1975), 226–27.

the Glorious Revolution in England, government was relocated in the will of the people. This was no small difference. If self-rule is abrogated, our legal tradition provides no other basis for law and government.

The twentieth century's belief in government power as a force for good has encouraged the practice of chasing after devils. Like a national emergency, a righteous cause can cut a wide swath through the law to more easily apprehend wrongdoers. In recent decades, both conservatives and liberals cut swaths through the law as they pursued drug dealers, S&L crooks, environmental polluters, Wall Street insider traders, child abusers, and other undesirables. Impatience, frustration, hysteria, political scapegoating, and greed have caused police, prosecutors, victims, and the plaintiffs' bar to grow weary of laws that protect those accused of crimes and negligence. The question is raised, "Why should the guilty have the benefit of law?" Sir Thomas More's answer (as presented in *A Man for All Seasons*) is that when the law is disregarded to better pursue the guilty, it is also taken away from the innocent. What are we to do, he asks, if those chasing after devils decide to chase after us? If the law is cast down, what protection do the innocent have? A little liberty taken here, a precedent there, and the Rights of Englishmen become history, a clear-cut area where once mighty oaks stood.

In this book, we blame the deteriorating reputation of American justice on the erosion of the Rights of Englishmen. We describe the safeguards provided by the Rights of Englishmen, the dangers that arise in their absence, the philosophical shift that brought about their erosion, and the continuing infringements of these rights in the interests of "higher causes."

In chapter 1, we contrast the protective nature of English law—the law as shield—with law that originates in the writ of the sovereign. In chapter 2, we show that even the powerful are defenseless against law when it is used as a weapon. Our understanding of and appreciation for these distinctions is the key to our continuance as a free society.

In chapters 3 through 10, we show Americans' growing vulnerability to injustice as prohibitions against crimes without intent, retroactive law, and self-incrimination are removed, along with restraints on prosecutorial powers. Each of these legal protections, which took centuries to achieve, has taken a ferocious beating in twentieth-century America. Today even wealthy and prominent Americans are less secure in law than unemployed English coal miners were in the 1930s.

This story of how the law was lost was thoroughly researched, and it benefited from reviews by legal scholars. Readers who wish to check quotes and context can turn to the bibliography or to the spring 2000 issue of *The Journal of the Georgetown Federalist Society* (Carolina Academic Press), where extensive excerpts of this book are published in law review format with copious footnotes. An overview of the argument was published in the *Cardozo Law Review*, Vol. 20, No. 3 (January 1999) under the title "How the Law Was Lost."

THE NEW ROBBER BARONS

IN THE DARK AGES, government officials used their police powers to enrich themselves. Powerful officials would seize travelers of means who passed through their jurisdictions and imprison them in castle dungeons until their ransom was paid. Those who practiced this rapacious behavior were known as robber barons.

Today in the United States their counterparts do the robber barons one step better: federal, state, and local law enforcement officers bypass the hostage-taking and simply seize property outright.

During the 1990s, hearings before the Judiciary Committee of the U.S. House of Representatives made public many cases of law enforcement officials who knowingly misapplied asset forfeiture laws to confiscate the life savings and property of innocent citizens.

One victim was Dr. Richard Lowe, a medical doctor in the small Alabama town of Haleyville. Dr. Lowe still charges $5 for an office visit, lives in a modest home, and drives a used car. In 1988 he consolidated his savings to establish a charitable account for a small private K–12 school that was on the brink of financial failure in his hometown. Dr. Lowe managed to transfer $900,000 to the school before the FBI seized his $3 million account.

Dr. Lowe had done nothing that would warrant the seizure of his life savings; the FBI and the U.S. Attorney had no cause to seize his money. (They simply took his money on the supposition that they could wear an old man out and force him to agree to a settlement that would allow them to keep some part of his assets. Dr. Lowe had to be hospitalized for stress and high blood pressure brought on by the seizure of his life's savings.)

As a youngster during the Depression, Dr. Lowe was scarred by bank failure. Consequently, over the course of his life he hoarded his cash. In 1990 his wife prevailed on him to take the cash that had accumulated in shoe boxes in his closet to the bank and add it to the school's account. When counted, the cash totaled $316,911.

In the United States today, law enforcement officials often automatically infer criminal activity from the presence of cash. As we will see in chapter 9, even $100 in cash is sufficient for police to presume illegal activity. Dr. Lowe's cash deposit was seized, along with his entire bank account. The bank president was indicted. The bank president's son was also indicted. Charges against the son were then dropped in exchange for the father's guilty plea to a trumped-up charge. Two years later Dr. Lowe was also indicted on trumped-up charges to pay him back for fighting to regain his money. Six years passed before the Eleventh Circuit Court of Appeals cleared Dr. Lowe and ordered the return of his money.

The U.S. attorney and the FBI were well aware that neither Dr. Lowe nor his banker were drug dealers or money launderers. But the law enforcement officials did not care. They used Dr. Lowe's cash hoard as "probable cause." They saw an opportunity in Dr. Lowe's cash and used a power bestowed by a short-sighted Congress to take Dr. Lowe's money.

Dr. Lowe lost six years of his old age to rapacious federal "law enforcement," in part because employees at other banks ratted on his cash deposit. Many people in the United States today seem unnervingly ready to report fellow citizens to government officials—a willingness that is characteristic of a police state.

In 1991, Willie Jones, a black nurseryman who did not have a credit card, paid cash for an airline ticket. His business and life were ruined by the actions of a callous airline ticket agent who alerted police that a ticket purchaser fit the profile of a drug dealer. Willie Jones was apprehended for carrying cash with which to stock his nursery, and his money was confiscated.

Most Americans are unaware of the police state that is creeping up on us from many directions. The Drug Enforcement Administration (DEA) maintains confiscation squads at major airports and has turned airline and airport employees into informers by awarding them 10 percent of confiscated assets. The ticket agent–informer who fingered the "suspicious" Willie Jones had already been paid thousands of dollars by the DEA for identifying other forfeiture candidates who had cash.

The DEA also maintains surveillance operations in hotels in New York, Miami, Los Angeles, and other cities. Hotel employees are paid to report guests who make multiple long-distance calls, have cash, and carry too little or too much luggage.

In 1991, Drug Enforcement Administration agents destroyed the gardening supply business of Michael and Christine Sandsness for selling perfectly legal grow lights used for indoor plants. The federal agents reasoned that grow lights were only purchased by people who intended to hide their cultivation of marijuana indoors. Thus the gardening supply business was determined to be facilitating illegal drug trade.

In 1993, Exequiel Soltero's restaurant business in a Seattle suburb was ruined after a paid government informant alleged that Soltero's brother, who owned no share in the business, sold a few grams of cocaine in the restaurant's men's room.

In 1997, fourteen employees traveling to Canada at company expense had their money seized at the border by U.S. Customs officials on the pretext that the aggregate cash in their possession (about $10,000) was evidence of a conspiracy to smuggle money.

Innocent people can lose their property for no other reason than reporting possible criminal activity to police. In 1998, the Red Carpet Motel in Houston, Texas, was seized by U.S. Attorney James DeAtley because motel employees reported suspicious behavior by room guests who appeared to be dealing in drugs. Mr. DeAtley reasoned that the motel had "tacitly approved" alleged drug activity by overnight guests because the motel did not charge enough for its rooms!

In the same year, electronics companies in California had operating cash seized because their purchasing agent, unbeknownst to the companies, was laundering stolen computer chips.

Law enforcement officials would not take such flimsy cases to court. The secret of their success is that they don't have to bring charges against the owners of seized property. The Comprehensive Forfeiture Act, passed in 1984, allows police to confiscate property on "probable cause"—the same minimal standard needed by police to justify a search. The law places the burden on the owner to prove that his confiscated property was not used to facilitate a crime.

House Judiciary Committee Chairman Henry J. Hyde has been struggling for years to rein in the power of police to confiscate property. The American Bar Association and the American Civil Liberties Union agree with Chairman Hyde that it is outrageous that the government can confiscate a person's property without convicting him or even charging him with a crime. Moreover, the property can remain forfeited even if the accused is acquitted of charges. Chairman Hyde has raised the question of whether the asset forfeiture laws have given birth to "an American police state."

The fate of multimillionaire Donald Scott answers in the affirmative. In 1992, Mr. Scott was gunned down and killed by thirty police officers led by a Los Angeles deputy sheriff who had a plot to confiscate Scott's 200-acre Malibu, California, estate for the U.S. Park Service.

Scott was killed because the law that protects us from tyrannical police actions has been lost to good intentions. Liberals chasing after white-collar criminals and environmental polluters, and conservatives determined to "save our children from drugs," have seriously eroded the protections once offered by law. Due process, the presumption of innocence until guilt is proven, the right to counsel, the prohibition against punishment based on presumption, and the ban on retroactive law have all fallen to good intentions.

Good intentions have transformed law from a shield for the innocent to a weapon used by police. Having lost the law, we have acquired tyranny. Americans are as yet unaware of their plight, because the U.S. population is large relative to the number of police and prosecutorial actions. If the confiscations suffered by Dr. Lowe and Mr. Jones were universal, the American people would rise up against these new robber barons. Instead, the random nature of the abuses is eating away at our rights and slowly acclimatizing Americans to tyranny.

The breakdown in the integrity of police and prosecutors is as serious as the breakdown in law. As this book goes to press, the Los Angeles Police Department is reeling from revelations of hundreds of cases of false evidence and wrongful convictions. The governor of Illinois has suspended executions in his state upon discovering that there were more innocent than guilty people on death row. Executions would resume, the governor said, when safeguards were in place to assure that people being executed were actually guilty.

How is it possible that police and prosecutors can be wrong more than half of the time on such a serious charge as murder?

Many people blame juries. But jurors must assume that police and prosecutors are committed to justice and are bringing legitimate cases—not cases based on tainted and fabricated evidence. Jurors assume that the evidence presented at trial is real, not made-up. Once the criminal justice system is perceived as a career-driven conviction mill, jurors lose confidence in the system.

In a multi-racial, culturally diverse society such as the United States, jurors' loss of confidence in the integrity of the justice system can produce outcomes that are marred by feelings of racial guilt on the one hand and racial loyalty on the other. A jury trial becomes a way to settle a score or to stand up to "the man." Justice ceases to exist. In its place arises "racial justice," "gender justice," and "class justice." Rights become unequal as victims' groups insist their members can only be sinned against and never commit wrongs themselves. When justice breaks down, the result is oppression, something that we all have an obligation to avert.

CHAPTER ONE

THE LAW AS SHIELD: THE RIGHTS OF ENGLISHMEN

FOUR YEARS INTO the "devil's decade" of the 1930s, a period of high unemployment, a series of articles in the London *Times* on depressed regions within England pierced the British conscience. Among the "Places without a Future" were the once prosperous coal fields of Durham in northeast England, which had a 37 percent unemployment rate.

County Durham wasn't a pretty picture. Herbert Pike Pease Daryngton, a member of the British House of Lords, wrote a letter to the *Times* saying that "your articles on 'Desolate Durham' are moving beyond words." Indeed they were. The coal pits, which had supported densely populated villages in which miners lived with their families in small row houses, were closed, leaving the inhabitants of entire precincts unemployed. A miner's weekly dole payment was the only thing standing between his family and starvation.

Economic life is always uncertain. At various times, stock market crashes and speculative busts have wiped out the rich, droughts and floods have ruined farmers, and when government mismanages monetary policy or technology makes an industry obsolete, the hardships for ordinary people can be extreme. Sometimes the hardships of famine are combined with the hardships of lawlessness, as in Somalia in 1992, a situation so bad that it prompted an American intervention from half a world away. But in 1934 the unemployed Durham coal miners, Lancashire textile mill workers, and Jarrow shipyard workers who marched on London were totally secure in law.

The legal security that the poor share with the wealthy is based on a set of principles known as the Rights of Englishmen. These rights serve as armor against capricious arrest, confiscation of property, and deprivation of life, limb, and liberty, and they protect every "Englishman" against predatory actions of government. The rights flow from a unique conception of law, but they were not handed down from above as natural law carved in stone. Rather, they are human achievements, fought for by those who believed in them.

Readers influenced by Marxist historians or immersed in the class warfare rhetoric of American politics may find it startling that the rich and the poor have the same legal rights. It is true that a person with more money can purchase better legal services than a person with less money, just as a person with more money can purchase more expensive clothes, housing, medical care, transportation, food, entertainment, and education for his children. The beauty of the English legal tradition lies in the elimination of legal, not economic, differences. Equality under law was achieved by eliminating class- or status-based legal rights. The laws apply equally to everyone regardless of income, wealth, or position.

The Rights of Englishmen are the product of a long struggle to establish the people's sovereignty over the law. The struggle began in England during the ninth century, when King Alfred the Great codified the common law. It moved forward with the Magna Carta in 1215, and culminated with the Glorious Revolution at the end of the seventeenth century. The idea that law flows from the people to whom it is accountable, and not from an unaccountable government, was the guiding vision of the Founding Fathers of the United States.

The Rights of Englishmen define the meaning of justice. The military, economic, scientific, and technological superiority of Great Britain and the United States helped to elevate the English concept of law above all others and to associate it everywhere with self-determination.

In the twentieth century writers influenced by Karl Marx have explained away this achievement. The law, they have explained, is merely an expression of the material interest of the ruling or capitalist class. Nikolai I. Bukharin, a lord of the new Soviet state and an expositor of this doctrine, soon after the 1934 march of the unemployed on London was to experience for himself the consequences of the brutal legal philosophy that he helped formulate (see chapter 2).

Historians have argued for decades about the reasons that this unique legal system was founded in England and carried to her colonies. But all agree that Englishmen have inherited a system of law that is predicated on respect for the individual and in which human dignity and freedom have flourished. In the rest of Europe, the operating legal assumption is that the "command of the King has the force of law," as Roman emperor Justinian's *Corpus Juris Civilis* stated. In contrast, the English legal system is conceived from the principle that law flows from the people. Rather than residing in the will of the sovereign, law reposes in the bosoms of the people.

As a distant province at the outer frontier of the Roman Empire, the British Isles only partly absorbed Roman culture. When in A.D. 425 Roman legions withdrew from Britain to defend the Eternal City, little of Rome remained. In the fifth century, the Angles, the Saxons, and the Jutes brought their own perspectives on law.

Victorian historian William Stubbs's *Constitutional History of England* traced the roots of the Rights of Englishmen to the community attitudes described in Roman historian Tacitus's first-century dispatch *Germania*. "Affairs of smaller moment the chiefs determine," Tacitus wrote in a key passage, but "about matters of higher consequence the whole nation deliberates."

Leaders of primitive German communities could rule only in accordance with ancient or "kindred" values. When an important issue faced the community, "the King or Chief is heard, as are others, each according to his precedence in age, or in nobility, or in warlike renown, or in eloquence; and the influence of every speaker proceeds rather from his ability to persuade than from any authority to command." With murmurs conveying displeasure, the brandishing of javelins reflecting favor, and "the most honorable manner" of signifying assent to various propositions through "applause by the sound of their arms," the community—the folk—expresses its will and the leaders carry out its wishes.

By the first century Rome's own republic had given way to the Caesars, and Tacitus has been accused of romanticizing the Germanic tribes who were pressing against Rome's frontiers. Nevertheless, Tacitus is an example of a civilized Roman who found much to admire in the accountability of Germanic law. When quarrels arose between members of a community, or when a person was charged with committing a forbidden act, "he was allowed to clear himself by producing twelve of his equals who were to swear with him that he was innocent." This reflected the assumption that the entire community, represented by the sworn men, and not a single judge, would determine whether an infraction occurred.

Stubbs postulated that the mighty oak of English liberties grew from this acorn planted in English soil by Germanic invaders. His thesis still commands respect. According to *The Western Experience: Antiquity to the Middle Ages*, published in 1974, "The connection between the later juries and parliaments and these barbarian traditions is admittedly distant, but certainly exists." Whatever their origins and complexity of development, the Rights of Englishmen stipulate a legal system that constrains the state and prevents law from being used as a weapon against the people. This is what it means to be secure in the law.

The economic depression that plagued England during the 1930s caused millions to lead economically insecure lives, but no Englishman could be hauled out of his house to a dungeon, put on the rack, and tortured until he incriminated himself. Between each Englishman and the government stand a few basic legal principles that prevent the government's use of the law as a weapon for oppression.

The most essential protection is the precept that there can be no crime without intent. This foundation of a just legal system is based on the presumption that people have a moral compass that allows them a choice between violating the law and obeying it. To make it easier to ensnare people, Caligula, the Roman tyrant, wrote his laws in small print and posted them on high pillars to prevent ordinary people from knowing the law. In contrast, basing crime on the accused's intent guards individual liberty by ensuring that people cannot be convicted for offenses that they did not intend to commit. As eighteenth-century jurist William Blackstone wrote in his *Commentaries on the Laws of England,* "An unwarrantable act without a vicious will is no crime at all."

The "vicious will" precondition for crimes, also known as *scienter* ("knowingly") and *mens rea* ("a guilty mind"), has broad implications. In order for a person to violate a law knowingly, he must know that the conduct is illegal. If the law is continuously changing or so vague that people have to guess at its meaning, a person cannot knowingly violate it. To be just, law must be certain. Moreover, unless law is certain, it cannot fulfill its purpose of commanding what is right and prohibiting what is wrong.

The requirement of intent rules out *ex post facto* ("after the fact") laws. One cannot have a "vicious will" to engage in conduct that was legal at the time the act took place. Noting that it is "cruel and unjust" to punish someone for having in the past done something that is only retroactively illegal, Blackstone stated the principle that "all laws must therefore be made to commence in futuro"—in the future.

To prevent arbitrary arrests, a warrant showing "probable cause" must be signed by a magistrate. The requirement of a warrant for an arrest protects the humble abode the way a moat and strong wall protect a castle. This protection is summed up in the common law maxim, "A man's house is his castle; even though the winds of heaven may blow through it, the King of England cannot enter it." This legal barrier that protects the sanctity of the individual is a central achievement of English jurisprudence. It means that the sovereign himself is subject to law. According to Blackstone, "The true liberty of the subject consists not so much in the gracious behavior, as in the limited power, of the sovereign."

Another of the Rights of Englishmen is the protection against self-incrimination. Without this right, a suspect could be put on the rack and tortured until he admits guilt. Besides the rack, other methods used to extract evidence by force included thumbscrews, legscrews, and a torture called strappado, a pulley that would hoist a person in the air by his wrists while heavy weights were attached to his feet. Blackstone was aghast at these practices that rated a "man's virtue by the hardness of his constitution, and his guilt by the sensibility of his nerves!" The injunction against self-incrimination ended English torture by the 1640s, more than a century before its demise elsewhere in western Europe. From its inception, the injunction included the corollary protection against torturing witnesses into providing evidence against others.

At Runnymede in 1215, King John signed the Magna Carta, which set out the framework for limitations on sovereign power. The Magna Carta asserted the security of every freeman in "the free enjoyment of his life, his liberty, and his property, unless declared to be forfeited by the judgment of his peers or the law of the land," as Blackstone summarized it.

These principles have had to be continuously defended against government encroachment. In the face of assertions of absolute royal prerogative during the reign of James I in the early 1600s, jurist Sir Edward Coke repeatedly appealed to the Magna Carta's statement that the king is constrained by the "law of the land." With the backing of Parliament, upon which the king was economically dependent, Coke, as chief justice, stood before James in Whitehall Palace in 1616 and insisted that the king could not halt the proceedings of a court case. "The stay required by your Majesty was a delay of justice and therefore contrary to law," Coke said. Coke later wrote in his *Institutes of the Laws of England* that the sovereign had to govern in conformity with the "due course and process of law." Later reduced to the two words, *due process*, Coke's phrase expressed the principle that the king must follow legal processes and procedures in governance and the administration of justice.

The law empowered Coke to stand up to the sovereign's claim of divine right. James removed him as chief justice, but Coke reappeared as a member of Parliament, where he had been Speaker of the House of Commons and a champion of free speech during the reign of Elizabeth I. Back in the Commons, Coke led the fight against James's attempts to constrain parliamentary powers:

> The privileges of this House is the nurse and life of all our laws, the subject's best inheritance. If my sovereign will not allow me my inheritance, I must fly to Magna Carta and entreat explanation of his Majesty. Magna Carta is the Charter of Liberty because it maketh freemen. When the King says he cannot allow our liberties of right, this strikes at the root.

In rage, James dissolved Parliament and had Coke arrested and sent to the Tower of London. Coke was charged with defrauding the king of funds relating to land holdings, but everyone knew that James's adversary was the law. Eleven months later Coke was freed after he was cleared by three justices, who declared that he "neither in law nor conscience was to be charged of any thing."

Coke returned again to Parliament and continued to defend law against encroachments by the king's government during the reign of James's son, Charles I. Coke championed a prisoner's right to a public trial, the writ of habeas corpus (a safeguard against illegal detention), the right of the accused against self-incrimination, and the right not to be jailed without cause. Desperate for more money than he could get from Parliament, Charles coerced loans from the upper classes, in violation of a statute dating from the fourteenth-century reign of Edward III that said, "Loans against the will of a subject are against reason and the liberty of the land." Charles imprisoned subjects who refused his demands or impressed them into involuntary servitude in the navy. When the courts failed to release five arrested knights who protested their illegal confinement, Coke led the fight for the Petition of Right of 1628, reiterating the principles of the Magna Carta in protest of the knights' treatment.

Due process requires that a prosecutor provide to a grand jury evidence that a crime occurred before a charge can be brought against an individual. Even before evidence is brought, the principle of prosecutorial discretion protects citizens from being targeted by those empowered to prosecute. Prosecutors have enormous discretion in choosing their cases, but the choice is constrained by the amount of available evidence and the act's level of criminality. If there is strong evidence that nine adults committed murders, some evidence that a schoolchild stole a loaf of bread, and speculation that a banker may have violated an arcane law, the prosecutor is not permitted to first chase after the schoolchild or the banker.

In addition, the prosecutor should not bring the full weight of the government against private individuals in searching for reasons to prosecute them. Armed with complete access to everything citizens do, creative prosecutors could find novel grounds for indictments against almost anyone. Prosecutors are supposed to deal with known crimes and not engage in fishing expeditions, looking for grounds on which to indict someone.

U.S. attorney general and later Supreme Court justice Robert Jackson said in 1940 that the most dangerous power of a prosecutor is that

> he will pick people that he thinks he should get, rather than pick cases that need to be prosecuted. With the law books filled with a great assortment of crimes, a prosecutor stands a fair chance of finding at least a technical violation of some act on the part of almost anyone. In such a case, it is not a question of discovering the commission of a crime and then looking for the man who has committed it, it is a question of picking the man and then searching the law books, or putting investigators to work, to pin some offense on him. It is in this realm—in which the prosecutor picks some person whom he dislikes or desires to embarrass, or selects some group of unpopular persons and then looks for an offense, that the greatest danger of abuse of prosecuting power lies. It is here that law enforcement becomes personal, and the real crime becomes that of being unpopular with the predominant or governing group, being attached to the wrong political views, or being personally obnoxious to, or in the way of, the prosecutor himself.

The role of the government in a criminal case is not only to be the plaintiff, but also to represent the defendant. As plaintiff, the government follows and presents evidence against the charged party. As the defendant's representative, the government must ensure that the subject accused of committing a crime is treated fairly, by respecting his rights throughout the judicial process. Only by exercising this dual responsibility can the government be an agent of justice. To uphold justice, the sovereign cannot stain itself by violating the law to bring a guilty person to justice. That is the majesty of law. Prosecutors who suborn perjury to convict innocent persons are evil incarnate. They desecrate the law.

U.S. Supreme Court justice George Sutherland summarized the dual role of prosecutors in 1934:

> The United States Attorney is the representative not of an ordinary party to a controversy, but of a sovereignty whose obligation to govern impartially is as compelling as its obligation to govern at all; and whose interest, therefore, in a criminal prosecution is not that it shall win a case, but that justice shall be done. As such, he is in a peculiar and very definite sense the servant of the law, the twofold aim of which is that guilt shall not escape or innocence suffer. He may prosecute with earnestness and vigor—indeed, he should do so. But, while he may strike hard blows, he is not at liberty to strike foul ones. It is as much his duty to refrain from improper methods calculated to produce a wrongful conviction as it is to use every legitimate means to bring about a just one.

Robert Jackson saw it the same way: "Any prosecutor who risks his day-to-day professional name for fair dealing to build up statistics of success has a perverted sense of practical values, as well as defects of character. . . . A sensitiveness to fair play and sportsmanship is perhaps the best protection against the abuse of power, and the citizen's safety lies in the prosecutor who tempers zeal with human kindness, who seeks truth and not victims, who serves the law and not factional purposes, and who approaches his task with humility."

The way our system is supposed to work, once a prosecutor obtains an indictment from a grand jury, the prosecutor then faces the additional hurdle of overcoming a presumption of the accused's innocence by presenting evidence that the accused is guilty "beyond a reasonable doubt" to a trial jury before an impartial judge. At his trial, the defendant is entitled to have an attorney present evidence in his defense and to poke holes in the government's case against him by confronting his accusers.

The right to confront adverse witnesses provides defendants the opportunity to puncture what otherwise might seem like airtight accusations against them. Out of the adversarial dialectic, truth would become apparent. In the face of charges of treason based on out-of-court statements allegedly made by Lord Cobham in 1603, Sir Walter Raleigh shouted in the London courtroom, "My Lords, I claim to have my accuser brought here face to face to speak." Raleigh continued, "Mr. Attorney, if you proceed to condemn me by bare inference, without an oath, without a subscription, without witnesses, upon a paper accusation, you try me by the Spanish inquisition. If my accuser were dead or abroad, it were something. But he liveth and is in this very house!"

Although Raleigh was convicted, the English viewed the trial as unjust for being based on "nothing more than presumption and surmise." One of the judges who heard Raleigh's case lamented on his deathbed that "the justice of England was never so depraved and injured as in the condemnation of Sir Walter Raleigh." In response to the injustices of Raleigh's case and other political trials, the evidentiary rule against the admissibility in court of hearsay evidence and the right to confront adverse witnesses arose.

Having juries and not government officials determine guilt or innocence also provides a check upon the justice of laws.

Juries could simply refuse to convict if they considered the law being enforced against their peer to be unjust. When a jury refused to convict William Penn of "tumultuous assembly" in 1670 (before he founded Pennsylvania), the trial judge imprisoned the jury, demanding that it reverse its verdict and convict the Quaker activist. The Court of Common Pleas soon issued a writ of habeas corpus ordering the jury's release from jail.

Parliament strengthened this prohibition of arbitrary arrest and imprisonment of individuals by state officials in the Habeas Corpus Act of 1679. Blackstone called the reform "that great bulwark of our constitution" and praised it as the "second *Magna Carta.*" The Great Writ, as it was known, required that those in custody be charged and detained lawfully.

Due process, no crime without intent, habeas corpus, no self-incrimination, no ex post facto laws, the right to counsel, the right to confront one's accusers, and the duty of prosecutors to serve truth make up the Rights of Englishmen. These rights transformed law from the prerogative of rulers into the protector of the people from arbitrary government power. This transformation also promoted justice, because it defined the purpose of the judicial process as the discovery of truth. In contrast, confessions and evidence obtained by torture on the rack have nothing to do with veracity and everything to do with a torture victim's desire to avoid pain and to stay alive and in one piece.

The injunction against self-incrimination ruled out the possibility of plea bargaining. Plea bargaining is akin to torture, because it can be used to extract false confessions from the accused so that they can avoid being tried on a more serious charge. Judges in seventeenth-century England refused to accept pleas in which people admitted minor offenses in order to avoid being charged with major offenses. Without a trial in which the government was forced to prove its case, false pleas would crowd out truth. Therefore, there could be no trial without proof that a crime occurred and evidence that the defendant committed it.

Concluding his summary of the "absolute rights of every Englishman," Blackstone said that "every species of compulsive tyranny and oppression must act in opposition to one or another of these rights, having no other object upon which it can possibly be employed." In other words, the opposite of the Rights of Englishmen is tyranny.

It was part and parcel of the individual's autonomy that property rights are "sacred and inviolable." Another right of Englishmen was the right to publicly petition and criticize the king—what we know today as First Amendment rights. If government broke free of these restraints, the "last auxiliary right of the subject," Blackstone said, is "having arms for their defense." The right to bear arms expresses the "natural right of resistance and self-preservation, when the sanctions of society and laws are found insufficient to restrain the violence of oppression." The law's affirmation of this right provides both psychological and physical checks on the tendency of governments to behave tyrannically.

Free from the worry of arbitrary abuses of government power, Englishmen could apply their creative energies to pursuits other than appeasing the government. In the *Wealth of Nations* and in his *Lectures on Jurisprudence*, eighteenth-century Scottish economist Adam Smith recognized that the security of people in the law made capitalism possible.

Before the Rights of Englishmen empowered people, the source of an individual's power was the number of armed men he could rally, or the difficulty of subduing a castle or keep. Because power was unequal, rights were unequal. The Rights of Englishmen ended the idea that might makes right. Until then, over the vast sweep of history, laws tended to consist of edicts or decrees by rulers. Nothing but the king's good nature prevented law from being a means of oppression. In contrast, the Rights of Englishmen restrained rulers and their minions by making government subject to law.

In a free society, law empowers Everyman against the arbitrary power of government. Englishmen are secure in the law, because the law is reposed in the bosoms of the people and not in the will of the state. Blackstone wrote that when executive power distorts the established law, it is incumbent upon Parliament to impeach and punish the conduct of the government's "evil and pernicious counselors."

The sovereignty of law also protects political leaders and government ministers. By depriving them of arbitrary power, it simultaneously protects them against arbitrariness whenever they lose a political dispute. The protections of free speech arose from the right, or, more specifically, the *obligation*, of royal advisers to advise the king freely and honestly without fear of reprisal. In this way a king could count on getting solid advice rather than the flattery of sycophants. This principle favoring the freedom of expression as a means of ascertaining truth grew beyond the king's privy counsel, to members of Parliament, and ultimately to every subject in the realm. Law's constraint on government set men free.

CHAPTER TWO

THE LAW AS WEAPON:
THE TRIAL OF
NIKOLAI BUKHARIN

THE LEGAL INHERITANCE that Englishmen receive as their birthright is more valuable than social position, wealth, or political office. Without law as a shield, almost everything else is devoid of value.

What does it mean to be rich or to hold a powerful position if a prosecutor can indict you without having any evidence that a crime occurred and then torture you until you admit to a crime that was not committed by you or by anyone, put you on trial without a lawyer, and accept no evidence from you except your admission of guilt? In the Soviet Union in the twentieth century, this was a fate suffered by many top-ranking Soviet officials—who themselves had the power of life and death over others—and commanding generals of the army.

To understand what it means to be without the protections provided by the Rights of Englishmen, consider the fate of Nikolai Bukharin, a high-ranking communist official. In the pitch blackness of the cold Moscow night of March 15, 1938, it would have been far better for Bukharin to have been an unemployed English coal miner.

Bukharin had been all that a communist ruler could be. Proclaimed by Lenin as the "golden boy of the revolution," the author of The ABC of Communism controlled the Soviet press from his Kremlin apartment. But the bullet that struck the back of his head on the evening of March 15 showed that he lacked the protection of law. Joseph Stalin, in his drive for supremacy, used the law as a weapon with which to kill Bukharin.

Two days after a "special commission" of the Central Committee voted in February 1937 that Bukharin should be "arrested, tried, and shot," Stalin's personal secretary called Bukharin with the message that he was to appear before the commission across the Kremlin yard from his apartment. Bukharin bid farewell to his sobbing wife, Anna Larina, and year-old son, Yuri. As Bukharin entered the building and moved to check in his overcoat, four guards surrounded him and took him straight to Lubyanka, a former insurance company headquarters that had become Moscow's most infamous political prison after the October 1917 revolution.

Minutes later, secret police entered Bukharin's apartment and demanded all of his papers, books, and articles, including letters he had received from Lenin. As his wife later wrote, "Everything was cleared out, down to the last scrap. It was all heaped into a huge pile in the study, a mountain of paper." Hours later, a truck pulled up. Police filled it with Bukharin's "mountain of paper" and, after cooking a meal of ham, sausage, and eggs for themselves in Bukharin's kitchen, drove away.

Bukharin, an esteemed member of the Soviet nomenklatura, could be arrested and his dwelling searched without cause because he lacked the Rights of Englishmen. Only five months earlier, *Pravda* had announced that Prosecutor General Andrei Vyshinsky's office had "failed to establish legal facts" against Bukharin. But facts were of no import. Thus, not even an incriminating note handwritten by Stalin describing his frame-up of Bukharin and found by Bukharin on the Kremlin floor was of any use to his defense. Bukharin's objective evidence of his frame-up counted no more than the lack of objective evidence that he had committed a crime.

The first question in English law enforcement is whether a crime—a violation of a known and definite public law—actually occurred. Rather than theory or speculation, there must be objective evidence that a crime took place. Second, there must be evidence linking the crime to the accused. Government prosecutors then have to persuade a jury. According to William Blackstone, the grand jury "ought to be thoroughly persuaded of the truth of an indictment, so far as their evidence goes; and not rest satisfied merely with remote probabilities: a doctrine, that might be applied to very oppressive purposes." If the grand jury, a "bulwark against the oppression and despotism of the Crown," is persuaded, it issues a "true bill"—an indictment—against the accused. After that, a trial jury must be persuaded of the truth of the indictment. As Blackstone wrote, "So tender is the law of England of the lives of the subjects, that no man can be convicted at the suit of the king of any capital offence, unless by the unanimous voice of twenty four of his equals and neighbours: that is, by twelve at least of the grand jury, in the first place, assenting to the accusation; and afterwards, by the whole petit jury, of twelve more, finding him guilty upon his trial."

Bukharin lacked these protections. As is now universally recognized, Bukharin (and the twenty lesser fallen notables of the new Soviet order who were tried with him) was innocent. The charges against Bukharin were spurious. He was accused of a conspiracy to overthrow the Soviet regime and to restore capitalism, charges allegedly stemming from a failed Bukharin plot to assassinate Lenin and keep the czar in power two decades earlier. A March 1, 1938, *New York Times* editorial said the charges were as if "twenty years after Yorktown somebody in power at Washington found it necessary for the safety of the State to send to the scaffold Thomas Jefferson, Madison,

John Adams, Hamilton, Jay and most of their associates. The charge against them would be that they conspired to hand over the United States to George III. Against such a background of unreason the new state trial begins in Moscow."

At Stalin's behest, Prosecutor General Vyshinsky crafted the incredible theory. It was simple to do, because he did not have to persuade a grand jury that a crime ever took place or a trial jury that Bukharin and his comrades were involved. For a year during which the secret police manufactured evidence by torture, Bukharin was kept in prison.

Prior to his arrest, Bukharin wrote a letter, "To a Future Generation of Party Leaders," which his wife memorized.[1] Writing from his Kremlin apartment's study, the communist theoretician described being "helpless" before "an infernal machine that seems to use medieval methods, yet possesses gigantic power, fabricates organized slander, acts boldly and confidently. . . . Since the age of eighteen," Bukharin said, "I have been in the Party, and always the goal of my life has been the struggle for the interests of the working class, for the victory of socialism. These days the newspaper with the hallowed name of *Pravda* [Russian for "truth"] prints the most contemptible lie that I, Nikolai Bukharin, wanted to destroy the achievement of October, to restore capitalism. This is an un-heard-of obscenity."

Lacking the Rights of Englishmen, Bukharin was indeed helpless before Stalin's "infernal machine." Protections against self-incrimination and coerced confessions did not exist. The Soviet "swallow"—a version of the medieval strappado torture method that tied the prisoner's hands and feet together behind his back before police hoisted him into the air—was commonly

---

[1]Following her twenty-year sojourn in Siberian prison camps, in 1961 Bukharin's wife gave her husband's testament to Khrushchev's Central Committee, where it was buried in Soviet archives until Gorbachev "rehabilitated" Bukharin in 1988.

used. Beatings, breaking bones, tearing off toenails, and crushing genitals were less complicated Soviet torture methods.

Not all torture methods inflicted immediate physical pain. One of the most systematic and effective methods of Soviet torture was the "conveyor belt." This method of breaking victims involved continuous rounds of questioning for hours, days, and weeks on end, all with little or no food or sleep and often interspersed with direct physical torture. Sometimes prisoners were drugged. These emotionally and physically fatiguing inquisitions would end only when the exhausted prisoner signed a confession.

To enhance the effectiveness of the conveyor belt, victims were subjected to psychological and moral pressures. The police would sometimes take the person on the conveyor to the impending shooting of another prisoner. The policemen would then tell the torture victim that only his confession could prevent the other prisoner's immediate death. Threats to family members were even more tormenting. Stalin's police would show victims pictures of family members and say that unless the victim confessed to everything and implicated everyone desired by the police, family members would be put to death. Bukharin stood up to the torture of his inquisitors for three months after his arrest. But he cracked when Stalin's agents cranked up the conveyor belt by promising the murder of his wife and infant son unless he testified against himself.

What English law rejected—rating "a man's virtue by the hardness of his constitution, and his guilt by the sensibility of his nerves"—served as the cornerstone of Soviet jurisprudence. As the *New York Times* editorialized on March 13, 1938, "If the indictment does not tell the truth and the defendants are confessing to crimes which they did not commit, we are plainly not living in the new human society of the Communist dream. We are back in the torture chambers of the Aztecs and Druids." Prosecutor General Vyshinsky, Stalin's grand theorist of confession, revealingly wrote that

"'I personally prefer a half confession in the defendant's own handwriting to a full confession in the investigator's writing,"' thereby creating the appearance that the confession was voluntary.[2]

When the show trial of Nikolai I. Bukharin, who had drafted the "general Party line" of the Soviet Communist Party, was staged, it had been well orchestrated and rehearsed. The stage set was grand. The great hall of the Soviet House of Trade Unions was formerly the ornate dining room of the czarist Nobles' Club, a three-story marble building with Corinthian columns. The immense hall retained the large crystal chandeliers and baby blue walls that were topped with a frieze of dancing girls.

On the morning of March 2, 1938, bells summoned the 300 spectators to the trial hall. Several uniformed secret police officers surrounded the prisoner's dock, a wooden box cheaply stained in brown, in the right front of the room. Behind the elevated judges' table covered with floor-length green baize, a blue velvet curtain opened, and the prisoners, "dictators, one-time commissars and one-time diplomats," filed in and sat down in four rows of chairs in the prisoner's dock.

A bailiff shouted, "The court is coming; everybody rise," and all did. Vassily V. Ulrikh, the rotund president of the Military Collegium of the Supreme Court of the USSR, followed by two fellow sitting judges and one alternate, burst through the velvet curtain. After the jurists wearing neat military uniforms sat down, the bailiff bid everyone else to do likewise.

Watching the grand entry of the jurists, Prosecutor General Andrei Vyshinsky stood behind a long table to the left of the judges' bench. With horn-rimmed glasses, a blue double-breasted suit, gray hair, and a distinguished forehead,

---

[2]Quoted in Robert Conquest, *The Great Terror: Stalin's Purge of the Thirties* (New York: Macmillan, 1968), p. 147.

Vyshinsky looked like a successful American lawyer. He gazed at the prisoners in the dock the way an eagle eyes its prey.

Between the prosecutor's desk and the prisoner's dock sat three defense attorneys. As the prisoners lacked any right to counsel, the defense lawyers were purely decorative.

Today the trial would be covered on CNN and Court TV, but in 1938 the entire world was watching through the eyes of a few news correspondents. Next to the courtroom, foreign correspondents were provided a room in which to type news stories and receive official comment. The international media also got a large blocked-off section in the courtroom. Another group receiving red-carpet treatment was the foreign diplomatic corps, whose most prestigious member was President Franklin D. Roosevelt's U.S. ambassador, Joseph E. Davies. During the trial, cigar smoke occasionally hung in the air near the ceiling in the back of the hall, a sign that Joseph Stalin had left his Kremlin suite, where the proceedings were being electronically relayed, to personally monitor the flexing of his steel grip around Bukharin's neck from a curtained window above the hall.

Besides the press and foreign VIPs, the trial hall was mobbed with hundreds of spectators, who were really part of the show. Most of the "incensed proletarians" in the trial hall were secret police employees tutored to act as angry workers. Vyshinsky was a master at igniting their derisive laughter.

The trial began with a reading of the fantastic indictment, covering an entire page in the *New York Times*, drawn from "confessions." Bukharin was linked to nonexistent foreign espionage involving the United States, Nazi Germany, Japan, China, Great Britain, and Poland, to assassinations and internal plots within Russia and the other Soviet republics, to hospital murders, to the destruction of food supplies, and to coup attempts.

Vyshinsky's plan for the rest of the trial was simple. With torture and family annihilation hanging over each prisoner, each defendant would plead guilty. The prosecutor general then planned to put each individual on the stand and walk through the details of his confession. He would intersperse the confessions with appearances by a few corroborating witnesses. After everyone had implicated Bukharin, Vyshinsky would put him on the stand for the trial's grand finale.

Once the reading of the indictment was finished, presiding judge Ulrikh asked each of the prisoners the same question: "Do you plead guilty to the charges brought against you?" Each prisoner in the dock replied, "Yes, I do," except Nikolai Krestinsky, a member along with Bukharin of Lenin's original politburo and a former Soviet ambassador to Germany, who defiantly declared, "I plead not guilty. I am not a Trotskyite. I have never been a member of the Rightist and Trotskyite Bloc, of whose existence I was not aware. Nor have I committed any of the crimes with which I personally am charged; in particular I plead not guilty to the charge of having had connections with the German intelligence service." Taken aback, Ulrikh repeated his question and received the same reply. Krestinsky said that he had confessed prior to the trial, but that he had lied and was now telling the truth. His intransigence shocked the entire court. Ulrikh swiftly completed his questioning of the other prisoners and abruptly adjourned the session.

Jarred by Krestinsky's stubbornness, when the session resumed, Vyshinsky called Sergei Bessonov, another Soviet diplomat in Berlin, to the stand. Bessonov followed his script and confessed to his alleged crimes. Bessonov smiled when Vyshinsky referred to Krestinsky's refusal to admit to these deeds. Asked why he was smiling, Bessonov replied that "the reason why I am standing here is that Krestinsky" implicated him. Vyshinsky then recalled Krestinsky to the stand. "I did not always tell the truth during the investigation," said Krestinsky. Asked why he would mislead the investigation, Krestinsky replied, "I simply considered that if I were to say what I am saying today—that it was not in accordance with the facts—my declaration would not reach the leaders of the Party and the Government." After a shocked hush from the audience, Krestinsky said that in his confession, he "did not speak voluntarily."

Krestinsky and Vyshinsky's sparring dominated international headlines the first day of the trial. That evening the Lubyanka conveyor belt was turned on to make sure the rest of the trial kept to Vyshinsky's script.

Even the least significant Englishman has the right to directly confront his accusers. Had Bukharin possessed this right, he might have uncovered that the Krestinsky who returned to the stand to retract his retraction was an actor playing the part that the real Krestinsky had refused to play.

Actors could never be hauled in as witnesses in English courtrooms, because that would taint the tribunal with fraud and thereby puncture the quest for truth. Without the Rights of Englishmen, there is nothing to prevent governments and prosecutors from using law to advance their interests. Before his own downfall, Commissar for Justice Nikolai V. Krylenko proclaimed that "in the specific nature of their functions there is no difference between the Soviet Court of Justice and the OGPU [secret police]. . . . Every Judge must keep himself well informed on questions of State policy, and remember that his judicial decisions in particular cases are intended to promote the prevailing policy of the ruling class and nothing else."[3]

He also expressed the political objectives of the Soviet court system: "Our court is an organ by means of which the directing vanguard of the proletariat, the working class as a whole, is building a new society. That is why its verdicts must be a definite instrument of political work, must be a definite instrument of educational, legal and political propaganda."[4]

---

[3]Quoted in Malcolm Muggeridge, *The Sun Never Sets: The Story of England in the Nineteen Thirties* (New York: Random House, 1940), p. 242.
[4]Quoted in Conquest, *Great Terror*, p. 270.

Once on the stand, Bukharin attempted to protect the lives of his wife and son with a general confession that took "full responsibility" for treasonous activities, but he cast aspersions on the specific charges against him. Presiding judge Ulrikh interrupted Bukharin at one point and said, "Yes, but you're going round and about; you're not saying anything about the crimes." After then going through a laundry list of crimes that he said he committed, Bukharin undermined his statement by saying that "confessions by the accused are not obligatory; confessions by the accused are a medieval principle of justice."

At the trial's conclusion, Vyshinsky demanded that Bukharin and his co-conspirators be "shot like dirty dogs." *Pravda* followed that line, declaring that "by exterminating without any mercy these spies, provocateurs, wreckers, and diversionists, the Soviet land will move even more rapidly along the Stalinist route, socialist culture will flourish even more richly, the life of the Soviet people will become even more joyous."

Six hours after adjourning the court, Ulrikh reconvened the tribunal to announce that Bukharin and the other defendants were sentenced to "the supreme penalty—to be shot, with the confiscation of all their personal property." There were no appeals. Within hours, Bukharin was dead. He had held power and position, but lacking law as a shield, even at his pinnacle he really had nothing.

CHAPTER THREE

HOW THE LAW WAS LOST

LEGAL PHILOSOPHERS HAVE approached the study of jurisprudence from different paradigms—for example, natural law versus positive law and legal formalism versus legal realism. In recent years legal paradigms have fueled public policy debates in America. In 1987 the nomination of a distinguished judge and legal scholar to the United States Supreme Court became entangled in a furious dispute between partisans of "judicial activism" and advocates of "original intent." For us, these paradigms are interesting but irrelevant.

The real question is whether law protects people from government or enables government to lord it over people. The English struggled long to achieve law that would protect people from arbitrary power. Once this was achieved and the sovereign was made accountable to law, the nature of government changed.

The control that democracy gave the people over government made them feel safe. Free from the unaccountable power of the sovereign, they ceased to perceive law as a threat. The questions arose: Since the government is ours and accountable to us, what is the purpose of a legal system that protects us from a power that we control? Doesn't the emphasis on individual rights preclude us from using our mechanism of government to achieve the greatest benefit for the greatest number?

Eighteenth-century British philosopher Jeremy Bentham answered in the affirmative and began a legal revolution in which people's rights would again become subservient to a politically defined greater interest. In this chapter we contrast William Blackstone's concept of law as the people's shield with Bentham's concept of law as a tool for socially engineering a higher level of happiness.

Most Americans are accustomed to thinking of law as a list of deeds that the government prohibits. This list is long. The *U.S. Code*, which contains all federal statutes, occupies 56,009 single-spaced pages. Its 47 volumes take up 9 feet of shelf space. An annotated version, which attempts to bring order out of chaos, is 36 feet long and has 230 hardcover volumes and 36 paperback supplements. Administrative lawmaking under statutes fill up the 207-volume *Code of Federal Regulations*, which spans 21 feet of shelf space and contains more than 134,488 pages of regulatory law. The *Federal Register* updates federal regulations daily. In 1994, its 250 volumes had a total of 68,107 pages. Federal law is further augmented by more than 2,756 volumes of judicial precedent, taking up 160 yards of law library shelving.

State and local governments also have laws, regulations, and judicial precedents. Tiny Rhode Island has 21,880 pages of statutory law supplemented by 22 thick volumes of interpretive regulations. The California Code is 11 yards long. The Golden State's 329 volumes of judicial opinions occupy 35 yards of shelf space. New York's code is 6 yards long. The Empire State's 929 volumes of judicial precedent fill 90 yards of shelf space.

This gigantic corpus, however, is not what Blackstone means by law. Little of value would be lost if these volumes disappeared overnight. What Blackstone means by law are prohibitions *on* government, not prohibitions *from* the government. According to Blackstone, law is a handful of principles that prevent the government from using the legal system as an instrument of oppression. What differentiates the fortunate few who live under Anglo-Saxon jurisprudence is not the number of laws—other nations have vast quantities of their own—but the requirement that law serve justice, not government.

In all other systems of jurisprudence, the government is presumed to define justice, thus leaving people vulnerable to government persecution. This is why the English legal system has, throughout the ages, been revered. At the end of his *Commentaries of the Laws of England*, Blackstone praised England's "laws and liberties" as "the best birthright, and noblest inheritance of mankind."

Blackstone's reverence for law as a guarantor of liberty resonated in hearts and minds in the colonies across the Atlantic. According to historian Daniel Boorstin, in American history "no other book—except the Bible—has played so great a role as Blackstone's *Commentaries on the Laws of England*." Boorstin concludes that "Blackstone was to American law what Noah Webster's speller was to American literacy." Edmund Burke declared in the House of Commons in 1775 that "in no country perhaps in the world is the law so general a study" as in America, where "all who read, and most do read, endeavor to obtain some smattering in that science." As proof, Burke reported that a prominent bookseller told him that Blackstone's *Commentaries* were a colonial American best-seller, nearly matching English sales.

Burke's point was underlined one year later when colonists penned their Declaration of Independence, essentially an affirmation of their rights as Englishmen that they felt King George III had trampled. "Even without Blackstone," Boorstin wrote, "the Americans surely would have fought their Revolution and doubtless would have preserved English institutions in America. But the convenient appearance of the *Commentaries* within the decade before the Declaration of

Independence made it much easier for Americans to see what they were preserving; and made it feasible to perpetuate those institutions in remote villages without trained lawyers or law libraries."

If King George III had behaved toward colonial Americans with the wisdom of Alfred the Great, Blackstone's *Commentaries* might have collected dust in Boston and Philadelphia book shops. But to people experiencing "repeated injuries and usurpations," Blackstone struck a chord with his description of the "absolute rights inherent in every Englishman" and his dramatic presentation of their "rise, progress, and gradual improvements." Backed by Blackstone, colonial Americans saw their struggle in the context of the epic struggle between the virtuous ancient constitution "concerted by Alfred" that guarded "public and private liberty" and tyrannical deviations from it. Blackstone said, "The liberties of Englishmen are not (as some arbitrary writers would represent them) mere infringements of the king's prerogative, extorted from our princes by taking advantage of their weakness; but a restoration of that ancient constitution, of which our ancestors had been defrauded." Blackstone detailed how through the ages courageous Englishmen fought to restore Alfred's constitution from servility to alien legal conceptions that William the Conqueror imported from Normandy in 1066. At that time, the Rights of Englishmen were "totally buried under the narrow rules and fanciful niceties of metaphysical and Norman jurisprudence." Blackstone detailed the drama through the ages—with the Magna Carta (1215), the Petition of Right (1628), and the Bill of Rights (1689)—that restored Alfred's constitution. When members of the Continental Congress signed the Declaration of Independence—pledging "to each other our Lives, our Fortunes, and our sacred Honor"—on July 4, 1776, they were infused with confidence that they, and not King George, stood with both feet firmly planted in English law.

The same year that Americans asserted their Rights as Englishmen in the Declaration of Independence, Blackstone's concept of law was attacked in an anonymous tract. The author was Jeremy Bentham, a vainglorious economist whose embalmed remains sit today in the University of London. In time, ideas from this pamphlet would spread across the Atlantic and gradually nibble away the basis of American liberty. But that would come later.

In December 1763 Blackstone stepped to the podium of his Oxford classroom to begin teaching his popular course—what academic department heads today would call a "cash cow"—for the tenth year. As England's foremost legal scholar spoke, two students who sat next to each other had totally different reactions. For one, Blackstone inspired reverent awe. For the other, Blackstone inflamed contemptuous disgust.

Samuel Parker Coke was enthralled with Blackstone's every word. His imagination soared with images of Alfred the Great consulting with England's wise men about customs from the past before restating the common law after defeating the Danes at Edington in 878. He envisioned himself standing at Runnymede when King John signed the Magna Carta in 1215. More than ever before, he appreciated the courage of his forebear, Sir Edward Coke, for reasserting the principles of the Magna Carta in parliamentary disputes with Charles I, culminating in the Petition of Right in 1628. He could feel the cool Channel breezes at Brixham in November 1688 when William III arrived from the Netherlands in the Glorious Revolution. William and Mary, his queen, ascended to the throne in exchange for recognizing the supremacy of Parliament and affirming the Bill of Rights.

For the young Coke, Blackstone eloquently described how law rests in the people and their sense of what is fair and just— the essence of the Rights of Englishmen. He saw how English law embodied the achievement and triumph of freedom in the ancient struggle against tyranny. As he carefully took notes,

Coke pondered how much better off he was than his cohorts who were studying law in Paris, Bologna, or Berlin. As an Englishman, the law was a shield he held instead of a sword a sovereign held. It was the Rights of Englishmen, rather than the king's good graces, that restrained England's sovereign authorities from doing harm.

Sitting next to Coke was his friend Jeremy Bentham, a sixteen-year-old prodigy and son of a wealthy London lawyer, who had already completed a bachelor's degree at Oxford and a year of legal study at London's Lincoln's Inn. When he was only five, Bentham's precocity earned him the nickname "Philosopher." In one of London's "logical disputations," in vogue in his childhood, young Jeremy defeated not only his opponent, but also the presiding moderator. He had also achieved fame for writing a Latin ode in honor of the accession of King George III.

To the diminutive Jeremy Bentham, Blackstone merely aroused antagonism by prattling about legal history, which Bentham dismissed as irrelevant mythology, reminiscent of the imaginary ghosts that had tormented his childhood. Bentham later wrote that he could not take notes during Blackstone's lectures because "my thoughts were occupied in reflecting on what I heard. I immediately detected his fallacy concerning natural rights; I thought his notions very frivolous and illogical." The notion of "natural rights" is the rationalization that philosophers such as John Locke put on the historical achievement of the English in making law accountable to the people.

Bentham derided it all as "nonsense on stilts." What Blackstone lauded as historic struggle and achievement that secured the Rights of Englishmen, Bentham lamented as the erection of new legal barriers that blocked government from doing good.

Back from Oxford at Lincoln's Inn, Bentham vented his gnawing disdain for Blackstonian law in an essay entitled "A

Fragment on Government," which was widely distributed in London in 1776. Because eighteenth-century Englishmen held Blackstone's *Commentaries* in the same high esteem as Shakespeare's plays and the King James Bible, Bentham's attack on Blackstone was anonymous. The "Fragment" caused an uproar in British legal and political circles because of both its shocking content and its "ungentlemanly" anonymity. Of course, the essay's disregard for honor and etiquette was in line with Benthamism's core—a slashing assault on all inherited values, institutions, and customs, especially as embodied in law. Bentham assailed Blackstone for glorifying the status quo: "He is the dupe of every prejudice and the abettor of every abuse. No sound principles can be expected from that writer whose first object is to defend a system."

Young Jeremy Bentham wanted to remake the world. Sitting in Blackstone's Oxford classroom, he quickly grasped that English law was a barrier. Liberty—what Blackstonian law secured—has always been a barrier to those who want to remake society. When law resides in the will of the people, the elites, who wish to proclaim their will from on high, lack power. To reverse this, Bentham determined that he would reinvent the millennia of English jurisprudence from his desk in his London study—in the same Westminster residence where the author of *Paradise Lost*, John Milton, had lived during Oliver Cromwell's mid-seventeenth-century interregnum.

In order to undercut Blackstone, Bentham ambushed English liberty. He derided it as a "fictitious legal entity." He found *liberty* and *liberal* to be mischievous words. The real issues, he declared, were happiness and security. What good is liberty, he asked, if the absence of government action means people are unhappy and insecure?

Bentham's "Fragment on Government" recognized the "jealous antagonists" of individual liberty and government, but in contrast to Blackstone, he sided with government. He did this by viewing liberty as the freedom of government from restraint, not the freedom of people from government. He insisted that "freedom in a government depends not upon any limitation to the Supreme Power." Rather than a restraint on government, Bentham considered law to be government's instrument for doing good. This reformulation posed no danger, Bentham stated, because the purpose of both government and law was to promote the "greatest happiness for the greatest number."

From Bentham's perspective, Blackstone made the individual count for too much, thereby frustrating the government's ability to act in the public's wider interest. Instead of the tyranny of the government, it was the tyranny of the individual whose petty individual rights stood in the way of the rational reconstruction of society.

Bentham spent the rest of his life evaluating almost anything and everything according to the "utilitarian principle"— the extent to which it promoted the "greatest happiness for the greatest number." Using his utilitarian razor, Bentham shaved the Rights of Englishmen out of English jurisprudence. As Gertrude Himmelfarb has written, "The principle of the greatest happiness of the greatest number was as inimical to the idea of liberty as to the idea of rights." Friedrich A. Hayek reached the same conclusion: "Bentham and his Utilitarians did much to destroy the beliefs which England had in part preserved from the Middle Ages, by their scornful treatment of most of what until then had been the most admired features of the British constitution."

Bentham wrote in the "Fragment" that "the age we live in is a busy age; in which knowledge is rapidly advancing towards perfection." Bentham had total confidence in his ability to construct a science of good government focused on promoting happiness and minimizing suffering. He believed that social engineering to enhance the greater good took precedence over the Rights of Englishmen. Historian David A. Lockmiller notes in his biography, *Sir William Blackstone*, that while

"Blackstone was a commentator on laws as they existed," Bentham "was the prophet of a new era" who audaciously "created a Heaven of his own and invited mankind to join him."

Bentham's "heaven" was a gulag. Historian Paul Johnson has described how Bentham "wanted to treat as criminals and *apprehend* people who were likely, because of their social and economic status, to fall into crime, whether or not they had committed one." Bentham suggested that these people be put into hundreds of "industry houses," where they would be reformed with heavy labor. Johnson says that "there were many respects in which Bentham's industry houses adumbrated the work camps set up in Hitler's Germany and Lenin's Russia over a hundred years later."

Bentham's influence as an English legal philosopher was entirely dependent upon the success of the English in making government accountable to law. Prior to the Glorious Revolution, the concept of government as an entity that could be trusted to devote itself to the happiness of its subjects would have been too strange for words. At Runnymede, King John did not defend himself as a promoter of the public interest. Any such claims would have fallen on deaf ears.

It is easy to impute good motives and draw up lists of good things that government could do if only there were no chains on its powers. For Bentham, the more power the government had, the more power it had to do good. This could make sense only to a people who had tied government down so that it could do them no harm. Blackstone viewed law as an assertion of the people's independence. Bentham thought this independence was foolish, because it obstructed the government's power to induce progress. He said, "Government is good in proportion to the happiness of which it is productive on the part of the body of the people subject to it."

Blackstone said to his students at the end of his lectures that "we have taken occasion to admire at every turn" the "ancient simplicity" of English law. But he did not stop there.

He also said, "Nor have its faults been concealed from view; for faults it has, lest we should be tempted to think it of more than human structure."

It was on this point that England's foremost jurist left his role as a chronicler of how the Rights of Englishmen were achieved and took on the role of a seasoned barrister imploring his students to heed his wisdom. Blackstone acknowledged the rage for modern improvement that lurked within each age, especially from those desiring "to show the vast powers of the human intellect, however vainly or preposterously employed." Beseeching his students to be patient, Blackstone said that English law's grounding in the values, customs, and traditions of the people ha[d] allowed the Rights of Englishmen to meet the "exigencies of the times." "We plainly discern the alteration of the law from what it was five hundred years ago, yet it is impossible to define the precise period in which that alteration accrued, any more than we can discern the changes of the bed of a river, which varies its shores by continual decreases and alluvions."

To reiterate his theme of patience and the importance of treading slowly, Blackstone said, "We inherit an old Gothic castle, erected in the days of chivalry, but fitted up for a modern inhabitant. The moated ramparts, the embattled towers, and the trophied halls, are magnificent and venerable, but useless. The inferior apartments, now converted into rooms of convenience, are cheerful and commodious, though their approaches are winding and difficult." As political scientist Herbert Storing observes, Blackstone "is careful to warn against reform that might loosen some apparently useless stone or weaken some inconvenient timber and cause the whole edifice, the pleasant apartments as well as the noble shell, vital damage."

Blackstone's lesson was lost on Jeremy Bentham, for indeed, impatience is the essence of Benthamism. One of Bentham's admirers, parliamentarian Henry Peter Brougham, who served as lord chancellor from 1830 to 1834, said that the age of law reform and the age of Jeremy Bentham were one and the same, as no one before him had ever seriously thought of adapting law to the task of promoting human happiness. Brougham concluded his accolade: "Not only was he thus eminently original among the lawyers and the legal philosophers of his country; he might be said to be the first legal philosopher that had appeared in the world." Brougham dismissed the champions from Alfred the Great to William Blackstone in the long struggle for accountable law as mere clerks concerned with perpetuating the law that they inherited, whereas he saw Bentham as a "legal philosopher" seeking to radically transform law into something new. Brougham's uninformed opinion became commonplace.

Bentham's advocacy of torture underscores the radical nature of his "legal philosophy." Torture is anathema to the Rights of Englishmen. Blackstone proudly declared that "trial by rack is utterly unknown to the law of England." Torture's absence from English jurisprudence long distinguished it from legal systems in the rest of Europe, where torture was a legally sanctioned instrument of investigation and adjudication. Holding the law in their hearts and minds, the English disdained the idea that they could ever be put on the rack. In contrast, across the English Channel on the European continent, people had no say in the matter, because the sovereign defined the law.

Jeremy Bentham advocated the legalization of torture, which, of course, would destroy everything for which English jurisprudence stood. But that was Bentham's aim. In his self-proclaimed role as an impartial "deontologist"—an expert on the maximization of aggregate happiness—he postulated that the systematic use of torture to extract evidence could contribute to the greater happiness of the greater number just as flowers in London parks and sport fishing did. Bentham blithely used his "felicific calculus"—the calculation of units of felicity—to assess everything, including mandatory chapel at Oxford.

Bentham defined torture as making a person suffer "any violent pain of body in order to compel him to do something or to desist from doing something which done or desisted from the penal application is immediately made to cease." Dispelling the "sentimental prejudice" against torture with the "dictates of reason and utility," Bentham concluded that "torture might be made use of with advantage." Just as "a Mother or Nurse seeing a child playing with a thing which he ought not to meddle with, and having forbidden him in vain pinches him till he lays it down," the government can promote security against crime by torturing suspects. Bentham dismissed dangers of sadistic impulses and false confessions to terminate unbearable pain. He believed judges could be as trusted to prescribe the proper degree of torture as they are to properly sentence the guilty. We hear much the same thing today from those who tell us we can trust prosecutors and police with wide latitude and discretion.

As much as Jeremy Bentham disliked William Blackstone, only with Blackstonian law taming government could Bentham credibly advocate torture. Commenting on Bentham's advocacy of torture, English legal historians W. L. Twining and P. E. Twining write that "apart from the enormous practical difficulties of devising workable safeguards, there is the perennial question of the extent to which one is prepared to *trust* those in authority." Bentham benefited from the fact that government is trustworthy only when the Rights of Englishmen are in place. The Rights of Englishmen are most appreciated when they are absent.

Tyranny was such a distant memory for Bentham that he did not take protections against it very seriously. Undercutting the legal achievements proscribing torture would restore tyranny quickly. Torture would, by definition, establish a class of torturers who were prone to violence and who would endanger society. Torture treats individuals as means to an end, rather than ends unto themselves who are shielded by the Rights of Englishmen. As Bentham casually dismissed Rights of Englishmen that prohibited torture, he likewise did away with other Rights of Englishmen. Richard Posner has summarized the implications of Bentham's "deontological" prescriptions:

> Bentham's assault on traditional language and the habits of thought encapsulated in it prefigured the totalitarian assault on language by Newspeak, Hitler, and the Soviet press. In his suggestions for prison reform, Bentham was a pioneer in developing techniques of brainwashing. He toyed with the idea of having everyone's name tattooed on his body to facilitate criminal law enforcement. Compulsory self-incrimination, torture, anonymous informers, abolition of the attorney-client privilege and of the jury, and depreciation of rights are other parts of Bentham's legacy to totalitarian regimes.

Blackstone's concept of law gave us the Rights of Englishmen. Bentham's concept undermined the Rights of Englishmen. For Blackstone, law was the people's shield. For Bentham, it was permissible for the government to trample the individual in the name of a "greater good." Blackstone respected property as an "absolute right, inherent in every Englishman." Bentham thought private property was merely a legally dispensable creation of the government. Blackstone thought law was grounded in the values and traditions of the people. Bentham thought law could be scientifically remade by the government in pursuit of "the greatest happiness for the greatest number." Blackstone revered juries and reviled the Court of Star Chamber, which Parliament had abolished in 1641 for its tyranny. Bentham hated juries and praised the Court of Star Chamber for its efficacy in securing convictions. For Blackstone, law was a shield held by the people against government. For Bentham, law was a sword wielded by government over the people for their own good.

Bentham believed in the wisdom and perfectibility of public administrators. Blackstone feared the government's "evil and pernicious counselors" and defended constitutional diffusions of power, while Bentham favored the consolidation of government authority. Blackstone was conscious of human fallibility. Bentham trumpeted the limitless powers of reason, especially his own. Blackstone was an incrementalist, Bentham a radical.

Surrounded by 70,000 pages of unpublished manuscript, Bentham died on June 6, 1832. But his legacy has continued. The history of English legal reform "in the nineteenth century is the story of the shadow cast by one man—Bentham," said A. V. Dicey, holder of Blackstone's Oxford chair from 1882 to 1909. The day after Bentham died, the first of England's reform bills crafted in his image received royal assent. Three days after Bentham's death, his utilitarian disciples, leading doctors, and medical students gathered in London's Webb Street School of Anatomy in order to observe the dissection of his body. It did not take long for Bentham's shadow to reach America, where his calculus would ultimately dissect the Rights of Englishmen out of U.S. law.

Over the decades Benthamite influences have eaten away at the Rights of Englishmen. There was never a radical frontal assault that overthrew these rights. Rather, it has been a piecemeal and incomplete process. Benthamite concepts were grafted, so to speak, onto the legal tree of liberty. Enough of Bentham has found its way into our law that we can no longer take for granted that we will be afforded the protections provided by the Rights of Englishmen. In the following chapters we show infringements of the rights that prevent government from using law as a weapon.

CHAPTER FOUR

CRIMES WITHOUT INTENT

FOREMOST AMONG THE Rights of Englishmen is the requirement that no one can be prosecuted for a crime without evidence that a crime has occurred and evidence that links the accused to the crime. If in 1938 Prosecutor General Andrei Vyshinsky had had to present evidence of a plot by Bolshevik leaders to overthrow their own revolution, it would have been impossible to indict Nikolai Bukharin, much less convict him.

Vyshinsky might have attempted to argue that some of Bukharin's statements and actions discouraged farmers from sowing and thus had the effect of disorganizing food production, just as a conspiracy would have. Such an exercise would count for naught in a court governed by Englishmen's rights, because in such a court there can be no crime without intent.

Although few people have the phrase "no crime without intent" on the tips of their tongues, the sense of fairness that it embodies resides in the hearts of people who have never heard of the Rights of Englishmen. The principle shields people from being criminally prosecuted for accidental or "innocent" acts. It prevents citizens from being held liable for actions that were made illegal after the fact. It prevents the government from persecuting people for transgressions whose illegality was unknowable. Under Anglo-Saxon jurisprudence, a prosecutor cannot put a person on trial based only on the prosecutor's suspicion or theory that a crime has occurred.

"No crime without intent" has long been the foundation of law in the English-speaking world. An ancient maxim of the common law is that "an act does not make one guilty, unless the mind be guilty." William Blackstone insisted that criminality requires a "vicious will" in addition to a forbidden act. Oliver Wendell Holmes acknowledged the importance of intent when he observed that "even a dog distinguishes between being stumbled over and being kicked." The objection to punishing unintended acts is instinctive and is summed up in the child's familiar exculpatory, "But I didn't mean to."

There is good reason for this long-standing consensus that crime requires intent. It is both unjust and inefficient to punish actions that are unrelated to criminal intent. Punishment implies moral blameworthiness, and the stigma of a criminal conviction is undercut when no distinction is made between intended and unintended behavior.[1] It is inefficacious to devote law enforcement resources to punishing conduct that is not intentionally criminal. If no crime was intended, punishment does not serve as a deterrent against future criminal behavior or protect society from a socially dangerous person. It merely diverts scarce resources from the pursuit of those who intentionally commit criminal acts to the pursuit of those who unintentionally stumble over the law.

Prosecuting crimes without intent shatters the moral authority of law and demeans the honest efforts of citizens to obey the law. Moreover, it destroys the security that law provides. Berkeley law professor Sanford H. Kadish wrote that if crime is separated from intent, "the criminal law would create insecurity in the general community when the central function

---

[1]This distinction is recognized, not undercut, by manslaughter. A fatal accident caused by an intoxicated driver implies a degree of negligence that borders on intent.

of the criminal law is to create that security." Prosecutors would have an unfettered discretion to prosecute or not to prosecute potentially every person in the community, and this "discretion would constitute an invitation to abusive and discriminatory exercise of authority against the disliked or the unpopular on political or other grounds." Security and liberty would be threatened. As Blackstone emphasized, tyranny is the inevitable alternative to the Rights of Englishmen.

As incredible as it may seem, in the United States the Rights of Englishmen have been eroded to the point that innocent Americans can find themselves in positions that resemble the plight of Nikolai Bukharin. In contemporary America, crimes no longer require intent. Prosecutors have invented new felonies to fit those who have been targeted. Accidents have been criminalized, and it has even become a crime to make a mistake when filling out regulatory forms required by government.

The Exxon Valdez

IN 1989, THE Exxon *Valdez* oil supertanker ran aground off the coast of Alaska in beautiful Prince William Sound. The resulting 11-million-gallon oil spill temporarily damaged the environment. Today, nature has recovered, thanks to an expensive cleanup by Exxon and nature's own recuperative powers. But the law, which was also devastated by the episode, has not recovered. The soiling of the pristine sound captured the public's imagination to such an extent that a far worse desecration passed unnoticed.

Exxon faced large cleanup costs and civil tort damages. But the U.S. Justice Department went beyond law and justifiable liability by bringing preposterous criminal charges against the oil giant. Eleven months after the *Valdez* hit Prince William Sound's Bligh Reef, a federal grand jury returned a five-count criminal indictment against Exxon Corporation and its wholly owned subsidiary Exxon Shipping Company. The indictment was absurd on its face. President George Bush's attorney general, Richard Thornburgh, acknowledged that the felony charges against Exxon made "a unique case which requires some innovative legal approaches which are never without risk." Whenever a prosecutor brags about his innovativeness, the Rights of Englishmen are under assault.

The government's "innovative legal approach" was to criminalize the accident. It is absolutely certain that America's largest oil company did not run the *Valdez* aground with the criminal intention of polluting the water and killing migratory birds. Yet, the Justice Department's criminal indictment assumed that Exxon did.

Two counts of the trumped-up indictment were magicked out of statutes—the Clean Water Act and the Refuse Act—designed to punish polluters. These acts make it illegal to discharge hazardous substances and refuse without a permit. They are designed to stop towns, cities, and businesses from using waterways as their garbage bins.

However, the explicit purposes of the statutes did not stop the Justice Department from claiming that $150 million of crude oil that accidentally spilled into Prince William Sound was "refuse matter," "thrown, discharged and deposited" by Exxon without a permit.

A third count charged Exxon with violating the Migratory Bird Treaty Act, which prohibits the hunting and killing of migratory birds without a permit. The Justice Department used the act to charge Exxon with spilling oil in order to kill birds without a license.

The two remaining felony counts of the indictment were drawn from the Posts and Waterways Act and the Dangerous Cargo Act, which require tankers to be manned by competent personnel. The government charged that Exxon "willfully and knowingly" employed people incapable of performing the duties assigned to them. According to the Justice Department, one of the world's largest companies purposely hired incompetent people to squander its profits and jeopardize its existence.

Criminalizing the accident permitted the Justice Department to use the Criminal Fines Improvement Act to extort a fortune from the corporation. Using a formula that multiplies fines to twice the amount of damages caused by "criminal activity," Thornburgh said that Exxon faced criminal liability in excess of $700 million, plus cleanup costs, restitution to fishermen and other aggrieved parties, and other fines.[2]

In a front-page story on March 1, 1990, the *New York Times*—no friend of oil companies—said that "the government faces a risky criminal trial based on untested legal principles." But in the Soviet Union in 1938, Joseph Stalin and Andrei Vyshinsky had tested these principles in the show trials used to destroy Nikolai Bukharin and other leading Bolsheviks. Following the path blazed by Stalin's chief prosecutor, the U.S. Justice Department charged Exxon with a nonexistent conspiracy to pollute Prince William Sound in order to kill migratory birds. As a result of this precedent, anyone involved in a car accident resulting in gasoline spilling into a stream or waterway faces potential criminal prosecution for an "environmental crime."

Despite the absurdity of the charges, Exxon lacked sufficient confidence in our crumbling justice system to go to trial. The company settled out of court. In exchange for dropping the felony counts, on behalf of the company Exxon chairman Lawrence Rawl entered a guilty plea on behalf of the company in federal court to the misdemeanor counts and committed his corporation to paying a $125 million criminal fine. Upon

---

[2]Such vast liability for misdemeanors underscores Blackstone's observation that the "gentler name" of misdemeanor crimes for "smaller faults" often can be deceptive.

accepting Rawl's plea, District Judge H. Russel Holland called Exxon "a good corporate citizen."

But good corporate citizenship requires resisting when zealous prosecutors misuse the law. As New York attorney Stanley S. Arkin put it, "Companies that stand up to prosecutors and fight them in court are performing a patriotic duty by resisting the arrogant and undeserved application of criminal law." We are all endangered when a wealthy corporation with law on its side feels impotent to prevent the criminalization of accidents.

The government's indictment of Exxon used a novel theory of liability as a rationale for raiding both Exxon Corporation's deep pockets and the purse of its subsidiary, Exxon Shipping. The owners of a corporation are traditionally shielded from liability under the corporate veil. To pierce the veil, the government defined Exxon Shipping as an "agent" of Exxon Corporation. However, as reported in the *Restatement of Agency*, under U.S. law "a corporation does not become an agent of another corporation merely because a majority of its voting shares is held by the other." If *United States v. Exxon* had gone to trial, the government would have had to prove, rather than assert, this "agency" relationship. Stephen Raucher wrote in the *Ecology Law Quarterly* in 1992 that the judiciary's "willingness to embrace the government's agency theory in this case marks the first time that criminal liability for the acts of a wholly owned subsidiary has been successfully employed in any reported environmental case." Raucher warns that the "expansion of agency concepts into realms once walled off by the corporate form" makes "parent corporations much more vulnerable to criminal prosecutions."

Novel theories of criminal liability created by prosecutors after the fact are becoming commonplace. The prosecution of savings and loan executive Charles Keating is another example.

The Case of Charles H. Keating, Jr.

CHARLES KEATING WAS the victim of an ancient injustice—a bill of attainder. He was convicted of a crime that did not exist until he was charged with it. The crime was not on the statute books but was pieced together by prosecutors from civil offenses and converted into a felony. Prosecutors and California Superior Court Judge Lance Ito—infamous for his mishandling of the O. J. Simpson murder trial—rewrote the law and transformed the civil tort doctrine of *respondeat superior,* in which a "master" is economically liable for the wrongdoings of his "servant," into a crime. Judge Ito embraced the prosecutor's "novel legal theory" that it did not matter that Keating neither knew about nor approved of the alleged acts of wrongdoing by his employees.

Keating was caught up in the finger-pointing that resulted when ill-considered federal policies caused the collapse of the nation's S&Ls and depleted the deposit insurance fund. Government policymakers did not want to take the blame for their expensive mistakes, so they shifted the blame to S&L owners. Keating, a high-profile owner of a California S&L, was a ready-made opportunity for ambitious California prosecutors.

Keating was the chairman of American Continental Corporation (ACC), a prosperous Arizona-based real estate development company that had purchased California's Lincoln Savings and Loan in 1984. Federal regulators had supported this sale with favorable financial terms, as they had done with many other thrift sales in the early 1980s.

In another arrangement common in the thrift industry and approved by federal and state regulators, ACC representatives sold ACC bonds in Lincoln branch offices. In compliance with securities laws, prospectuses issued with these bonds, which the SEC had approved, stated in capitalized boldface type that the bonds were not insured by the Federal Savings and Loan

Insurance Corporation. Moreover, the front page also warned that "no dealer, salesman or any other person has been authorized to give any information or to make any representation in connection with this offering other than those contained in this Prospectus and any Prospectus Supplement, and if given or made, such information or representations must not be relied upon as having been authorized by the Company."

Despite these disclaimers and the government's approval of the sale of ACC bonds in Lincoln branches, when the bonds collapsed in value after the real estate market collapse of the late 1980s, prosecutors found a scapegoat in Charles Keating. The real estate market collapse, which decimated both ACC and Lincoln, was caused by negligent U.S. policymakers. Most economists attribute the fall in real estate values to ill-conceived monetary and tax policies. The crisis was exacerbated by the 1989 Financial Institutions Reform, Recovery and Enforcement Act (FIRREA). As Treasury Secretary Nicholas F. Brady testified before the Senate Banking Committee on May 23, 1990, FIRREA helped produce "not only higher-than-expected losses but also an increase in the population of savings and loans that will require attention." With the stroke of President George Bush's pen, many successful thrifts were ruined.[3] Lincoln, listed by *Forbes* as the nation's second most prosperous thrift in 1987, became the symbol of the S&L crisis two years later.

---

[3]FIRREA required S&Ls to change the way they accounted for goodwill on their balance sheets. This not only made bad economic sense, but abrogated the government's contracts with healthy S&Ls that had agreed to take over insolvent thrifts. On August 30, 1995, the U.S. Court of Appeals for the Federal Circuit recognized FIRREA's destruction of these contracts and ruled that the federal government cannot renege on its solemn contractual obligations and is "liable for breach of contract where its legislation is directed at repudiating prior contractual agreements." This ruling was affirmed in 1996 by the Supreme Court.

The day before Keating's trial, Keating's prosecutors eagerly awaited the testing of their "novel legal theory." In an August 1, 1991, *Wall Street Journal* article titled "Keating Trial Is Testing Ground for a Controversial Legal Theory," prosecutors admitted that their theory was a "hybrid" that combined "legal exceptions to two common notions—that guilt requires intent to commit a crime and that people are responsible only for their own acts."

There was much anger and emotion in Judge Ito's courtroom as the prosecution presented its case. Many elderly and unsophisticated ACC bondholders testified that unscrupulous salesmen had lured them into buying the bonds with assurances that they were insured by the government. No evidence was presented that Keating personally did anything wrong. The prosecution brought no evidence whatsoever that Keating, who had never sold a single ACC bond, knew that salesmen had fraudulently misrepresented the safety of the financial instruments or sold them without first giving a customer a prospectus.

Rather than dismissing the case, however, Judge Ito permitted prosecutors to draft a new crime that would mesh with their lack of evidence and thereby ensure a conviction. University of Chicago law professor and corporate law expert Daniel R. Fischel has written that by acquiescing to the prosecutors, "Judge Ito created a crime out of thin air tailor-made for Charles Keating, a crime for which nobody in the history of California had ever been prosecuted." The U.S. Constitution, as Professor Fischel notes, prohibits "ex post facto crimes, crimes created after the fact to prosecute particular individuals. This basic safeguard was intended to protect the rights of unpopular individuals—individuals just like Charles Keating—from the arbitrary imposition of power by the government responding to powerful interest groups or mob hysteria." Charles Keating was incarcerated despite the fact that his crime could not be found in California's statute books.

When a California appellate court upheld Judge Ito's legislative drafting, the court admitted that no legal precedent existed for it: "This appears to be a case of first impression on the aiding and abetting theory for this particular Corporations Code section." Rather than setting Keating free, however, the court upheld Keating's conviction on the basis of language added to a 1993 California corporate fraud statute by the California legislature after Keating's conviction in order to codify the novel theory used to prosecute Keating. Keating thus was a victim of an unconstitutional application of ex post facto law, which in turn was rubber-stamped by an unconstitutional bill of attainder passed by the legislature. Prosecutors, judges, and legislators all produced a scapegoat, and law was corrupted by those sworn to uphold it.[4]

The Case of Clark Clifford and Robert A. Altman

KEATING'S UNPOPULARITY MADE him vulnerable. However, popularity and status provide no protection from prosecutorial abuse. Ask Clark Clifford, the dean of the Democratic Party's establishment, who for years provided wisdom and stability for Democratic policymakers. Clifford came to Washington in 1945 as World War II was ending, after a brief but thriving career as a St. Louis lawyer. When fellow Missourian Harry Truman became president after Franklin Delano Roosevelt's

---

[4]In 1996, after Keating had served 4 ½ years in jail, federal district judge John G. Davies declared his conviction to be a violation of *mens rea* and the constitutional prohibition of ex post facto law and ordered his release.

death, Clifford accompanied former St. Louis banker James K. Vardaman, Jr., to the White House, where Vardaman served as Truman's naval aide. Clifford was Vardaman's assistant.

Clifford quickly caught Truman's attention. Before long, Clifford had Vardaman's job, and he soon became Truman's White House Counsel. When the Cold War began, Clifford drafted the first outlines of Truman's doctrine of Soviet containment. He became a close friend of Truman. Over the objections of Secretary of State George Marshall, Clifford persuaded Truman to recognize the fledgling state of Israel. He also redesigned the presidential seal. In 1947, the *Saturday Evening Post* dubbed Clifford "Assistant President of the U.S.A." Clifford became legendary for strategizing Truman's come-from-behind victory over Republican Thomas E. Dewey in the 1948 presidential election. In adulating cover stories, *Time* and *Newsweek* lauded Clifford as Truman's most creative advisor.

Clifford left the White House in 1950 and formed his own law firm, where he became the Washington attorney of choice for corporate America in the postwar era. Billionaire Howard Hughes, AT&T, Phillips Petroleum, Firestone Tire and Rubber, IBM, McDonnell-Douglas, Knight-Ridder, Du Pont, and scores of other blue-ribbon clients kept Clifford on lucrative retainers, because he, more than anyone else, knew the people who made Washington tick. Clifford was the first D.C. lawyer to earn over $1,000,000 per year. Whenever Fortune 500 companies faced rough waters on the banks of the Potomac, Clifford served as their lifeguard. He also served on numerous corporate boards.

For decades, politicians (including two rival senators in the 1950s named John F. Kennedy and Lyndon Baines Johnson) sought out Clifford's advice. Clifford directed Kennedy's presidential transition team and then served as his private lawyer. He reorganized Kennedy's national security structure after the Bay of Pigs fiasco. When the Vietnam conflict overwhelmed President Johnson's defense secretary, Robert McNamara, Johnson appointed Clifford to the post. Clifford thus presided over the cabinet department he had helped design as Truman's advisor. Jimmy Carter asked Clifford to serve as his special envoy to the Middle East in the wake of the Soviet invasion of Afghanistan.

When Democratic socialite Pamela Digby Churchill Hayward Harriman—later President Bill Clinton's ambassador to France—held a Georgetown party in 1991 to celebrate the publication of Clifford's memoirs, *Counsel to the President*, a 400-person Who's Who of the Washington elite attended. Clifford signed 200 copies of his book that evening. Limousines delivered such political luminaries as Senators Edward Kennedy, Claiborne Pell, and Chris Dodd, House Speaker Tom Foley, and Representative Patricia Schroeder. William Safire of the *New York Times* and Katharine Graham, owner of the *Washington Post*, joined in honoring the pillar of Washington's "permanent government." Former first ladies Jacqueline Kennedy Onassis and Lady Bird Johnson paid tribute to Clifford and his memoirs by telephone.

Being a prince of the American establishment could not, however, shield the octogenarian Clifford and his wunderkind law partner and protégé, Robert Altman, from the theories of ambitious prosecutors. On July 29, 1992, Manhattan District Attorney Robert Morgenthau called a press conference to announce that a grand jury had indicted Clifford and Altman for bank fraud relating to alleged bribes that they had accepted for keeping secret the alleged ownership of First American Bankshares by the Bank of Credit and Commerce International (BCCI). "Today's indictment spells out that this massive fraud was not just a criminal fraud scheme," Morgenthau declared, "but a sophisticated and corrupt criminal enterprise, organized from the top down to do just this—

accumulate money and gain power and prestige that the money provided." Later that same day, U.S. Justice Department officials announced a similar indictment of the two lawyers on federal charges. Attorney General William Barr said that Clifford and Altman had "enriched themselves through secret financial arrangements with BCCI, which resulted in millions of dollars of profits to them, and then conspired to keep those arrangements from the federal regulators."

After pleading not guilty in a New York City courtroom, the superlawyer who played poker with Harry Truman and Winston Churchill the night before Churchill's famous "Iron Curtain" speech had his fingerprints taken. "They do it two or three times on every single finger," Clifford later recalled. He was then photographed for mug shots before being recorded as a charged felon and released without bail.

Clifford's personal assets were immediately frozen. When he tried to pay the chauffeur who drove him to the airport to fly back to Washington with a credit card, the card was rejected because of the asset freeze. He later suffered the embarrassment of having a check to his lawn boy bounce. Altman's assets were also frozen. To pay their lawyers, doctors, personal staffs, or other basic expenses, Clifford and Altman had to appear before a judge to get permission to use fragments of their own money.

The spurious nature of the charges against Clifford and Altman were evident from Morgenthau's admission after the indictments were returned that the supposed fraud "had virtually no direct cost to citizens of the United States." Just as Morgenthau had no evidence of any victims, he had no evidence that a crime had occurred—just a theory. The theory itself was based on rank speculation.

The charges did not arise from complaints from First American's many depositors. In contrast to hundreds of financial institutions across the country during the 1980s, First American was successful, primarily because of Clifford's and

Altman's stewardship. Besides improving bank services and expanding into new markets, creative television advertisements in which Clifford appeared persuaded thousands of customers to switch their bank accounts to First American. Consequently, bank assets grew from $2.2 billion to more than $11 billion. To this day, no federal or state regulatory authority or independent authority has ever found any evidence of money laundering or other financial improprieties at First American. Neither U.S. taxpayers nor depositors lost a cent during Clifford's and Altman's nine-year tenure.

Despite an investigation that cost taxpayers over $20 million, once the prosecutors' rhetoric dissipated, the indictments merely theorized that several legal and unremarkable individual transactions that Clifford and Altman had engaged in were linked by a massive conspiracy of fraud and bribery.

In contrast to murder mysteries that begin with investigators examining a dead body for clues or examining solid evidence of a killing, in this case no evidence existed that a crime had occurred or that Clifford and Altman had committed one.

Morgenthau took four months to present his theory, dressed up with forty-five witnesses and 300 exhibits that told no criminal tale. Judge John A. K. Bradley found that there was nothing to Morgenthau's bribery theory. He declared, "A careful review of the voluminous testimony and documentary evidence submitted by the people reveal no evidence of the existence of any agreement or understanding by Altman with anyone along the lines pleaded in the indictment."[5]

What had occurred was that Clifford and Altman had financed purchases of First American shares with a bank loan.

---

[5]Because Clifford had suffered a massive heart attack prior to the trial, over the objection of prosecutors his trial was severed from Altman's. After Altman was acquitted, the New York charges against Clifford were dropped. The U.S. Justice Department ultimately dropped its indictment of the two lawyers due to the absence of evidence.

The transaction was handled by the blue-chip New York law firm of Wachtell, Lipton, Rosen & Katz. The stock's subsequent sale netted Clifford $2.9 million and Altman $1.3 million, and the prosecutors interpreted this capital gain as a bribe for First American's purchase in competitive bidding of the Bank of Georgia.

Washington lawyer Richard O. Cunningham described Morgenthau's case in the August 5, 1993, *Wall Street Journal* as "an edifice built on myths, misunderstandings and self-contradictory testimony presented by questionable witnesses."

The case against Altman was so weak that his defense rested before calling any witnesses. The jury soon announced its verdict of acquittal.

However, the fact that the attempted frame-up of Clifford and Altman failed should not blind us to the fact that the indictment itself discarded the sacred right of Englishmen that shields citizens from indictments based on speculation. That an establishment figure like Clark Clifford can be indicted on the basis of a prosecutor's speculation should cause every American to shudder.

In the aftermath of O. J. Simpson's acquittal for murder in October 1995, commentators such as Michael Lind of the *New Republic* have called for the abolition of the jury system. Lind says that it is "time to junk" the ancient Anglo-Saxon institution, which he derides as "barbaric." On the contrary, Robert Altman's acquittal underscores the jury's critical importance as a check on tyranny. Barbara Conry, the jury foreman, said later, "I felt insulted by the prosecutor's case." Another juror, IRS employee Ricardo Palacio, told reporters that Altman "was innocent from the start, from the very first witness."

A lingering question from the Clifford and Altman travesty is how many other defendants did Robert Morgenthau successfully frame during his long tenure as a New York prosecutor? If there is a fault with the jury system, it is that prosecutors are not punished for bringing phony charges and suborning perjury to "prove" them. The jury in the Altman trial should have been allowed to express its contempt for Morgenthau's case by indicting him. Few things are more despicable in a free society than public officials who misuse their power and abuse citizens.

If prosecutors were to bear a risk similar to medical malpractice for bringing unjustified cases to court, there might be a more efficient use of prosecutorial resources. Novel theories of criminality would lose their attraction, and prosecutors might focus their attention on crimes for which they had real evidence. Until reforms are implemented to crack down on corrupt prosecutors, citizens less prominent than Clark Clifford can be prosecuted on the basis of theories.

The Case of Benjamin Lacy

CONSIDER, FOR EXAMPLE, the grim tale of the U.S. Justice Department's frame-up of a seventy-three-year-old apple juice producer, Benjamin Lacy, in Linden, Virginia. The story begins on October 7, 1994—one month before the Democratic Party lost its forty-year control of Congress—at the confirmation hearing of Lois J. Schiffer, President Bill Clinton's nominee as assistant attorney general for environmental and natural resources. To get confirmed, Ms. Schiffer had to promise to Democratic senators that she would round up some small-business white-collar criminals.

Most businessmen are honest; they have to be to maintain the trust of suppliers, customers, and employees. If prosecutors need to fill a quota of white-collar criminals, they must find businessmen to frame. Dispensing with the principle that there can be no crime without intent has made it easier for them to fill their quotas for categories of crimes.

In Mr. Lacy's case, mistakes he made in filling out waste-water report forms became in the hands of prosecutors evidence of a conspiracy to mislead the government with fraudulent information. Federal prosecutors theorized that Lacy's mistakes were evidence that he was covering up the pollution of a stream. However, they did not present any evidence of pollution and kept out of court evidence that the stream was not polluted. The pollution aspect of the case turned on the prosecutor's surmise, not on any factual evidence.

The mistakes on Mr. Lacy's reports can be explained, but not by a conspiracy. The reports were due before the written results could come back from the testing lab, so the lab would read the results over the phone, and they would be entered on the forms. On a few occasions over a multi-year period, incorrect numbers were entered. The vast majority of the reports were accurate, and there was no evidence of systematic misreporting in order to cover up unlawful behavior.

However, the facts fell to the prosecutors' theory, and innocuous mistakes were treated as fraud despite the absence of any purpose. As the stream itself is pristine, Mr. Lacy's conviction is akin to convicting a person of murdering someone who everyone knows to be alive and well. What happened to Mr. Lacy can happen to anyone now that the principles of *mens rea*—no crime without intent—and *actus rea*—evidence of a criminal act—have been breached by prosecutors.

The Attack on Mens Rea

THE LOSS OF the Rights of Englishmen did not happen overnight. Just as shifts of arctic glaciers cannot be detected by the untrained eye but compound together over time to build pressure for sudden avalanches of ice, the threats to the Rights of Englishmen have been forming for decades. In his nineteenth-century treatise *New Commentaries on the Criminal*

Law, Joel Prentiss Bishop explained infringements of the principle that "there can be no crime, large or small, without an evil mind" as temporary events: "The calm judgment of mankind keeps this doctrine among its jewels. In times of excitement when vengeance takes the place of justice, every guard around the innocent is cast down. But with the return of reason comes the public voice that where the mind is pure, he who differs in act from his neighbors does not offend."

In the twentieth century, however, judges have chiseled enough exceptions to the precept that this right of Englishmen has become a shadow of its former self. In 1910, the Supreme Court permitted the criminal prosecution of Minnesota's Shevlin-Carpenter Lumber Company for cutting down timber on state lands without a valid permit. A state official had renewed the permit but had no authority to do so. In what Stanford law professor Herbert L. Packer called "an example of constitutional adjudication at its worst," the Supreme Court unanimously rejected the company's appeal to the ancient precept that there can be no crime without intent. Justice Joseph McKenna argued that "public policy may require that in the prohibition or punishment of particular acts it may be provided that he who shall do them shall do them at his peril and will not be heard to plead in defense good faith or ignorance."

Twelve years later the Supreme Court ruled that intent was not a necessary ingredient in the commission of a criminal act if the law's purpose is the "achievement of some social betterment." In 1943 the Supreme Court upheld a conviction of the president of a pharmaceutical distribution company for shipping adulterated products in interstate commerce because a shipping clerk accidentally put old labels on two boxes of prescription drugs sent to medical doctors. The drugs were safe, and the old labels hardly differed from new labels—the name of one ingredient changed. The Court ruled that legislation dealing with actions that endanger the lives and health of people "dispenses with the conventional requirement for criminal conduct—awareness of some wrongdoing."

Three justices dissented, stressing that "it is a fundamental principle of Anglo-Saxon jurisprudence that guilt is personal and that it ought not lightly to be imputed to a citizen who, like the respondent, has no evil intention or consciousness of wrongdoing."

Justice Felix Frankfurter justified the Court's decision by appealing to faith in the fairness of government agents: "The good sense of prosecutors, the wise guidance of trial judges, and the ultimate judgment of juries must be trusted. Criminal justice necessarily depends on 'conscience and circumspection in prosecuting officers.'"

Frankfurter's confidence in prosecutors was, perhaps, justified in the 1940s. Only three years before, Attorney General Robert Jackson had given a speech underscoring the moral imperative that prosecutors pursue justice rather than "statistics of success." Only then is the citizen's safety secure, Jackson stated. Six decades have passed since Jackson's famous speech. Jackson's twenty-one successors have not succeeded in keeping alive his eloquent emphasis on the principle of prosecutorial fairness. Instead, attorney general after attorney general, Republican and Democrat, has given countless speeches bragging about successes in getting convictions. The quest for justice and solicitude for fairness toward citizens is a forgotten topic at the Department of Justice.

The twentieth century has witnessed decimation of *mens rea* in the chambers of the Supreme Court. "The onus for the erosion of *mens rea* rests on the courts," wrote Herbert L. Packer in his 1962 *Supreme Court Review* article, "Mens Rea and the Supreme Court." Justice Robert Jackson, who gained familiarity with totalitarian corruption of criminal law as the Nuremberg prosecutor of Nazi war crimes, attempted to contain the erosion in 1952. But the swath cut through the law by predecessors was too large.

Jackson did succeed in getting the Supreme Court to unanimously reverse the conviction of a man wrongly accused of stealing government property. Joseph Edward Morissette, a World War II veteran, was deer hunting on uninhabited wooded land in Michigan in December 1948. During the war, the air force had used part of the land as a bombing range, dropping simulated bombs on various targets. Following the test bombings, the metal remains of simulated bombs were rounded up and thrown into heaps to rust. The air force abandoned the region and the remains after the war. Morissette took some of the abandoned bomb casings to Flint, Michigan, where he sold them for $84.

Zealous prosecutors succeeded in getting Morissette convicted for "unlawfully, willfully and knowingly steal[ing] and convert[ing]" property of the United States in the value of $84. He was subject to either two months' imprisonment or a $200 fine. The Supreme Court's reversal of Morissette's conviction hinged upon the fact that the trial judge had rejected his defense that he believed that the casings were cast-off and abandoned and that he did not intend to steal any property. "That is no defense," the trial judge insisted upon ruling that Morissette could not explain his innocent mistake to the jury.

Jackson's thirty-page opinion gave a history of *mens rea*, emphasizing its importance. He wrote, "The contention that an injury can amount to a crime only when inflicted by intention is no provincial or transient notion. It is as universal and persistent in mature systems of law as belief in freedom of the human will and a consequent ability and duty of the normal individual to choose between good and evil." He rejected the government's position that Morissette's intent was irrelevant:

> The Government asks us by a feat of construction radically to change the weights and balances in the scales of justice. The

purpose and obvious effect of doing away with the requirement of a guilty intent is to ease the prosecution's path to
conviction, to strip the defendant of such benefit as he derived
at common law from innocence of evil purpose, and to cir-
cumscribe the freedom heretofore allowed juries. Such a
manifest impairment of the immunities of the individual
should not be extended to common-law crimes on judicial
initiative.

Mr. Morissette won his case, but as so often happens,
others in his position did not. In the 1957 case of *Lambert v.
California*, Justice William O. Douglas demonstrated the sorry
condition of what was once considered "a sacred principle of
criminal jurisprudence" when he cavalierly dismissed William
Blackstone: "We do not go with Blackstone in saying that 'a
vicious will' is necessary to constitute a crime."

Harvard legal scholar Henry M. Hart, Jr., was horrified by
the destruction of *mens rea*. In a 1958 article, "The Aims of the
Criminal Law," published in *Law and Contemporary Problems*,
Hart said that the Warren Court's increasing concern about
criminal procedure was meaningless without *mens rea*. He
asked,

> What sense does it make to insist upon procedural safeguards
> in criminal prosecutions if anything whatever can be made a
> crime in the first place? What sense does it make to prohibit
> ex post facto laws (to take one explicit guarantee of the
> Federal Constitution on the substantive side) if a man can, in
> any event, be convicted of an infamous crime for inadvertent
> violation of a prior law of the existence of which he had no
> reason to know and which he had no reason to believe he was
> violating, even if he had known of its existence?

The indictments of Ben Lacy, Clark Clifford, Robert
Altman, Charles Keating, and Exxon attest to the injustice that

results when the precept that "there can be no crime without intent" is abandoned. More Americans seem destined to experience the use of law as weapon.

CHAPTER FIVE

RETROACTIVE LAW

THE *MENS REA* REQUIREMENT rules out ex post facto laws, because if an act was legal when it took place, the actor could not have intentionally engaged in illegal conduct. If Nikolai Bukharin had had protection against retroactive laws, his alleged acts prior to the October Revolution would have been irrelevant to the question of whether he had violated Soviet law, because no such sovereign law existed at that time.

Retroactive law is anathema to the Rights of Englishmen. Henry de Bracton, a twelfth-century English jurist, said that in every case "time is to be taken into account, since every new law ought to impose a form upon future matters, and not upon things past." Sir Edward Coke restated Bracton's counsel in the oft-repeated maxim that "A new state of the law ought to affect the future, not the past." Because it is "cruel and unjust" to punish someone for an act that was not illegal at the time it was committed, William Blackstone said that "all laws must therefore be made to commence" *in futuro*—in the future.

Retroactive law also offended popular sensibilities. In *Leviathan*, Thomas Hobbes listed the maxims "Where no civil law is, there is no crime" and "Nothing can be made a crime by a law made after the fact" as precepts of a just commonwealth. Even before the addition of the Bill of Rights, the U.S.

Constitution forbade both Congress (Article I, Section 9) and the states (Article I, Section 10) to enact ex post facto laws.

These prohibitions were bulwarks of the American constitutional order. The Philadelphia essayist Rusticus wrote in the September 7, 1785, *Freeman's Journal* that "ex post facto laws are poison to free constitutions, and pregnant with calamity to the community." On October 21, 1787, Tench Coxe wrote in his pamphlet *Examination of the Constitution for the United States of America*, "Laws, made after the commission of the fact, have been a dreadful engine in the hands of tyrannical governors. Some of the most virtuous and shining characters in the world have been put to death, by laws formed to render them punishable, for parts of their conduct which innocence permitted, and to which patriotism impelled them. These have been called *ex post facto laws*, and are exploded by the new system."

Paley's Principles of Moral Philosophy, a popular primer in the eighteenth century, stated,

> If laws do not punish an offender, let him go unpunished; let the legislature, admonished of the defect of the laws, provide against the commission of future crimes of the same sort— The escape of one delinquent can never produce so much harm to the community, as may arise from the infraction of a rule, upon which the purity of public justice, and the existence of civil liberty essentially depend.

The prohibitions against retroactive law remain in the Constitution's text, but they are not legally enforced. Retroactive liability is alive and well. The damage began in 1797, when the Supreme Court avoided interfering with the Connecticut legislature's resolution of an estate conflict by asserting in *Calder v. Bull* that the ex post facto clauses applied only to criminal, not civil, statutes.

The Court undoubtedly viewed monetary losses from retroactive civil liability to be less harsh than imprisonment or execution for ex post facto crimes. But as Oliver Wendell Holmes observed, a man's property "can't be displaced without cutting at his life." In 1829, Justice William Johnson, upset at being trapped by the "unhappy" precedent "that the phrase 'ex post facto,' in the constitution of the United States, was confined to criminal cases exclusively," protested *Calder v. Bull's* ruling. Justice Johnson accurately noted that "the policy and reason of the prohibition to pass ex post facto laws, does extend to civil as well as to criminal cases" and traced the simultaneous usage of the principle from ancient Rome throughout English history to America's founding.

Despite scholarly support for Justice Johnson's position, such as University of Chicago law professor William Winslow Crosskey's definitive 1947 *University of Chicago Law Review* article, "The True Meaning of the Constitutional Prohibition of Ex-Post-Facto Laws," *Calder v. Bull's* false distinction continues, tricking unwary aspiring lawyers as they are taking the bar exam. Over the years, some Supreme Court justices have tried to ameliorate the unfairness of this inconsistency, but without lasting success.

Justice Stephen Field said in the 1866 *Cummings v. Missouri* decision that the ex post facto law clause cannot be evaded by "giving a civil form to that which is in substance criminal." The Court then struck down a Roman Catholic priest's conviction for preaching without having taken Missouri's post–Civil War oath that required all people in positions of "honor, trust, or profit" to deny ever rebelling against the Union "by act or word." Field noted that "it was no offence against any law to enter or leave the State of Missouri for the purpose of avoiding enrollment or draft in the military service of the United States, however much the evasion of such service might be the subject of moral censure."

Missouri's oath requirement therefore constituted an ex post facto law, because it imposed a punishment for an act not punishable at the time it was committed.

However, the fact that retroactive civil laws have been overturned in certain circumstances as infringements of due process has not restored the force of law to the constitutional prohibition against ex post facto law. In 1994, the Supreme Court upheld a retroactive tax increase enacted in December 1987. Justice Antonin Scalia lamented that "the reasoning the Court applies to uphold the statute in this case guarantees that *all* retroactive tax laws will henceforth be valid."

Little has changed since Charles B. Hochman's 1960 survey in the *Harvard Law Review*, "The Supreme Court and the Constitutionality of Retroactive Legislation." Hochman concluded that the constitutionality of a retroactive statute depends upon a variety of policy considerations that are based on nebulous measures of the public interest. Until *Calder v. Bull*'s rank expediency is overruled, subjective policy will continue to uphold retroactive civil liability, with disastrous results for citizens.

Superfund

DISRESPECT FOR THE prohibition against retroactive, or ex post facto, liability was evident in a lame-duck session of Congress in November and December 1980. Ronald Reagan had just swept President Jimmy Carter out of the White House and Republicans into control of the U.S. Senate on a platform of lower taxes, strong defense, and less burdensome government regulation. The *Washington Post* predicted that "new Republican strength in the Senate" would "doom toxic Superfund." Indeed, one of the bill's sponsors, liberal senator John C. Culver (D-Iowa), had just been defeated in the GOP tidal wave. Carter's environmental goal, "the so-called 'superfund' to finance cleanup of toxic waste dumps is apparently dead," the *Post* reported. But then something happened.

President Carter asked Senate Minority Leader Howard Baker (R-Tennessee) to exempt Superfund (the popular name for CERCLA—the Comprehensive Environmental Response, Compensation, and Liability Act) from his decision to keep all controversial bills off the Senate floor until the new Congress. Republican leadership cooperated with the defeated Democrat and helped enact the most far-reaching retroactive legislation in our history. Lawmakers chose to grandstand on an issue and gave no thought to the fundamental rights of Americans. Superfund has done little for the environment, but it is responsible for massive injustices and a growing disrespect for law.

Troubled by the "Superfund Superrush," a *Wall Street Journal* editorial warned that "the superfund bill may even be, as its proponents have it, the most important environmental legislation of the Eighties. But if so, it's worth spending the time to get it right. We certainly do not need one last gasp of the open-ended, no-costs-barred approach the electorate rejected in turning out this Congress and voting in a quite different one." A *Washington Star* editorial cautioned that "the frenzied atmosphere of a lame-duck session is not the climate in which to translate urgency into law." But these caveats were lost in the fray.

The Reagan transition team was, publicly at least, silent on the issue. Former EPA economist Fred L. Smith, Jr., wrote in 1988 that "President-elect Reagan might well have prevailed upon Senate Republicans to block this bill. For whatever reason, he did not." Perhaps Reagan's advisors feared beginning his administration with an issue that Democrats could use to portray Republicans as unconcerned about the environment.

Superfund has been widely criticized by the judges faced with interpreting it. Judicial opinions refer to CERCLA as "a hastily drawn piece of compromise legislation, marred by vague terminology" and as "hastily and inadequately drafted" with a "sketchy" or "non-existent" legislative history. And for good reason.

The bill was the product of private and off-the-record discussions between twenty-five to thirty senators representing different interests and with varying understandings of what was being accomplished. The compromise bill lacked traditional records such as committee reports, bill markups, or hearing transcripts. Frank P. Grad summarized CERCLA's shrouded origins in his treatise, *Environmental Law:*

> Although Congress had worked on "Superfund" cleanup of toxic and hazardous waste bills, and on parallel oil spill bills for over three years, the actual bill which became Public Law No. 96-510 had virtually no legislative history at all, because the bill which became law was hurriedly put together by a bipartisan leadership group of Senators—with some assistance of their House counterparts—introduced and passed by the Senate in lieu of all pending measures on the subject. It was then placed before the House, in the form of a Senate amendment of the earlier House bill. It was considered on December 3, 1980, in the closing days of the lame duck session of an outgoing Congress. It was considered and passed, after very limited debate, under a suspension of the rules, in a situation which allowed for no amendments. Faced with a complicated bill on a take-it or leave-it basis, the House took it, groaning all the way.

One groaning congressman was William Howard Harsha (R-Ohio), who declared after noting the bill's inconsistency and ambiguity on the simple question of liability, "This bill is not a Superfund bill—it is a welfare relief act for lawyers."

At 9:45 A.M. on December 11, 1980, Jimmy Carter opened the signing ceremony in the White House Cabinet Room. In addition to praising the bill's main sponsors, Senators Jennings Randolph (D-West Virginia) and Robert Stafford (R-Vermont) and Representative James Florio (D-New Jersey), the lame-duck president lauded Minority Leaders Howard Baker and John Rhodes (R-Arizona) "for making this a bipartisan project, succeeding in this effort even after the election of this year." Carter also honored DuPont chairman Irving Shapiro, whose support had neutralized initial industry opposition. Before picking up his pen, Carter said that he took "great pleasure" in signing Superfund into law and declared the legislation a "landmark in its scope and in its impact on preserving the environmental quality of our country." Carter said that the "most important" aspect of the bill was that "it enables the Government to recover from responsible parties the costs of their actions in the disposal of toxic wastes." This statement has proven to be pure fantasy.

Several members of Congress had urged passage of the bill by referring to "ticking time bombs" of toxic waste, but the real time bomb was CERCLA's acidic impact on the protection against retroactive liability. His House colleagues did not want to hear it when Representative David Stockman (R-Michigan) warned that Superfund meant that someday soon they would "receive a letter from a company in their district that has just received a $5 million or $10 million liability suit that was triggered by nothing more than a decision of a GS-14 that some landfill, some disposal site, somewhere, needed to be cleaned up and, as a result of an investigation that his office did, he found out that that company contributed a few hundred pounds of waste to that site 30 years ago."

CERCLA essentially declared that the EPA would identify hazardous toxic waste dumps for cleanup across the country. Receipts from a special tax on crude oil, imported petroleum products, and basic chemicals, as well as general revenues, would finance a $1.6 billion "Superfund" to underwrite EPA's cleanup of the dumps. Then, applying the "polluter pays" principle, EPA would recover cleanup costs from so-called responsible parties. But the statute never demarcated who these liable parties might be. Environmental lawyer Karin Oliva wrote in the July 1995 *Southern California Law Review* that "the most notable and detrimental result of the compromise was the absence of a clear definition of the parameters of liability."

Reagan administration lawyers encouraged courts to fill this liability void with "strict, joint and several, retroactive liability"—though these words do not appear in the statute. This meant total, rather than proportionate, retroactive liability for parties who were connected with the waste dumps in any way prior to the passage of Superfund, regardless of the legality of their actions at the time they occurred. In 1991, George Clemon Freeman, Jr., chairman of the business law section of the American Bar Association, said Superfund's retroactive liability is "without any precedent in the civilized or uncivilized world." Moreover, as Freeman wrote in the February 1995 *Business Lawyer,* "It is ironic that it was the Reagan administration's EPA that persuaded a number of courts to engage in judicial activism by marching into the void where Congress feared to tread."

Alfred R. Light begins his 1991 treatise, *CERCLA: Law and Procedure,* with this observation: "To understand the Superfund Act, first purge your mind of conventional notions of justice." To make his point, Light hypothesizes that in the early nineteenth century Benjamin Franklin gave Thomas Jefferson a French pot made of iron and copper, which Jefferson stored in an underground compartment at Monticello, near Charlottesville, Virginia.

During the Civil War, valuables were stored in the pot. But Union cavalry led by Phil Sheridan invaded Monticello and seized the pot. Sheridan gave a receipt to one of Jefferson's servants attesting to the pot's change in title. The pot made its way to Fort McNair, in Washington, D.C., where it was stored for more than a century in a concrete shed near military stables. The pot did not rust and maintained perfect condition.

In the late 1970s, excavations near the stables found significant quantities of "Agent Purple," a hazardous substance used in the Vietnam conflict, in the ground. How it got there no one knew, but the pot was considered to be refuse, and it was identified as having once belonged to Jefferson.

Professor Light then asks whether the EPA could hold former president Jefferson (or his heirs) totally liable under the 1980 Superfund law for the cleanup of "Agent Purple's" hazardous waste dump on the grounds that a pot that had once belonged to him had found its way into a contaminated site. Light answers his own question: "Under well-established CER-CLA precedents, Jefferson loses his motion" to dismiss the lawsuit. He adds, "Some real-life CERCLA fact situations rival this fantasy in apparent absurdity." CERCLA, Light says, simply throws out "the basic principles of fair play and substantial justice underlying the American system of jurisprudence."

Superfund has made it economically dangerous to own land, finance its purchase, or insure assets that can be linked in any way to waste sites. University of Chicago Richard Epstein says that Superfund's imposition of retroactive liability "makes it an act of heroism to purchase a site, or worse still, to accept it as a charitable gift." A September 2, 1993, *Washington Post* editorial, "Time to Reform Superfund," said that Superfund is "generating intolerable injustices" that give "a bad name to a good cause."

Superfund has cleaned up few sites, but it has enriched lawyers[1] by ruining many small businesses and depleting the life savings of many ordinary people who could be connected, however remotely, with waste disposal practices that were legal at the time they occurred. It has also hurt shareholders in large

---

[1] A 1994 General Accounting Office survey of Fortune 500 corporations, "SUPERFUND: Legal Expenses for Cleanup-Related Activities of Major U.S. Corporations," found that litigation expenses eat up roughly one-third of Superfund cleanup costs. A 1993 *Time* article labeled Superfund sites "The Lawyer's Money Pit."

companies, banks, and insurance companies that have been arbitrarily assigned retroactive liability by federal bureaucrats and courts.

For example, banks that foreclosed on businesses linked to waste sites have been held liable, as have insurance companies that insured truck fleets. The liability is so broadly defined that anyone who used a contaminated site, regardless of whether their refuse was a contaminant, is forced to pay damages. One sign painter had to pay because wood scrap from his signs found its way to a site. A contractor was forced to pay because his broken bricks were found on a site later declared to contain hazardous waste.

The same happened to a pizzeria, identified by its discarded cardboard boxes. The archdiocese of Newark, New Jersey, bought a piece of vacant land in order to expand its cemetery and found itself involved in a $25 million lawsuit over decades-old waste found on the site.

EPA's effort to pin cleanup costs on a New Jersey gas company for a site polluted in the 1880s, one hundred years before the passage of the Superfund law, has created the new field of "insurance archaeologists." These specialists attempt to unearth how liability might be assigned on the basis of leases held by corporate predecessors who had no idea that they were violating a law that would be passed a hundred years after their time.

Private creditors of bankrupt companies often bear the Superfund cleanup costs, because courts have given EPA claims priority status that trump private claims in bankruptcy proceedings. Gas stations and automobile dealerships have been held liable for cleanup costs stemming from past disposal of old motor oil and batteries. Landlords have been held liable for not preventing acts of tenants before the actions became illegal.

In the EPA's ever expanding quest for "deep pockets," employees of waste disposal companies have been interrogated by government lawyers in order to conjure up memories of the sources and destinations of trash they supposedly hauled decades before. EPA treats these vague recollections as suffi cient evidence of absolute liability. One concrete materials company in Madera, California, never sent oil or anything else to the Purity Oil Superfund site and has documents to prove it. The company used its waste oil for dust control in its concrete yard and donated any excess to local farmers for use between vineyard rows, a common practice. Yet the government is holding the family-owned firm liable for the cleanup of as much as 48,000 gallons of oil based on the assumption that the company must have used the site.

An iron and metal works in Milwaukee, Wisconsin, has been declared a "potentially responsible party" for the cleanup of a toxic landfill, because the name of the firm's president was listed in the address book of a deceased landfill operator. Although the landfill closed in 1975, one former employee thinks the iron and metal works was a hauler. The iron and metal works occasionally purchased scrap metals from the landfill, rather than depositing waste there, but EPA lawyers remained intransigent, forcing the firm to settle for $15,000 after spending $50,000 in legal expenses. An individual in Wyoming found himself a potentially responsible party because he had sold bags of dog food and seed and had accepted a third-party check as payment. He was caught in Superfund's liability web because the check had been issued by a battery-cracking plant, retroactively deemed to be a polluter, that ultimately was bankrupted by CERCLA.

A log hauler in Tacoma, Washington, faces $1 million of liability because in the late 1970s the company used smelter slag in its operations on rented land. At that time, the slag was considered to be an environmentally safe, practical, and cost-effective product, but EPA now considers it to be a hazardous pollutant. Because the rented parcel was after the fact defined to be part of a large Superfund site, the company has been forced to contribute $145,000 toward cleanup after spending $160,000 in legal fees. Speaking for many small business people who are subject to EPA legal extortion, the log hauler's vice president said, "It's impossible to operate a small business if the potential liability exists retroactively for actions that are lawful, ethical and generally accepted practices when they are performed."

Congress permitted Superfund to snap the constitutional pillar against retroactive law because of public hysteria over toxic wastes that stemmed from the "discovery" in 1978 that the Love Canal housing development in Niagara Falls, New York, was built over a toxic waste dump. The canal itself had been dug in the 1890s by entrepreneur William Love as part of a failed hydroelectric project. During World War II, Hooker Chemical, a subsidiary of Occidental Petroleum, thought that because the canal's clay-lined walls were leakproof and the area was sparsely populated, it would be an ideal place for a chemical dump. Between 1941 and 1953, Hooker deposited 21,800 tons of chemical waste into the 3,200-foot-long ditch. The U.S. Army also disposed of toxic chemicals into Hooker's dump during this period.

In the postwar baby boom, the Niagara Falls School Board eyed the site as an inexpensive location for a new school and exerted pressure on Hooker to relinquish the property or face condemnation under the writ of eminent domain. In 1952, Hooker donated the property for $1 to the school board along with a written warning that the buried chemical wastes might prove harmful if the canal's clay walls and cover were broken. In 1957, before the school board sold part of the site to a housing developer, Hooker protested.[2] As reported in the November 8, 1957, *Niagara Gazette*, Hooker's lawyer, Arthur Chambers, acknowledging "a certain moral responsibility in

---

[2]Because of these warnings and Hooker's compliance with "available knowledge and industry practice at the time," a federal court rejected New York State's attempt to fine Hooker Chemicals $250,000 in punitive damages in 1994. "In general, given the state of scientific knowledge and the legal principles of that time," District Judge John T. Curtin ruled, Hooker "did not exhibit the degree of recklessness which would warrant a punitive damages award."

the disposition of the land," warned the board that the land near the canal site was "unsuitable for construction in which basements, water lines, sewers, and such underground facilities would be necessary."

After decades of exactly such construction, noxious substances began seeping out of the ground in the late 1970s, catalyzing mass media hysteria. Actress Jane Fonda visited the area. With tears streaming from her eyes, she called for the evacuation of local residents. In October 1979, public television ran a documentary, *A Plague on Our Children*, which featured a Love Canal segment. *Today, Sixty Minutes, The MacNeil-Lehrer Report, Donahue*, and *Good Morning America* followed suit. The EPA leaked bogus reports warning of human cancer risks and chromosome damage in the region. In May 1980, President Carter declared an emergency at Love Canal and ordered the relocation of 700 families and earmarked $15 million in federal grants and loans for relocated Love Canal residents. Love Canal quickly symbolized a national toxic waste crisis. As Carter EPA administrator Douglas M. Costle recounted in 1985, "Love Canal became so powerful in the national consciousness we were able to pass the superfund bill even after Carter was defeated, and that's an extraordinary action to do in a 'lame duck' administration."

The rush to pass Superfund ignored the fact that the alleged health risks at Love Canal were exaggerated. As Marc K. Landy, Marc J. Roberts, and Stephen R. Thomas noted in their 1994 study, *The Environmental Protection Agency: Asking the Wrong Questions from Nixon to Clinton*, during the Love Canal crisis, "a scientific Gresham's Law was at work. Poorly constructed, poorly presented studies drove out more careful and scrupulous research." The dire warnings in faulty reports captured headlines, but their refutations did not. "Then, as now," the authors state, "no reliable epidemiological studies showed that area residents were subject to greater health risks than the population at large." A June 13, 1980, *Science* article,

"Love Canal: False Alarm Caused by Botched Study," stated, "In the opinion of many experts, the chromosome damage study ordered by the EPA has close to zero scientific significance." A June 19, 1981, *Science* article, "Cancer Incidence in the Love Canal Area," stated that "data from the New York Cancer Registry show no evidence for higher cancer rates associated with residence near the Love Canal toxic waste burial site in comparison with the entire state outside of New York City."

And so the scientific story has continued. A 1991 study by the National Research Council "kicked the chair out from under the toxic-waste emergency," wrote Gregg Easterbrook in *A Moment on the Earth: The Coming Age of Environmental Optimism*, by debunking the purported relationship between proximity to toxic wastes and cancer. Indeed, supposedly unsafe Superfund sites have become wildlife preserves. In 1992, liberal congresswoman Patricia Schroeder (D-Colorado) proposed declaring the Rocky Mountain Arsenal—a Superfund site—a national wildlife refuge because the former military explosives manufacturing center had become home to eagles, peregrine falcons, white-tail and mule deer, pheasants, and geese. According to Easterbrook, environmental activists worked to scuttle Schroeder's bill, because green lobbyists realized that making a "deadly place" a sanctuary for endangered species would expose the successful hoax.

Huge sums of money paid by innocent people have not made the world an environmentally safer place. W. Kip Viscusi and James T. Hamilton observe in a Summer 1996 *Public Interest* article, "Cleaning Up Superfund," that Superfund's "cleanup expenditures have not delivered much reduction in risk." Justice Stephen Breyer's 1993 book, *Breaking the Vicious Cycle*, criticizes costly EPA standards that require, in effect, sites to be so clean that children can safely eat the dirt. A New Hampshire EPA cleanup required a $9.3 million expenditure so that children would be able to eat without harm small amounts of dirt daily for 245 days per year. But even worse than the economic waste is the damage to our legal system. Superfund has separated liability from blame and destroyed the connection between law and justice.

It is foolish to think that this return of tyranny can be confined to civil offenses. Already prosecutors are using novel theories to create retroactive criminal offenses in total defiance of the constitutional prohibition of ex post facto law. Exercising this power prosecutors have transformed courts of law into torture chambers.

CHAPTER SIX

REINVENTING TORTURE

THE FUNCTION OF justice is to serve truth. The moral authority of a justice system depends on its achieving this goal. Consequently, the foremost task of a justice system is to establish the truth or falsity of the charges levied against the accused. The sincere concern with justice kept truth foremost in the minds of seventeenth-century English jurists. Matthew Hale, for example, insisted that truth should never be "choak'd and suppress'd" and that the justice of legal processes depended on their reliability in "searching and sifting out the truth."

The emphasis on truth protects the innocent. The aversion against sentencing an innocent person is well expressed by the ancient legal maxim that "it were better to acquit twenty that are guilty than to condemn one innocent." This is why the justice system is not designed for the convenience of prosecutors and police. Conviction is made difficult in order to protect the innocent. As we will see, the safeguards that protect the innocent are bypassed by plea bargains.

The quest for truth is rarely mentioned as the primary purpose of the justice system today. Cracking down on crime, increasing conviction rates, prosecuting elusive white-collar criminality, giving law enforcement the "tools it needs," putting more police on the streets, righting economic wrongs, and remedying discrimination are the ends of justice today. Rarely do we hear pundits pondering whether or not legal procedures enhance the "true and clear Discovery of Truth."

The quest for truth became the focus of trials in the seventeenth century because English courts wanted no part in sentencing innocent people to death or subjecting them to public humiliation. They respected people's reputations, and English judges wanted no innocent blood on their conscience or their tribunals. Their abhorrence of convicting the innocent was reinforced by the religious beliefs of the age, such as accountability before God in the afterlife, and bad experiences with arbitrary judicial practices, such as Star Chamber proceedings in which due process and evidentiary standards were absent.

This fear of convicting the innocent reflected the insight, gained from experience, that when evidence and witnesses are subjected to the light of a public trial, people who were previously considered to be obviously guilty can sometimes be revealed to be completely innocent. When this happened, it did not take much imagination for individual jurists, lawyers, members of the jury, and citizens at large to see themselves in the shoes of the person whose name had been besmirched with false accusations. These sobering moments elevated in their minds the role of law as a shield against injustice.

When the focus of justice is the pursuit of truth, often those found guilty can respect the process that led to their convictions. The respect that a fair trial shows to those who have breached societal norms can promote their rehabilitation. This contrasts with the manipulation of the plea bargaining system, which promotes cynicism and alienation.

Only if the legal system actively seeks truth can society carry out the retributive and punitive aspects of justice. Otherwise, innocent people who do not deserve retribution will be treated unjustly. Moreover, if punishment is meted out bureaucratically, without concern for genuine guilt or innocence, the legal system loses its majesty.

When trials serve truth rather than the convenience of those who control law, torture and negotiated guilty pleas are excluded from the justice system as neither practice has anything to do with truth.

Preemptive guilty pleas were distrusted and inherently suspect because they created a presumption of coercion and torture and violated the maxim that "No man is bound to accuse himself"—*Nemo tenetur seipsum accusare*. Revering truth, English judges were loathe to accept guilty pleas, and they urged prisoners to retract them. Jurists presumed that only duress, torture, or unethical promises of leniency would cause a defendant to forsake a trial.

English justice contrasted with the situation in continental Europe, where, as Leonard Levy writes in *The Origins of the Fifth Amendment: The Right Against Self-Incrimination*, confessions coerced by torture "became the crux of the trial." An executioner in the German duchy of Zerb was reported in a Leipzig disputation in 1733 to have invented an instrument "which would wring a confession out of the most hardened and robust." In opposition to such brutality, legal reformers on the Continent praised England for the "goodness of her laws" that rejected torture.

English jurists recognized that a guilty plea could be provoked by needs other than the alleviation of a bad conscience. Perhaps the plea was a fraud, prompted by a bribe in which someone who was poor took the fall for the guilty party in exchange for money or advancement for his family. Maybe a minor accomplice was taking the full blame for the major acts of another who was still at large and whose wrath the minor accomplice feared. Maybe the prisoner had been confined without food and was merely seeking nourishment. Or perhaps he had been physically tortured or abused and was seeking relief. Maybe threats had been made against his wife, children, or estate. Guilty pleas in the absence of trial prevented the judicial search engine from finding out what actually had happened, thus impeding the pursuit of truth. The easy convenience of a guilty plea had the stink of malfeasance.

Jurists also took a jaundiced view of confessions that accompanied testimony against supposed accomplices. Blackstone considered the charges to be unreliable, merely "false and malicious accusations of desperate villains" that provided little "benefit to the public by the discovery and conviction of real offenders." Thus, as Albert W. Alschuler concluded in the January 1979 *Columbia Law Review*, English courts would have condemned today's practice of soliciting testimony against others in exchange for reduced charges or a lenient sentence. After studying London court records, legal historian John Beattie reported, "There was no plea bargaining in felony cases in the eighteenth century."

In the United States today, plea bargaining has displaced trial by jury as the dominant method of criminal dispute resolution. According to Justice Department statistics, 90 to 95 percent of all federal, state, and local criminal cases are settled by plea bargains.[1]

Plea bargaining has ominous implications for the Rights of Englishmen. Yale law professor and medieval legal historian John Langbein says, "The parallels between the modern American plea bargaining system and the ancient system of judicial torture are many and chilling."[2] Defendants who insist upon exercising their constitutional right to a jury trial risk a substantially increased sentence if they are convicted, and this sentencing differential alone is enough to make plea bargaining

[1]Kathleen Maguire and Ann L. Pastore, eds., *Sourcebook of Criminal Justice Statistics 1994*. U.S. Department of Justice, Bureau of Justice Statistics (Washington, D.C.: U.S. Government Printing Office, 1995), pp. 461–63, 483–86.
[2]John H. Langbein, "Torture and Plea Bargaining," *University of Chicago Law Review* 46 (Fall 1978): 8.

coercive. The hated maxim of medieval glossators (the legal theorists of torture)—*Confessio est regina probationum* ("Confession is the queen of proof")—has replaced the jury trial for the vast majority of criminal cases.

Truth is the plea bargaining process's greatest casualty. Yet, the justice system's movers and shakers—prosecutors, judges, defense lawyers—show little concern for truth. This is apparent from how the plea bargaining process works. Terror, not truth, is its hallmark.

The prosecutorial power to bring charges against a person is an awesome power. It is intimidating to those on the receiving end, who are often frightened when they experience the power of the state arrayed against them. Even people who have confidence in the system can be nervous and anxious about it.

People's ability to withstand anxiety varies. Some people thrive under pressure and stand up well. Others cannot stand the unknown and act to end the uncertainty. For people who like to control their own fates, plea bargaining is a way to escape the stress. It permits defendants to participate in shaping the charges against them as well as the punishment, and it spares them the expense of lawyers' fees for a jury trial.

For people who aren't good advocates for themselves and who are likely to fare poorly on the witness stand, a plea bargain can be a compelling option. Their confidence in their innocence has to contend with their general lack of self-confidence. Accustomed to losing arguments, they may "cop a plea" to avoid the risk of more serious punishment.

Truth is shoved aside by plea bargaining. Many Americans who are alarmed by high crime rates are critical of plea bargains because they believe that pleas let criminals off too lightly, with slaps on their wrists, thus subverting the deterrent effect of punishment. Whenever more serious crimes are reduced for lesser offenses, the justice system signals that punishment can be reduced with a plea. Thus, both deterrence and truth suffer when a lesser crime is invented in a plea bargain to take the place of the serious crime that was in fact committed. We sympathize with the public's dislike of plea bargaining, but we believe the problem is more serious than reduced deterrence.

Plea bargaining gets away from the facts. First, as is widely recognized, justice is not done when premeditated murder, for example, is reduced to a lesser charge. But, more fundamentally and perhaps less obvious, plea bargains corrupt the prosecutorial function by severing it from the discovery of truth.

The practice of having people admit to what did not happen in order to avoid charges for what did happen creates a culture that, as its develops, eventually permits prosecutors to bring charges in the absence of crimes. As a little yeast leavens the whole loaf, systematized falsehoods about crimes corrupt the entire criminal justice process.

Plea bargaining became common for pragmatic reasons, such as crowded court dockets. Given the number of crimes and the resources allocated to the justice system, it is impossible for the courts to try all the cases and comply with the constitutional requirement of a speedy trial. Plea bargaining thus evolved as an ad hoc compromise. It would have been better to increase the resources of the justice system.

Plea bargaining puts the defendant at the mercy of his lawyer's negotiating skills instead of the judgment of a jury. Ostensibly, both the defense lawyer and the prosecutor prepare the case for trial by examining physical evidence, interviewing witnesses, and scheduling court dates. In reality, however, the defense and prosecution are scoping out the strengths of their relative positions in order to arrive at a deal.

A subtle dialogue proceeds in a game of lawyer's poker. Maybe the defense attorney has a reputation for being formidable at trial. The club sitting on the defense attorney's shelf is the threat "We'll see you in court." But whenever the defense lawyer lifts the club, the prosecutor knows that his counterpart may well be bluffing. Neither side really wants a trial. Trials are costly and uncertain, take too much time and work, and interfere with everything else on each lawyer's "to do" list. Even a defendant who wants a jury trial may be pressured to the contrary by a disinclined lawyer.

In effect, collusion is going on between the prosecution and defense, and the defendant learns that if he will plead guilty to a lesser charge, the prosecution will not try to convict the defendant on the charge for which the defendant was arrested. Pressures on a defendant can be overwhelming. They are well illustrated, for example, by the defendant who told the judge (*North Carolina v. Alford*, 400 U.S. 25, 28, 1970), "I ain't shot no man, but . . . I just pleaded guilty because they said if I didn't they would gas me for it."

Many times the offer is too good for even an innocent person to resist. A person accused, already stressed out in a world of job insecurity, corporate downsizing, unsafe streets, financial worries, and family tensions, might agree to a plea just to put an end to the additional stress of dealing with the justice system.

The risks of a jury trial can appear too great to all parties. An array of unknowables increases the uncertainty of trial. Questions loom for the defendant: for instance, How good is my lawyer and how irritated will my lawyer be if I reject the plea? Some defense lawyers dislike the confrontation of trials and prefer using their skills in negotiation to butting heads with prosecutors. They hesitate to damage their relationship with a prosecutor with whom they may be negotiating future pleas.

Trials are time-consuming for defense lawyers and drain energy from the law firm that could otherwise be devoted to other clients. Moreover, a lost trial can hurt the lawyer's reputation, but a plea resulting in a reduced charge does not. The prosecutor knows this and takes it into account in arriving at an offer. Similarly, the defense attorney knows that the prosecutor cannot take every case to trial and has pressures from the judge not to let the court docket build.

Defendants assess whether they can afford to keep on paying lawyers during a trial. An indigent defendant with a public defender may wonder if the public defender, who is dependent on the court to assign him cases, has the inclination to mount a spirited defense. Judges contending with crowded dockets are inclined to assign cases to public defenders who are content to settle cases with pleas instead of taking them to trial.

In effect, coercive pressures push all parties to a settlement in which the accused admits to having committed a fictional offense in order to avoid being tried for a real one. The crime that is punished is in fact created by negotiation. Thus, the process works to create a lie that can be accepted by all parties, including the judge, who perfunctorily asks the defendant to state that no deals prompted the plea.

It is only a short step from creating a fictional crime out of a real one to creating a fictional crime out of thin air. The step isn't taken all at once. When the option of plea bargaining first surfaces, it is considered by everyone involved as a way of meting out punishment in a timely way. But with the passage of time, several things happen. As plea bargaining takes over from jury trials, little police work is tested in a courtroom before judge and jury. Prosecutors lose touch with the quality of the police investigative work that is the basis of indictments, and the police learn that their work has no more chance of a courtroom test than one in ten or one in twenty. Gradually the incentive to find a suspect becomes more compelling than the incentive to find the guilty person.

As time passed, prosecutors came to realize that serving justice is incidental to their careers and that their conviction rate is their performance indicator. A prosecutor's conviction rate can be built up by plea bargains. Ambition takes on new meaning as prosecutors learn that they can make political careers for themselves by targeting high-profile issues and high-profile people.

Plea bargaining permits prosecutors to build cases on speculation rather than on evidence. This is especially true for business and financial crimes, which are often vaguely defined and murkily understood. The prevalence of doubtful cases is also affected by social attitudes toward big corporations and Wall Street. The beliefs that "business is theft" and that white-collar crimes go undetected creates a presumption of guilt against such defendants that protects a prosecutor's trumped-up charges from public scrutiny. This strengthens the hands of prosecutors who use leaks to the media to pressure a high-profile target into a plea.

Of course, not all prosecutors indict phony cases, but some do—just as some people who were in fact innocent were tortured until they falsely incriminated themselves. Bad things do happen. Plea bargaining has unquestionably made it easier for prosecutors to abuse their power. It is to these implications we now turn.

Plea bargaining permits prosecutors to draw up indictments for which they have little or no evidence. News of a forthcoming indictment is leaked to the press to put pressure on the accused by tarring him in the eyes of his friends, family, employer, coworkers, and the general public. The charges may be largely made out of thin air, but the prosecutor benefits from the public's presumption that the prosecution has a case.

The defendant is told by his lawyer, who is often a former prosecutor, that even if a jury throws out the bulk of a massive indictment, one or two counts alone may carry severe penalties. The prosecutor can compound the pressure by leaking rumors to the press that the indictment will be expanded and that the accused's friends and family members are also being investigated. Associates of the defendant are approached by government agents, supposedly "investigating," but in reality spreading intimidation and terror.

Newspaper and television reports are based on anonymous leaks from the prosecutor's offices, preceded by the phrase "According to sources familiar with the investigation." The accused's spouse and children might find themselves criticized and ostracized by playmates, acquaintances, and fellow church, synagogue, or club members. Prosecutors declare that they will push for "maximum penalties" involving long prison sentences and huge fines. They might threaten freezes or forfeiture of the accused's assets unless the accused "cooperates" with the government. It can become too much to bear.

The resolve to keep one's name clean gives way to the desire to end a Kafkaesque travail. The prosecutor's unethical tactics might cause the defendant to give up any expectation of a fair trial. At this point, he calls his lawyer and gives his okay to working out a deal.

The lawyer assures the accused that a wise choice has been made and promises to push for a good deal. The defense lawyer, known in the trade as a "fixer," may have already been sounding out prosecutors for their conditions for a deal. The defense lawyer then leaves word with the prosecutor that the plea negotiations have been fully authorized by the defendant. The prosecutor reports the good news to the local district attorney or the regional U.S. attorney. The publicity-hungry D.A. looks forward to trumpeting another victory against crime at a press conference on the courthouse steps.

The real poker game then begins. Neither side wants to go to trial and risk a loss. The prosecutor fears losing before a liberal judge or a skeptical jury. He may have concerns about whether the accused in fact did any of the things the indictment charges. In court, this veil might be ripped. For the defense lawyer, trials require concentration and harder work than negotiating with prosecutors in a conference room. Much preparation and uncertainty go into facing the complexities of trial and relating to jurors who might be paranoid about crime or biased against the defendant. Thus, the symbiotic relationship between defense lawyers and prosecutors nurtures cooperation rather than conflict.

Against this backdrop, the lawyers, all of whom have sworn to uphold the Constitution, broker a deal. They negotiate a listing of crimes of a lesser nature that the defendant might have committed rather than the counts listed on the indictment. In exchange for dropping some charges, the defendant might agree to testify against other people on the prosecutor's hit list or go undercover to entrap prosecutorial targets into committing crimes. In order to get a guilty plea the prosecutors will promise a reduced prison sentence, incarceration in a less onerous prison, probation instead of incarceration, or lesser fines.

Once the agreement is drawn up between the lawyers, the prosecutor increases the public pressure, playing bad cop, while the defendant's lawyer encourages his client to accept the terms of the deal. The prosecutor might leak details of the plea negotiations to the press in order to stir up public concern that the defendant is getting off lightly. This permits the prosecutor to respond with a sometimes fabricated announcement that the grand jury is considering expanded charges against the defendant. This, in turn, prompts the defense attorney to stress the advantage of a quick plea.

By now, even the strongest and wealthiest people can begin to feel beaten down. Facing physical and psychological pressure akin to torture, the defendant accepts the deal, agreeing to plead guilty and waiving the constitutional right to a trial. The risk and cost of going to court seem too high. The prosecutors seem unconcerned with the truth of the case, and the government's power to make life miserable is fearsome and intimidating. Better to make the best of a bad situation than to increase the risk.

In a courtroom, crowded perhaps with tearful family members, concerned friends, and news reporters, the accused steps before the judge to give his guilty plea. The procedure might be delayed for a few minutes as the defense attorneys and prosecutors adjust the written statement of admitted offenses, called a "statement of facts," in order to tailor them to fit sentencing factors or other cases on the prosecutor's docket. Even as they come as witnesses to the plea, the defense and prosecution often are still at work negotiating the "facts."

Before accepting the plea, the judge asks the defendant for assurance that the plea was voluntary and that no deals prompted it. The judge's acceptance of the assurance underscores the complicity of all parties in the evasion of truth. As Stanford law professor Lawrence M. Friedman notes in *Crime and Punishment in American History*, the charade is a farce, "an out-and-out lie." Judges, clerks, defense lawyers, prosecutors, the defendant, and court reporters are all parties to the lie. We cannot base crime and punishment on made-up offenses and expect honesty to remain at the heart of the prosecutorial process.

By making facts malleable, plea bargaining enables prosecutors to supplement weak evidence with psychological pressure. This weapon plays a central role in their calculus. One of the masters of this art, Rudolph Giuliani, rode it to the mayoralty of New York City. While U.S. attorney for Manhattan, he boasted in congressional testimony (February 1987) that in his experience the major difference between so-called white-collar criminals and real ones is that the former "roll a lot easier." The criminal charges create "a conflict between what they appear to families, friends, co-workers, and what they're doing in the secret part of their life. It tends to move them toward confessing, putting it all behind them."

Giuliani's chilling words echo the belief of Cesare Beccaria, an eighteenth-century Italian legal theorist, that torture measures an individual's sensitivity to pain, not his guilt. Just as a medieval torturer assessed "the muscular force and nervous sensibility of an innocent person" in order to "find the degree of pain that will make him confess himself guilty of a given crime," the modern prosecutor wields the instrument of psychological torture.

Whenever a defendant "cops a plea," freedom is jeopardized along with justice. Alexander Hamilton in the *Federalist Papers* called trial by jury the "very palladium of free government." With nine out of ten cases never reaching trial, the door is opened to coercive prosecutors in the mold of Andrei Vyshinsky.

The Case of Michael Milken

GIULIANI RECOGNIZED THAT the extraordinary successes of financial upstart Michael Milken made him vulnerable. The success of his financing schemes created enormous Wall Street envy, and the use of junk bonds in hostile takeovers of corporations angered influential corporate executives. Giuliani had another ally in the ambiguousness of financial infractions. For example, "insider trading" is a regulatory creation, undefined by statutory law, that permits prosecutors to define the offense as it suits their purpose. The presumption of the man in the street was that Milken became super-rich so fast that he must have been crooked. This presumption made Milken a vulnerable target for trial in the media. It is not our purpose here to show that Milken was innocent of the charges. (Milken's innocence is examined by University of Chicago law professor Daniel Fischel in his book, *Payback: The Conspiracy to Destroy Michael Milken and His Financial Revolution.*) Here we use the Milken case to illustrate the extraction of guilty pleas by the modern instruments of torture.

Milken was a hugely successful innovator who single-handedly revolutionized financial markets. He developed a new approach to corporate finance that undercut decades of accumulated human capital. Early in his career, Milken used his mathematical genius and human intuition to study corporate financial statements, their links to the product marketplace, and the history of financial markets. He found that traditional methods of assessing the risk of corporate bonds had little connection to actual future performance and a company's ability to pay off future debt obligations.

Milken found that new companies and those able to restructure themselves often performed better than companies with investment-grade ratings that were based on past successes. Acting on this insight, Milken financed companies that traditional Wall Street investment bankers wouldn't touch. Previously, growth firms with promising futures lacked easy access to capital, because they didn't fit the profile used by commercial banks and institutional investors, who would only finance companies that had investment-grade credit rankings. Milken changed this by invigorating the high-yield bond market. Nicknamed "junk bonds" because of their uncharted credit histories, these bonds gave investors yields that were disproportionate to the risk. Household names like MCI, CNN, McCaw Cellular, Barnes & Noble, Stone Container Corporation, Time-Warner, Safeway, and Mattel were all Milken junk bond financings.

Milken's huge earnings and the profits of his employer, Drexel Burnham Lambert, ruffled Wall Street feathers. Drexel was regarded by its peers as a second-tier firm that was getting rich too fast. By 1986 it was Wall Street's most profitable firm, with revenues in excess of $4 billion and earnings of $545.5 million. Even worse, Milken operated out of Los Angeles, and New York City's establishment was skeptical of tinseltown's morals.

When not working at his X-shaped desk, Milken spent his time with his family and his philanthropy. Situated on the West Coast, he was not well known in Manhattan circles. He also neglected to build political alliances and to acquire protectors by making political contributions. Milken gave his money to organizations that help poor black children.

The liberal media did not see Milken as a "do-good" Democrat, but as the personification of Reagan-era "greed." Giuliani once bragged that by giving negative treatment to his prosecutorial targets, "the media does the job for me."[3] The Reagan administration was untroubled by Milken's travail because his prosecution was seen as a counterpoint to the charge that Republicans favor the rich.

The press shilled for Giuliani and never took a hard look at the charges. Numerous *Wall Street Journal* articles under the bylines of reporters James B. Stewart, Daniel Hertzberg, and Laurie Cohen cited unnamed government sources ("according to people familiar with the government's investigation") to create a sordid tale of "the greatest criminal conspiracy the financial world has ever known." In *Barron's*, Benjamin Stein derided the junk bond market as a "Ponzi scheme," and Connie Bruck branded Milken and his associates as the "Cosa Nostra of the securities world."

Michael Milken had the law on his side, but that wasn't enough. To this day, no evidence exists that Milken ever committed any crimes or engaged in any conduct that had ever before been considered criminal.[4] Giuliani's assistant U.S. attorney John Carroll admitted as much. At Seton Hall Law School in April 1992, Carroll said that in the Milken case "we're guilty of criminalizing technical offenses. . . . Many of the prosecution theories we used were novel. Many of the statutes that we charged under . . . hadn't been charged as crimes before. . . . We're looking to find the next areas of conduct that meets any sort of statutory definition of what criminal conduct is."

Milken was subject to the whims of regulators and prosecutors who criminalized regulatory infractions. Indeed, the Securities and Exchange Commission has categorically refused

---

[3]Quoted in Alan Dershowitz, Introduction to Fenton Bailey, *Fall from Grace: The Untold Story of Michael Milken* (New York: Birch Lane Press, 1992), p. xix.
[4]Daniel Fischel, *Payback: The Conspiracy to Destroy Michael Milken and His Financial Revolution* (New York: HarperCollins, 1995), p. 158.

to define insider trading—an alleged Milken offense—on the grounds that defining the offense would reduce their discretion in bringing the charge.[5] Ignoring the constitutional protection against ex post facto law, government bureaucrats made up the law as they went along in order to fashion a net with which to catch Milken.

To create the appearance of hardened criminal activity in the financial arena, Giuliani staged a stormtrooper assault on the financial firm Princeton/Newport involving fifty federal marshals outfitted with automatic weapons and bulletproof vests. The media-hungry prosecutor also staged the public handcuffing of two New York investment bankers on their trading floor. Although both Princeton/Newport and the investment bankers were later exonerated, Giuliani's media stunts served to turn public sentiment against white-collar defendants and to intimidate individuals into becoming government witnesses.

The biggest crime in the Milken case was committed by prosecutors. It is a felony to leak grand jury testimony, but the government used leaks to build pressure on Milken. In March 1989, Milken was indicted on ninety-eight counts of securities fraud and racketeering. When he failed to cooperate with a plea, the media was told of an expanded "superseding indictment" that apparently never existed.[6]

Resorting to a tactic that has never been approved by the U.S. Supreme Court, federal prosecutors threatened to indict

---

[5] This point has been widely noted by legal commentators such as George Mason Law School Dean Henry Manne, author of *Insider Trading and the Stock Market*. Henry Manne, "For Milken, Verdict First, Trial Later," *Wall Street Journal*, 13 February 1990. *See also*, L. Gordon Crovitz, "The SEC Overstepped When It Made Insider Trading a Crime," *Wall Street Journal*, 19 December 1990; Fischel, *Payback*, pp. 57–61.
[6] In eighteen *Wall Street Journal* stories following the initial indictment, Laurie Cohen reported that Milken would imminently face an expanded superseding indictment of between 160 and 300 additional counts.

Milken's younger brother Lowell unless Milken pled guilty. "A brother for a brother," U.S. Attorney General Dick Thornburgh quipped to his deputies. Lowell Milken was a "sort of ready chip in the negotiations," boasted Carroll to the law students. To rub in the reality of the threat, FBI agents were dispatched to hound Milken's ninety-two-year-old grandfather.

To make it hard for Milken to resist, a RICO (Racketeer Influenced Corrupt Organizations Act) charge was added to the indictment. This would permit prosecutors to freeze Milken's assets. To end his travail, Milken agreed to plead guilty to six counts that were not part of the indictment but were invented by his lawyers.

Milken's sentencing judge, Kimba Wood, called a special sentencing ("Fatico") hearing in order to allow the government to present its strongest counts against Milken (apart from the six to which he pled guilty). Reaching deep into its arsenal of insider trading, racketeering, bribery, and stock manipulation charges and armed with the advantages of a lower burden of proof and lower evidentiary hurdles than would be required in a genuine trial, the government still failed to convince the judge that Milken's "crimes" exceeded his plea.[7] The judge had to stretch to assess Milken's market "damages" at $318,082— hardly the foundation of a multi-billion-dollar fortune or evidence of a vast financial conspiracy.

Neither Milken nor his lawyers expected that he would receive a prison sentence for six charges that never before had carried time behind bars. Prosecutors had given the impression that all they sought was a face-saving plea. No one had ever been charged with aiding and abetting the filing of a false S.E.C. 13(d) schedule by another party, nor with aiding book-

---

[7]Ivan Boesky (a real insider trader who gave sources suitcases of cash) arranged a deal with the government to trap Milken, but his evidence was not used because prosecutors realized that Boesky lacked credibility as a witness.

keeping and record violations by another broker, nor with failing to disclose an attempt to recoup expenses from a portfolio manager. Yet the inexperienced judge, persuaded by prosecutors, aided and abetted the criminalization of petty civil charges by giving Milken an unprecedented ten-year sentence, which she thereafter reduced to two years.

The passage of time has made Milken an appreciated rather than despised figure. A September 30, 1996, cover story in *Fortune* acknowledged his extraordinary vision:

> The fact is, while you can disagree on whether Milken was a saint or a sinner during his 1980s heyday, you simply can't argue anymore about the singular importance of the junk-bond market he created. "We securitized business loans," Milken says, and he's right. And look, too, at the businesses he backed with his junk bonds! He was present at the creation of the cable industry and the cellular industry. Milken's junk bonds made it possible for MCI to compete with AT&T. He backed companies like Turner Broadcasting and McCaw Cellular because he saw something others didn't. Yes, this is the party line we've been hearing from Milken apologists for years, but that doesn't make it any less true.

If government coercion can "roll" a billionaire, Democrat, Jewish financier who was one of the country's most productive economic resources, what *can't* it do to a poor, black, inner-city youth or a middle-class citizen? If Michael Milken's billions could not protect him from prosecutorial frame-up, ordinary citizens have only their anonymity for protection.

Just as Michael Milken's high-priced Washington, D.C., attorney, Robert Litt, urged Milken to plea bargain with Litt's pals and former colleagues in Giuliani's office, public defenders give the same advice to their court-assigned poor clients. Like Bukharin's "attorney" in Moscow, who was an agent of Vyshinsky, public defenders have little incentive to zealously defend their clients in a scrappy fight for justice. Prosecutors know that false arrests and poor evidence do not threaten their careers, because public defenders almost invariably "rescue" their cases by advocating pleas.

WWOR-TV news reporter Barbara Nevins Taylor, in a September 7, 1996, *New York Times* article, described the pressure put on Eric Washington, an acquaintance of hers from a Brooklyn housing project, to plead guilty to a robbery the nineteen-year-old insists he didn't commit.

Eric got into a fight with a man to whom he had sold a dog, but who refused to pay him. The man claimed that Eric assaulted him and took the money while another man held a gun. No gun or any of the money was ever found. Based on the man's allegation, Eric and his codefendant were later arrested. Although Eric wasn't charged with wielding the gun, the D.A. refused to split the case. After the grand jury hearing, the accuser missed two appointments with prosecutors. If the case had gone to trial, Eric would have been acquitted due to the unreliability and dearth of evidence.

Eric, however, unable to raise bail and thus held in the miserable and dangerous Rikers Island prison awaiting trial, was a prime candidate for a coerced plea. Sure enough, prosecutors offered a deal, promising release from prison and entry into a job-training program in exchange for a guilty plea. Obviously, Eric was under pressure to cop a plea from a criminal justice system that was unconcerned about his guilt or innocence.

All too often, citizens believing themselves innocent are faced with just such a devil's choice. Columbia law professor H. Richard Uviller, a former prosecutor and defense attorney, writes in his 1996 book, *Virtual Justice: The Flawed Prosecution of Crime in America*, that "more innocent people are in prison on their own guilty pleas, I suspect, than by false verdicts of conviction."

Corporations are even more susceptible than individuals to pressure from ambitious prosecutors. By using press leaks, prosecutors can generate pressure on a company from institutional investors, outside directors, shareholder activists, class action lawyers, and Wall Street analysts.

Adeptly playing these groups against the company, in October 1996 the U.S. Justice Department fined agribusiness giant Archer-Daniels-Midland $100 million for allegedly fixing prices in agricultural product markets that a federal judge had, in 1991, determined could not be fixed because of the presence of large buyers who negotiate the prices that they pay. As every economist is taught, price fixing requires buyers without market power and a few producers who share common interests. Even then the situation is unstable, as each producer can gain market share by cutting prices.

In ADM's case, the markets for fructose, lysine, and citric acid were dominated by large buyers whose enormous purchases effectively set prices, making ADM more of a price taker than a price fixer. Moreover, all of the evidence shows a collapse in price—the opposite of price fixing. In 1991, when ADM entered the market, the lysine price fell to $1.08 per pound. In 1992, the price was 82 cents; in 1993 it was 90 cents, $1.14 in 1994 and $1.02 in 1995. As the low-cost producer, ADM was able to undersell its competitors and gain 40 percent of an expanded market. The company would not benefit from a price-fixing agreement that would limit its market share. Facts, however, had nothing to do with the case.

The government used an ADM executive who was subsequently convicted of defrauding ADM to create evidence of price fixing. ADM's downfall began when the company played it straight with authorities in November 1992. Mark Whitacre, head of ADM's BioProducts Division, reported that an employee of Ajinomoto, a Japanese competitor, offered to sell ADM product information for $10 million. ADM's top management immediately notified the FBI of Whitacre's report of the illegal offer. When ADM insisted that Whitacre be interviewed by the FBI, Whitacre reportedly had a fit of consternation and objected.

His protests notwithstanding, Whitacre was forced by ADM to meet with the FBI. Within two months of his interview with the FBI about the alleged Japanese offer, Whitacre had signed a secret agreement with Byron G. Cudmore, first assistant U.S. attorney for the Central District of Illinois, to "act in a covert capacity" as an agent against ADM "solely at the direction and under the supervision of agents of the FBI and this office." In exchange for providing evidence of criminal conduct, the government granted Whitacre immunity. While serving as the FBI's in-house agent, Whitacre used his executive position to orchestrate meetings with competitors that were scripted and videotaped by the FBI. The government case rested solely upon these tapes.

The tapes were tainted by the government's own dirty hands in fabricating a case. Moreover, during the period that Whitacre was under the sole direction of the FBI, he embezzled $10 million from ADM, according to evidence from lawsuits and FBI affidavits. ADM suspects that the Japanese proposal Whitacre reported was another of his schemes to bilk the company. Perhaps his interview with the FBI regarding the alleged Ajinomoto contact turned up potential charges against him, or Whitacre may have sold the bureau on a story of ADM wrongdoing in order to throw the FBI off the scent of his own misdeeds. Whatever happened during his FBI interrogation, Whitacre ended up being a government agent with a charter to act out a crime on the government's behalf. It was the FBI, and not ADM, that had the original idea of the price-fixing meetings.

Revelations of Whitacre's embezzlement threw the government off guard after the press had dutifully reported his participation in, but not his organization of, the price-fixing meetings. Concerned that Whitacre's lack of credibility would be exposed in a courtroom, the government resorted to bully tactics to increase the pressure on ADM to cop a plea. The FBI assigned eighty agents to raid the homes of thirty of the company's executives and leaked to the press that indictments of ADM and its officials were forthcoming. Alluding to medieval thumbscrews, a September 13, 1996, *New York Times* article began, "It's white-knuckle time at Archer-Daniels-Midland Co."

The article included the telltale signs of prosecutorial leaks: "people with knowledge of the inquiry" and "people with knowledge of the situation said." Similar stories soon popped up in the *Chicago Tribune, Wall Street Journal,* and *Los Angeles Times* and included references to anonymous sources "close to the case." Each story included a unique twist based on the anonymous leaks, but each conveyed the theme that ADM should settle quickly or suffer worse consequences. The government also announced that ADM's Japanese competitors were going to join Whitacre in testifying against the American firm. Of course, this "evidence" was also tainted by the self-interest of the foreign conglomerates.

The government was apparently bluffing. The indictment promised for Tuesday, September 17, 1996, never came forth. Prosecutorial energies weren't focused on a grand jury indictment. The leaks were intended to elicit pressure on ADM's management from third parties unhappy with share price declines caused by the rumors. Outside directors, fearful of their own potential liability, forced the company to settle the case.

The outside directors reassured themselves that with $2.5 billion of liquid assets on hand, a $100 million settlement with the prosecutors was a good deal. Sure enough, ADM's stock went up as soon as the deal was announced, making $500 million for its shareholders from an immediate jump in share price.

The deal was good for outside directors and for the prosecutor whose name recognition was boosted by the record fine. But the deal was bad for some of the company's executives, for American business, and for our system of justice. Most people will assume that ADM is guilty because it paid the fine, not that it copped a plea to end its directors' discomfort.

Prosecutors again learned that pressure tactics are more efficient than court cases, and that they can use the media, outside directors, Wall Street stock analysts, institutional investors, and shareholder activists to bring company officials to settlement, guilty or not.

If the government actually has evidence worthy of an indictment, it will indict rather than use leaks of a forthcoming indictment to coerce a plea. When prosecutors focus on real crime, rumors of indictment threaten evidence and hurt chances of apprehending suspects. Plea bargains, however, depend on pressure tactics, not on evidence. With the ubiquitous plea bargain, prosecutors have reinvented torture.

CHAPTER SEVEN

TURNING LAWYERS INTO GOVERNMENT SPIES: THE DEMISE OF THE ATTORNEY-CLIENT PRIVILEGE

PEOPLE CONFIDE IN their lawyers, secure in the attorney-client privilege. With legal roots going back to ancient Rome, the attorney-client privilege guarantees the confidentiality of interactions between client and attorney and ensures that a person's lawyer can aggressively defend him against the government. If the government had access to the communications between a client and his lawyer, the lawyer would be nothing but a government agent, like Soviet defense attorneys whose official role was to serve as adjuncts to the prosecution.

English lawyers revered the attorney-client privilege. For William Blackstone, it was elementary that "no counsel, attorney, or other person, entrusted with the secrets of the cause by the party himself, shall be compelled, or perhaps allowed, to give evidence of such conversation or matters of privacy, as came to his knowledge by virtue of such trust and confidence." Francis Bacon declared that "the greatest trust between men and men, is the trust of giving counsel."

Besides serving as a point of honor, because a gentleman would never reveal secrets that were reposed in him, the "inviolable" and "sacred" privilege ensured that the client would have confidence, ease, and freedom to be frank and completely open with his attorney "alter ego," who was navigating the client's way through the complex legal thicket. Wise jurists recognized that the attorney-client privilege promoted equality before the law and efficiency in the administration of justice, because without it "a man would not venture to consult any skillful person, or would only dare to tell his counselor half his case." The result would be convictions resulting from a lack of access to legal knowledge, not from wrongdoing.

Jeremy Bentham despised the attorney-client privilege. He thought there was nothing immoral or treacherous about a lawyer betraying the confidences of his clients. "The conviction of delinquents is the end of penal justice," Bentham wrote. Deterring the guilty from seeking legal advice, therefore, wouldn't hinder justice, while the innocent would have nothing to fear from their attorneys' disclosures of their confidences. Reminiscent of his disdain for the protection against self-incrimination and his corresponding endorsement of torture, Bentham declared that with the abolition of the attorney-client privilege, "the professional lawyer would be a minister of justice, not an abettor of crime."

Although the attorney-client privilege withstood Bentham's nineteenth-century diatribes, Benthamite arguments are eroding it in the United States as we enter the twenty-first century. Alarm over prosecutorial pressures on defense lawyers to provide evidence against their clients prompted University of Colorado law professor Kevin R. Reitz to write in the *Duke Law Journal* (December 1991) that "under current law, it could be a serious mistake for a suspect in a criminal case to obtain counsel. . . . Obtaining a lawyer is a bit like inviting a government agent into the defense camp."

Similarly, San Antonio defense attorney Gerry Goldstein, president of the National Association of Criminal Defense Lawyers, has written, "Before long, lawyers will have to issue an 'attorney general's warning' sort of like the surgeon general's warning on cigarettes: Consulting a lawyer could be dangerous to your safety."

Unfortunately, these statements cannot be dismissed as hyperbole. The attorney-client privilege has eroded to the point that aggressive defense lawyers have trouble defending even themselves against unethical prosecutors. Alexis de Tocqueville believed that American lawyers would never tolerate oppression. Knowing their legal rights, he wrote, they would fight back, and a government that oppresses lawyers would find "them to be enemies all the more dangerous."

The success of the government's shakedown in 1990 of the blue-chip Wall Street law firm Kaye, Scholer, Fierman, Hays & Handler suggests that the pugnacious spirit that Tocqueville sensed among early-nineteenth-century attorneys has dissipated. Today, win-at-all-costs government prosecutors can crack pillars of the legal establishment by implementing asset freezes.

Kaye, Scholer, a prosperous and well-heeled 400-attorney firm, whose partners enjoyed an average income of $660,000 in 1990, found itself faced with frozen assets and a $275 million lawsuit for failing to assume an alleged public responsibility to inform on its client. The government claimed that the firm should have disclosed to thrift regulators adverse and damaging evidence against its client, Charles H. Keating and his Lincoln Savings and Loan Association.

Prominent legal ethicists, such as Yale's Geoffrey Hazard, noted that convenience for the government's prosecutions can never take precedence over the attorney-client privilege and that Kaye, Scholer was bound by legal duty not to be a snitch for the prosecution. But the government didn't need legal ethics on its side; it had raw power. In addition to freezing the firm's assets, the government froze the personal assets of each of the 400 partners. Since only a few of the partners had handled the Keating case, the government was able to build pressure to settle from the other partners. Other pressures came from the firm's other clients, who feared guilt by association, and from banks that threatened to cut off credit crucial to the firm's ability to meet its payroll.

These pressures enabled the government to win the day. Kaye, Scholer promptly settled the case out of court for $41 million. This case did not, strictly speaking, overturn the attorney-client privilege, because the law firm admitted to no wrongdoing. However, by settling instead of fighting the case, the firm allowed regulatory officials to infringe upon the attorney-client privilege. The settlement did not establish the precedent that firms must snitch on their clients, but it did establish the precedent that the government can freeze an attorney's assets in an attempt to force him to betray his client. An attorney who keeps confidence with his client can be made to pay for doing so.

Defenders of the Office of Thrift Supervision's attack on Kaye, Scholer argue that the firm could have challenged both the asset freeze and the merits of the lawsuit in court but did not, with the implication being that the law firm found the government's case too compelling. Of course, if the government's legal case had been so compelling, the asset freeze would have been unnecessary. The purpose of the freeze was to disrupt the personal and professional lives of 400 lawyers in order to force a settlement and win the government's point.

The New York City Bar Association found that the government misused its power to coerce Kaye, Scholer to capitulate. The bar association said, "In the case of Kaye, Scholer, OTS confronted the firm with the choice of settling promptly or going out of business. The effect of this order apparently has been to deprive Kaye, Scholer of its right to defend itself in court on the merits." The bar report concluded that the asset freeze order is "of questionable constitutionality," that it "clearly went beyond a reasoned response and threatened the financial viability of the firm," and that the unilateral power to freeze assets without a judicial hearing destroys the "chief guarantee of our liberties, due process and judicial review of government power." Without the protections of a judicial hearing prior to a freeze, "government regulators may use the power to freeze assets not to prevent their dissipation or to recoup the fruits of crime or fraud, but to force a law firm to settle without regard to the merits." Of course, the same pressure can be felt by any defendant, not just a law firm.

The government's newly gained power to freeze assets of attorneys who refuse to turn state's witness against their clients effectively destroys the attorney-client relationship. A proper defense of a citizen from an attorney's point of view can be seen as "misleading" or "concealment" from an aggressive regulator's or prosecutor's perspective. As the bar association put it,

> The line not to be crossed may be so vague, and so subject to selective enforcement, that the attorney may not wish to come anywhere close to the line and thereby risk financial ruin. The attorney is put on notice that a vigorous defense, or indeed the use of any aggressive or hardball tactics at all, may result in an attachment of the firm's assets, well beyond the fees earned in a particular matter. It is the client who will suffer the chilling effect.

Assistant Attorney General Stuart M. Gerson tried to defend the government's action by claiming that Kaye, Scholer was, in Bentham's words, "an abettor of crime" and had helped Keating commit fraud by withholding information. But the question of whether or not there *was* fraud was the legal question in dispute. In effect, government lawyers were acting as judge and jury before the issue could be honestly addressed in court. Moreover, in 1993 a New York appellate court exonerated Peter Fishbein, the Kaye, Scholer partner whose alleged misconduct was the basis for the government's action. Legal scholars, however, have not exonerated the government for its misconduct. The Code of Professional Responsibility provides that "a government lawyer . . . should not use his or her position or the economic power of the government to harass parties or to bring about unjust settlements or results." Chasing after Charles Keating, the U.S. Department of Justice utterly ignored its professional responsibility to the law and acted as a tyrant. University of Chicago law professor Daniel Fischel concludes that the government's "unilateral and unjustified imposition of the asset freeze, which coerced Kaye, Scholer into settling the government's groundless charges, was a clear violation of this ethical principle. It's unfortunate the government was never held accountable."

The coercion used by the government against Kaye, Scholer is just the latest of a number of steps taken by the federal government to exempt itself from the normal rules of our legal system. Under policies originally promulgated during the Bush administration and reaffirmed by the Clinton administration, the Justice Department has released its litigators and attorneys from the obligation to follow state ethical rules that prevent lawyers from directly communicating with adversaries in the absence of their counsel. This rule prevents those trained in the law from taking advantage of those who aren't. In order to win its cases, the government has side-stepped ethics and has exempted its attorneys from the state ethical rules. In other words, the federal prosecutor can fight dirty in court, but the defendant's attorney is bound by strict ethical norms.

Oliver North's attorney, Brendan Sullivan, astonished a meeting of the Federalist Society in 1992 when he revealed that Independent Counsel Lawrence Walsh had subpoenaed him to testify against his client before a grand jury. Sullivan appeared before the jury armed with pocket copies of the

Constitution to give to its members to remind them of his rights and those of his client, and at some risk of being held in criminal contempt he courageously refused to talk. In the face of Sullivan's refusal to violate the attorney-client privilege, the special prosecutor backed off.

North was lucky to have a zealous attorney in his defense. However, what if Walsh had used an asset freeze on Sullivan's law firm to force Sullivan to cooperate with the prosecution of his client? That might not have deterred Sullivan from his duty, but it would undoubtedly sap the zeal of many defense lawyers.

Walsh's tactics are not unique. Max Stern and David Hoffman wrote in the *University of Pennsylvania Law Review* in 1988 that "prior to 1980, federal prosecutors generally believed that lawyers were *not* potential sources of information in criminal investigations. Subpoenas to lawyers were rare and the government was generally not successful in enforcing them." However, "law and order" Justice Department officials in the Reagan administration were more concerned with convicting criminals than with defendants' rights. "They reexamined traditional assumptions about attorney subpoenas as they formulated aggressive approaches to criminal investigation. They concluded that prosecutors had wrongly assumed this investigative technique to be unavailable." An explosion of subpoenas to lawyers to testify against their clients followed. Paradoxically, some conservative lawyers, who professed anger at Walsh's harsh treatment of Sullivan, had a hand in promoting identical abuses as Justice Department lawyers.

The attorney-client privilege was further damaged when the Supreme Court narrowed the interpretation of the Constitution's Sixth Amendment right to the "assistance of counsel" in "all criminal prosecutions." In 1989 the Court said that pretrial asset forfeitures do not transgress the Sixth Amendment's right to counsel even when the forfeiture prevents a defendant from being able to pay the defense lawyers. Justice Harry Blackmun, joined in dissent by Justices William Brennan, Thurgood Marshall, and John Paul Stevens, objected that "it is unseemly and unjust for the government to beggar those it prosecutes in order to disable their defense at trial." Blackmun said that in addition to spending vast sums of money to try those accused of crime, the government is now "free to deem the defendant indigent by declaring his assets 'tainted' by criminal activity the government has yet to prove." Moreover, Blackmun warned, "The government will be ever tempted to use the forfeiture weapon against a defense attorney who is particularly talented or aggressive on the client's behalf—the attorney who is better than what, in the government's view, the defendant deserves."

Just as Justice Department lawyers are not loath to put the convenience of their prosecutions ahead of the Rights of Englishmen, neither are they reluctant, as the next chapter will show, to bring federal discrimination suits against citizens who attempt to defend their property values by enforcing in state courts residential zoning covenants. The U.S. government has become a bully that uses brute force to get its way, regardless of the legal principle or constitutional right that stands in its way.

CHAPTER EIGHT

PRIVILEGE TRUMPING RIGHTS

AMONG THE COMPLAINTS the American colonists listed in the Declaration of Independence was that King George III "has erected a multitude of New Offices, and sent hither swarms of Officers to harass our People, and eat out their substance." The same imagery describes the behavior of federal agents from the Department of Housing and Urban Development (HUD) and the Department of Justice in their investigation, interrogation, and prosecution of citizen groups that take legal steps to prevent the location in their neighborhoods of commercially operated group homes. A home is most Americans' biggest investment, and many homeowners have experienced a reduction in property values when federal agencies have disregarded local zoning and covenants and coerced homeowners into accepting commercially operated facilities that destroy neighborhood integrity. The fact that group homes operate under contracts funded with the homeowners' tax dollars adds insult to injury.

When Berkeley, California, residents Alexandra White, Joseph Deringer, and Richard Graham learned that a taxpayer-funded homeless shelter was to be located in their neighborhood, they exercised their First Amendment rights of free speech to inform their neighbors and organize a protest. They soon found HUD investigators pounding on their doors and threatening them with jail terms and $50,000 fines unless they turned over to HUD documents that HUD could allege to be evidence that the Berkeley residents had violated the Fair Housing Act by opposing the homeless shelter.

The Fair Housing Act forbids citizens to refuse to sell or rent their homes to members of the legally privileged group known as "protected minorities." It does not say you cannot protest the location of a group home or halfway house next door in order to protect your property values. But to zealous federal bureaucrats intent on remaking the law, there is no difference between opposing the location of a commercially operated group home in your residential neighborhood and refusing to sell a house to a protected minority.

By rewriting the Fair Housing Act, these bureaucrats intentionally subvert the Constitution. In addition to protecting the freedom of speech, the Constitution's First Amendment guarantees "the right of the people peaceably to assemble, and to petition the Government for a redress of grievances." This clause protects the rights of citizens to address public officials in legislative bodies. It also protects citizens who are seeking the redress of their legal rights in court.

The Right to Petition the Government and seek the redress of grievances has ancient roots in English law. Biographer P. H. Helm writes that one reason ninth-century English King Alfred uniquely earned the title "The Great" was his insistence that all subjects had the right to "ride to the king" as his code put it, to resolve disputes.[1] Alfred's resolve led to the hallowed maxim that "everyone deserves his day in court."

William Blackstone lauded the English "right appertaining to every individual, namely, the right of petitioning the king or

---

[1] P. H. Helm, *Alfred the Great: A Biography* (1963; Reprint ed., New York: Barnes & Noble, 1995), pp. 11, 116.

either house of parliament for the redress of grievances." This right is buttressed by the principle that imprisonment and "prosecutions for such petitioning are illegal." He contrasted the English solicitude for the redress of grievances with the discouragement of such petitions in imperial Russia.

In Russia, "czar Peter established a law, that no subject might petition the throne, till he had first petitioned two different ministers of state. In case he obtained justice from neither, he might then present a third petition to the prince; but upon pain of death, if found to be in the wrong." Putting petitioners in jeopardy of death had an intimidating effect. As a consequence, "no one dared to offer such third petition; and grievances seldom falling under the notice of the sovereign, he had little opportunity to redress them."

The United States in the late 1990s is taking on some of the attributes of czarist Russia and losing those of Blackstonian England. Ill winds bringing regulatory oppression blew beyond Berkeley to San Diego, California, where, as San Diego Mayor Susan Golding told the U.S. Senate in 1996, citizens wanted to speak against the placement of commercially operated group homes in their residentially zoned neighborhoods, but the citizens feared being investigated and prosecuted by HUD and the Department of Justice.

Golding wanted to assure her constituents that they had nothing to fear and that their right to testify freely before their local elected officials was inviolable. But she was aware that the federal government had succeeded in bringing the full force and power of the U.S. government against individual homeowners in other cities. "There was nothing I could do," Golding recalled. She told the senators that she had had to ask herself if she "was still living in the United States of America because I remember being told when I was growing up that that's what happened in the former Soviet bloc, that you couldn't speak your mind, that you couldn't tell people how you felt."

Citizens who seek legal redress in the courts can find themselves harassed by unethical federal lawyers. In Bakersfield, California, five citizens were sued by the U.S. Justice Department for merely going to a state court to successfully enforce a deed restriction against commercial businesses being located in their residential neighborhood. In this case, the business was a Medicare-funded commercially operated warehousing operation for the mentally impaired. There was no reason the facility had to be located in a protected residential neighborhood, and a California state court issued an injunction. This brought in Assistant U.S. Attorney for Civil Rights Deval Patrick, who even tried to have a state judge deposed on the theory that as a resident of the neighborhood he had conspired with the judge who issued the injunction to discriminate against the disabled, a federally protected category of people.

The residents of Bakersfield were merely protecting their property values and the quality of their lives, not engaging in a conspiracy to discriminate. "The government is arguing that anyone who defends their property rights must be a bigot," noted Victor J. Wolski, their attorney. Whenever Americans have said, "We are a residential neighborhood, not a business district; please respect the zoning," the U.S. Department of Justice's Division of Civil Rights appears with a lawsuit threatening massive, bankruptcy-inducing fines. As part of the intimidation, citizens must hand over their federal and state tax returns, bank account statements, liability insurance policies, income and wealth statements, records of contacts with their lawyers, and, as in Bakersfield, California, lists of "each person who attended any meeting" of residents seeking to protect their neighborhood.

At a Senate hearing on September 18, 1996, Senator Carol Moseley-Braun, a black Illinois Democrat, described Assistant Attorney General Patrick's tactics as "gestapo techniques" that "run roughshod over citizens, over communities." When the

Illinois city of Palatine tried to block the location of a group home for recovering drug users next to an elementary school, federal agents descended on the neighborhood and spent three months questioning more than a hundred citizens for alleged housing discrimination. The Feds even prevented the city authorities from inspecting the group home for fire code violations.

In the federal executive branch's view, group shelters for protected categories are immune to local zoning restrictions and covenants, enabling commercial operators or government entities to locate such facilities wherever they want without legal accountability to local officials or neighborhood residents. Mayor Golding of San Diego pointed out that because of the threat of federal harassment of citizens and their elected officials, local communities are unable "to govern these business activities in a manner consistent with the rules applied to other types of private enterprise. As an example, we have a care facility for juvenile offenders that has recently located within one of our single family neighborhoods without city approval—resulting in unnecessary community conflict with adjacent families over the unacceptable behavior of the juveniles living in the facility."

The most troubling—and most ignored—aspect of such intimidation of citizens is the absence of statutory basis for the power exercised by HUD and Justice Department officials. Most commentators who have studied these cases have focused on balancing the supposed imperatives of "fair housing" against the chilling infringements of free speech, the power of localities to enforce zoning restrictions or regulate businesses, and the right of citizens to enforce contractual covenant and deed restrictions in state courts.

Many commentators do not protest the federal government's tactics, because they oppose restrictive covenants for civil rights reasons and zoning for economic reasons. But it is not zoning or covenants that are at stake. The government is misusing civil rights statutes to deprive citizens of zoning protections that have been upheld by the Supreme Court (see Justice George Sutherland's 1926 *Euclid v. Ambler Realty Company* decision). Libertarians are entitled to argue against zoning and to seek through persuasion the repeal of property restrictions. But they invite tyranny when they do not protest the government's use of force to intimidate people into not exercising their legal rights to petition the government. Alleged shortcomings of zoning are no excuse for winking at bureaucratic assertions of power.

The federal crackdown on residential neighborhood restrictions on behalf of protected groups has created privilege in law. The federal government does not intervene on behalf of a commercially operated bakery or dry cleaner that seeks to locate in a neighborhood restricted to residential use.

The protected group shelter business is legally unique because of the privileged status of its customers. Operators of lucrative group homes are exempt from laws that apply to other commercial businesses because of the privileged legal status asserted in behalf of protected groups by federal officials.

Shelter operators are well aware of this fact. Fully aware that HUD and the Department of Justice will defend them, they use their legal privileges to avoid otherwise generally applicable legal norms. A February 13, 1997, legal memo prepared for Kathryn Meyer, senior vice president for legal affairs at New York City's Beth Israel Medical Center, lays out a strategy for silencing the opposition to group homes in neighborhoods across the country.

Beth Israel wanted to service an additional 250 heroin addicts in methadone clinics at 25th Street and Second Avenue on New York City's East Side. Community groups were outraged, since 1,200 addicts were already getting treatment in the neighborhood. Moreover, in a signed agreement

Beth Israel had promised Manhattan's "Community Board Six" that the taxpayer-financed hospital wouldn't assign patients lacking community roots into the neighborhood. Pulling together a list of HUD and Justice Department precedents from across the nation, Beth Israel's lawyers concluded that the hospital could get away with breaching its contract by recasting the issue as a discrimination case. The legal brief noted that neighborhood opposition could successfully be prosecuted as a "classic instance of intentional, disability-based discrimination," just as HUD and the Justice Department had done elsewhere.

Beth Israel's legal memo shows how easy it has become to turn the normal exercise of constitutional rights into "discriminatory behavior":

> Resistance to the offer of transfer to these 200 patients appears to have as its source a profound distaste for patients on methadone maintenance treatment. A neighborhood activist entitled a recent column he authored: "No More Methadone Patients for This Area." Writing in the same local paper, a neighborhood resident criticized members of the local community board who, on a procedural motion, had voted not to consider a motion to criticize Beth Israel for the possible patient transfer: "Their votes supported the intrusion of more drug addicts into our neighborhood, thereby increasing the threats to our children, seniors and quality of life." Most recently, Community Board 6, whose geographic area encompasses the 25th Street treatment site, issued a strongly worded statement criticizing Beth Israel for planning the patient transfer.

The memo concluded by insisting that Beth Israel "must be cautious not to serve as an accomplice to any illegal discriminatory behavior by a public entity and/or public officials." In other words, thanks to federal misapplication of civil rights law, the hospital could break the agreement.

Because of Beth Israel's bad faith behavior, New York City Council member Antonio Pagan (D-Manhattan) resigned from the hospital's community relations task force in March 1997, concluding that "the hospital has acted in an insincere manner in its negotiations and has no intention of honoring the community's wishes or its longstanding agreements." Pagan called the negotiations a "total farce." "This community already has more methadone patients than any other in New York State," Pagan said, "but despite that, Beth Israel is dead set on giving us more regardless of what agreements they must break to accomplish it."

Before being elected to New York's city council, Pagan was the executive director of Coalition Housing, a nonprofit housing development corporation that provided affordable housing for the poor. He also was a founder and director of the Hispanic AIDS Forum. Over the years, he has often witnessed how the mantra of "disability discrimination" has, in his words, "been used to suppress taxpayers' voices and in so doing violate their constitutional rights under the First Amendment to the Constitution."

In congressional testimony in September 1996, Pagan said that group home operators systematically manipulate the wrongful interpretation of "anti-discrimination law" by federal bureaucrats to get unfair advantages and stifle neighborhood opposition to their designs: "They dangle HUD and the Justice Department as their sword and these two agencies are but too eager to comply in the charade." Federal bureaucrats at these agencies know that if they can silence New Yorkers, they can intimidate citizens in other cities with ease.

James Madison declared that "the censorial power is in the people over the Government, and not in the Government over the people." Because of the tyrannical behavior of HUD and the Department of Justice, this precept of our republic no longer holds true. Bureaucrats routinely use federal power that lacks statutory basis to violate the constitutional rights of U.S. citizens, and nothing is done about it.

CHAPTER NINE

FORFEITING JUSTICE

AT 8:36 A.M. ON October 2, 1992, thirty armed members of an "entry team" led by Los Angeles deputy sheriffs John Cater and Gary Spencer broke down the front door of multimillion-aire Donald Scott's home on his 200-acre estate in Malibu, California, and shot him dead. Mr. Scott was not on the FBI's most wanted list. He was holding no one hostage. He had committed no crime, and he had defied no summons. He was shot dead because Mr. Spencer had targeted Scott's estate for asset forfeiture on trumped-up drug charges.

Mr. Scott's oceanfront property with scenic vistas and a spring-fed waterfall was bordered on three sides by federal park land. For more than a decade, park personnel had coveted Scott's beloved "Trail's End" as a Yosemite by the Pacific. But Scott, sixty-one years old, multimillionaire, and heir to a vast European chemical and cosmetic fortune, did not want to sell.

Mr. Scott's murder was called "self-defense," but Ventura County District Attorney Michael D. Bradbury was suspicious enough to investigate. He uncovered a conspiracy to confiscate Mr. Scott's property. The idea seems to have originated with Deputy Sheriff Gary Spencer, who recruited Charles Stowell, a special agent of the Drug Enforcement Administration, by telling him that 3,000 marijuana plants were rumored to be on the property. At a subsequent meeting, Spencer arranged for Stowell to fly over the property to confirm the presence of the

#67, 66

Be a... ...ue

theory of...

" " Cle... ...on the Mandate

you seek.

#44 Focus quickly on crucial

Text and tell where To find it

marijuana. From an altitude of 1,000 feet without binoculars, Stowell claimed to have spotted 50 plants.

Spencer then arranged for Forest Service and other agents to search the property on foot. They reported that the property was clean. This did not deter Spencer. He did not need proof that marijuana plants were being grown on the property, only the presumption known as "probable cause," and he had that with the rumors (which he may have made up himself) and Stowell's "spottings."

The next step was a search warrant. Once a constitutional protection against unfounded accusations, the Fourth Amendment's warrant requirement is today a meaningless formality in which judicial officers rubber-stamp almost all searches, no matter how unreasonable.[1] As Mr. Bradbury later noted, this "search warrant became Donald Scott's death warrant."

Despite abundant testimony and evidence that the Scotts were open and friendly and posed no threat, Spencer mounted a SWAT operation involving nine state and federal enforcement agencies. Instead of knocking on Scott's door, showing the search warrant, and inspecting the property, the SWAT team broke into the house unannounced. Awakened from sleep by the noise, a confused Scott stumbled from his bedroom with rifle in hand and was cut down with a barrage of shots.

Needless to say, no evidence of marijuana or drugs of any kind was found. Bradbury, however, did discover that the entry team was armed with property appraisals of Scott's estate. The *Los Angeles Times* reported that Spencer had planned the raid for more than a year and had bragged that if only 14 marijuana plants were found, he could seize the estate. According to the *Times*, "Spencer had also told Park Service Ranger Tim

---

[1] No one ever asked Spencer why one of California's richest men with a large independent fortune would be engaged in the commercial cultivation of marijuana.

Simonds that the Sheriff's Department might give the property to the Park Service."

Despite Bradbury's report and extensive news coverage, the conspiracy to deprive Scott of his property that ended by depriving him of his life went unpunished. In chasing after drug dealers, a great swath has been cut through the law, leaving law-abiding citizens exposed to arbitrary, capricious, and unconstrained actions of law enforcement officers.

Scott's property could be targeted for seizure in this trumped-up way because policymakers lost their patience with the tension in law between protecting the innocent and punishing the guilty. Reining in drug dealers has become more important than safeguarding the innocent. Indeed, the law's protective shields are seen through a Benthamite lens as barriers to justice. One who saw it this way was William French Smith, attorney general in the Reagan administration. In his memoir, *Law and Justice in the Reagan Administration*, Smith stressed the need "to maximize the risk to those who engage in criminal acts." Another was Congressman Dan Lungren (R-California), chief sponsor of the legislation that expanded forfeiture powers in the 1980s. On the House floor, Lungren said, "Let us give law enforcement every single tool" to chase after drug traffickers.

As policymakers saw it, the drug trade was too profitable to be deterred by "the traditional criminal sanctions of fine and imprisonment." They argued that the way to deter drug trafficking was to seize the property of those suspected of drug crimes. The result was the Comprehensive Forfeiture Act of 1984, which radically expanded government forfeiture powers. The statute began, "The following shall be subject to forfeiture to the United States and no property right shall exist in them." Subsequent paragraphs listed the forms of personal property that could be confiscated on presumption alone that it was connected to drugs. This list included "aircraft, vehicles, or vessels, moneys, negotiable instruments, securities, firearms, raw materials, products, or equipment, controlled substances, parapher nalia, and books, records, and research." The paragraph that ultimately cost Donald Scott his life declared forfeitable "all real property, including any right, title and interest (including any leasehold interest) in the whole of any lot or tract of land and any appurtenances or improvements, which is used, or intended to be used, in any manner or part, to commit, or to facilitate the commission of, a violation of the subchapter."

There are major legal atrocities in the wording of this act. The presumptive seizure of property permitted by the act inflicts punishment without proof. It reverses the presumption of innocence that is the basis of our criminal justice system. The act contravenes another of the fundamental Rights of Englishmen—no crime without intent. An owner's property can be seized if a trespasser, unbeknownst to an owner or over his objection, uses it to "facilitate" the commission of an offense. The horror stories that this act has left in its wake are all obvious consequences of its literal meaning.

From Law to Plunder

WITH "PROBABLE CAUSE," law enforcement officers can seize property, and the statute gives them incentives for seizure. The proceeds are not deposited into the general government treasury. Instead, law enforcement agencies retain the proceeds. Whenever more than one government law enforcement agency, whether federal, state, or local, is involved in a seizure, the attorney general is authorized to divvy up the seized property based on the "degree of direct participation" in "the law enforcement effort resulting in the forfeiture." The 1984 forfeiture provision's reach was expanded in 1986, 1990, and 1992 to include proceeds from money laundering, financial institution fraud, and motor vehicle theft. Today the forfeiture provision, which targeted drug trafficking, covers 140 other federal criminal offenses. Scores of similar state and local forfeiture laws have been added to the books.

The forfeiture provision was intended to leave suspected drug traffickers unprotected by the traditional safeguards of criminal procedure. But this cannot be done without also leaving the innocent unprotected. By permitting punishment without indictment, prior to conviction, and despite acquittal, property rather than crime has become the target. Whatever the amount of drug trafficking profits that has been snared by the forfeiture laws, law enforcement officers and prosecutors have learned that it is easier to go after people's property than to bring indictments against them for criminal activities. Some of them have also learned that it is just as easy to go after the property of the innocent as it is to go after the property of the guilty. This is exactly what happened once forfeitures became a source of budgetary funds for law enforcement agencies and Justice Department officials began to encourage the use of forfeiture. In 1990 a Justice Department memo for U.S. attorneys stressed, "Every effort must be made to increase forfeiture income during the remaining months of 1990." The opportunity to augment budgets has skewed the efforts of law enforcement toward asset seizure and away from the apprehension and prosecution of criminals.

The Comprehensive Forfeiture Act of 1984 has been good for prosecutors and police, who now drive seized luxury cars in place of government-issue automobiles. Gold Rolexes have replaced Timexes, and seized cash finances tennis and health club memberships for law enforcement personnel.[2]

---

[2]See generally, W. John Moore, "Crime Is Paying Local Dividends," *National Journal*, 25 February 1989; Richard Miniter, "Ill-Gotten Gains; Abuse of Asset-Forfeiture Statutes," *Reason* (August 1993); Michael Isikoff, "Drug Raids Net Much Valuable Property—and Legal Uproar," *Washington Post*, 1 April 1991; John Enders, "Forfeiture Law Casts a Shadow on Presumption of Innocence," *Los Angeles Times*, 18 April 1993; Stephen Labaton, "Seized Property in Crime Cases Causes Concern," *New York Times*, 31 May 1993; Mike O'Callaghan, "War on Drugs Hitting Innocent Citizens," *Consumer Finance Law Quarterly Report* (Fall 1993): 380; Andrew Schneider and Mary Pat Flaherty, "Presumed Guilty: The Law's Victims in the War on Drugs," *Pittsburgh Press*, 11–16 August 1991.

Messrs. Smith and Lungren acted negligently when they crafted the "forfeiture weapon" without due regard to the incentives that it creates. Forfeiture gives law enforcement an incentive to foster the drug trade in order to benefit from it. Because of this, law enforcement is unlikely to give up the budgetary independence provided by asset forfeiture by driving drugs off the streets. The old way of benefiting from the drug trade—bribery—endangered the police and has been replaced with this form of "tax farming."

Forfeiture Indifferent to Guilt or Innocence

NEW INCENTIVES FOR law enforcement are just one unintended consequence of the 1984 act. Another is the plunder of the innocent. Fair housing laws have taken away landlords' discretion in choosing renters. Yet, if a suspected drug dealer or drug user is among the landlord's tenants, the owner's building can be seized. Retired army colonel Melvin Hanberg lost his California rental property because one of his tenants was alleged to be a drug dealer. An eighty-year-old black woman lost her motel because a prostitute used a room with a customer.[3] Helen Hoyle, a seventy-year-old black woman in Washington, D.C., lost her home because of police suspicion that one of her grandchildren once had drugs in the house.[4]

These travesties have occurred because the 1984 law targets property, not crime. Moreover, the law does not target only the property of presumed drug traffickers, but *all* property that "is used in any manner or part to commit or to facilitate the commission" of an offense. This includes the smoking of marijuana. Thus, owners have lost their boats when lessees

---

[3] James V. DeLong, *Property Matters: How Property Rights Are under Assault—and Why You Should Care* (New York: Free Press, 1997), p. 276.
[4] Nkechi Taifa, "Civil Forfeiture vs. Civil Liberties," *New York Law School Law Review* 39 (1994): 97–98.

have used drugs onboard. Donald A. Regan of Montvale, New Jersey, lost his car when he gave a lift to someone who, unbeknownst to Regan, had drugs in his possession. Leonard W. Levy's book *A License to Steal* is full of horror stories that illustrate the gestapo-like application of the asset forfeiture laws.

The forfeiture act disconnected crime from intent and punishment from crime. Neither Colonel Hanberg nor the elderly black woman was suspected of drug trafficking or prostitution. It is bad enough that the law permits police to strike at people through their property, not only prior to indictment and conviction, but without either. It is worse that even those who are acquitted cannot recover their property without proving that there was no "probable cause" for the seizure of their property. The forfeiture law totally ignores the presumption of innocence that is the foundation of our legal system. The law permits the police to strike at innocent third parties simply because a trespasser or lessee brings drugs onto their property or a thief uses a car stolen from them to "facilitate" a drug transaction.

House Judiciary Committee chairman Henry Hyde (R-Illinois) describes how undercover agents arrange for their drug purchases to take place in valuable buildings and on expensive tracts of land in order to maximize forfeiture income.[5] The theory is that the physical site "facilitates" the illegal transaction and is thereby a party to the crime, allowing its seizure. Under the existing application of the law, your home and everyone else's can be confiscated simply by an undercover agent arranging for a drug transaction to take place on your front lawn or in your driveway. Police seized Gary and Kathy Bergman's South Dakota home because it was visited by a friend who brought along a marijuana plant. Joseph and

---

[5]Henry Hyde, *Forfeiting Our Property Rights: Is Your Property Safe from Seizure?* (Washington, D.C.: Cato Institute, 1995), p. 31.

Frances Lopes lost their home when a mentally disturbed son planted marijuana in their backyard.

When asked about the injustice done to Mr. and Mrs. Lopes, Marshall Silberberg, the U.S. prosecutor who seized their house, snorted that the family should "be happy we let them live there as long as we did." Stefan D. Cassella, an official in the asset forfeiture division of the U.S. Justice Department, justifies the seizure of property from innocent parties on the grounds that otherwise nothing is accomplished for the government.

Under criminal forfeiture laws, frozen property belonging to the accused cannot be seized prior to conviction. Thus, the property is protected by the same protections that the law affords the person. This was dramatically altered by the 1984 legislation, which permits property to be seized on "probable cause." Unlike an arrest warrant, determination of "probable cause" is constrained only by the discretion of the police officer or prosecutor—an extraordinary delegation of lawmaking power. Thus Deputy Sheriff Gary Spencer could independently target Donald Scott's property. In September 1992, former New York City Police Commissioner Patrick Murphy testified to Congress that asset forfeiture has "created a great temptation for state and local police departments to target assets rather than criminal activity." Mr. Murphy noted that "seized cash will end up forfeited to the police department, while seized drugs can only be destroyed."

Murphy gave the example of a police department that set up roadblocks and relieved motorists of their cash on the grounds that there was probable cause that sums in excess of $100 indicated an intention to buy or sell drugs.

Once such victim was Selena Washington. She was stopped while driving south on I-95 in Florida. She had $19,000 from a home insurance settlement for hurricane damage and was on her way to purchase construction materials to repair her home. The police officer seized her $19,000 on the presumption that it was drug money and drove off without even taking her name. With the aid of an attorney and proof of insurance settlement, she was able to recover $15,000 by agreeing that the police could keep $4,000.[6]

Selena Washington's case demonstrates the impotence of the "innocent owner's defense" that allegedly protects the innocent from asset forfeitures. More evidence that the act hangs the innocent out to dry is provided by two *Orlando Sentinel* reporters who reviewed 1,000 videotaped police highway stops in Volusia County, Florida, in 1992 and concluded that the police had used pretexts to confiscate tens of thousands of dollars from motorists. Only four of the motorists managed to get all of their money back.[7]

The "innocent owner's defense" that is a part of some of the forfeiture statutes has proved to be a very feeble defense. The innocent owner must prove a negative in court and establish by the preponderance of evidence that he neither knew about nor consented to the misuse of his property by the alleged wrong-doer. The burdens of proof, filing and response deadlines, bond-posting requirements, and other procedural rules are all heavily tilted in favor of the government, especially when people can neither post bond nor pay a lawyer because their property has been seized and they are without financial means. Innocent owners also face police and prosecutorial threats of indictment as co-conspirators if they challenge the seizure of their property.

Often the safest and easiest course is to walk away from the property. This is the usual decision when the cost of proving the property's innocence exceeds its value, as in the seizure of small amounts of cash and older cars. Even in the relatively few cases in which owners succeed in recovering their property, it is often a Pyrrhic victory. Air charter operator Billy Munnerlyn

---

[6]Leonard W. Levy, *A License to Steal: The Forfeiture of Property* (Chapel Hill: University of North Carolina Press, 1996), pp. 2–3.
[7]David Heilbroner, "The Law Goes on a Treasure Hunt," *New York Times Magazine*, 11 December 1994, 70–73.

spent nearly $100,000 trying to recover his Learjet. When his jet was finally returned to him, it had been ripped apart in a futile search for drugs. The cost of restoring the aircraft was beyond his remaining means. Munnerlyn declared bankruptcy and took a job as a truck driver.[8]

The evidence is abundant that as a result of forfeiture laws, the police have become more corrupt than the Sheriff of Nottingham. Instead of condemning these unjust practices, U.S. attorneys and legal scholars defend them. At a 1993 debate at the University of Chicago Law School, Assistant U.S. Attorney Elizabeth Landes argued that it was permissible to infer drugs from the presence of cash. Conservative legal columnist Bruce Fein says that the innocent must be sacrificed in order to catch the guilty and that forfeiture is necessary as a counterweight to Miranda and other "protective features of criminal justice." The blindness of many conservatives to the dangers of asset forfeitures contrasts remarkably with their strenuous objections to the takings of private property by wetlands and endangered species regulations, and by rent control and zoning statutes.

With the forfeiture laws, policymakers have stripped away the protections that guarantee the presumption of innocence by redefining felonies as civil actions. This was once tried earlier, in 1886, when prosecutors tried to seize property of E. A. Boyd by applying civil statutes to a criminal offense. Since the liberty of a person is not at stake in a civil case, the government is permitted lower standards of proof. In *Boyd v. United States*, the Supreme Court firmly blocked prosecutors from pursuing people through their property. The Court said that if the government thought Mr. Boyd committed the crime of smuggling, prosecutors should prosecute him for smuggling, not forfeit his property in a civil suit. Moreover, if Boyd were acquitted of the crime of smuggling, the government was

---

[8]Charles Oliver, "A Forfeiture of Civil Liberties? Government Confiscating Assets of Guilty and Innocent," *Investor's Business Daily*, 7 March 1995.

forbidden to come back and seize the goods in a civil proceeding. Any alternative, Justice Joseph P. Bradley declared, "may suit the purposes of despotic power, but it cannot abide the pure atmosphere of political liberty and political freedom."

Justice Bradley warned that a return to tyranny would result from end-running the constitutional safeguards of criminal procedure by permitting citizens to be attacked through their property. The American Revolution cast off royal "writs of assistance," which placed "the liberty of every man in the hands of every petty officer." Bradley warned that tyrannical law often has its origin in slight deviations from permissible procedure:

> It may be that it is the obnoxious thing in its mildest and least repulsive form; but illegitimate and unconstitutional practices get their first footing in that way, namely, by silent approaches and slight deviations from legal modes of procedure. This can only be obviated by adhering to the rule that constitutional provisions for the security of person and property should be liberally construed. A close and literal construction deprives them of half their efficacy, and leads to gradual depreciation of the right, as if it consisted more in sound than in substance. It is the duty of courts to be watchful for the constitutional rights of the citizen, and against any stealthy encroachments thereon.

In 1928 Justice Louis Brandeis said that *Boyd* "will be remembered as long as civil liberty lives in the U.S." Paradoxically, the asset forfeiture law of the Reagan administration has effectively killed civil liberty in the United States. Conservatives, chasing after drug dealers, ignored and negated the constitutional prohibition against striking at a man through his property. Today *Boyd* is dismissed by legal scholars as mere "property worship."[9]

9Akhil R. Amar, *The Constitution and Criminal Procedure: First Principles* (New Haven: Yale University Press, 1997), pp. 22–25.

The ability to punish people as criminals without having to indict and convict them takes law enforcement back to a distant time prior even to the use of torture. Torture was an instrument used to produce evidence or confession at a trial; at least the importance of the trial was recognized. No such recognition can be found in the Comprehensive Forfeiture Act of 1984.

The asset forfeiture regime has contravened multiple Rights of Englishmen: the right to be innocent until proven guilty, the right not to be punished until guilt is proven beyond a reasonable doubt, the right to be free from unreasonable searches and seizures, the right not to be deprived of property without due process of law, the right to be free from excessive and disproportionate punishment, the right to the assistance of counsel, the right against self-incrimination, and the right to equal protection of the law. Rather than being protected by law, Americans hold their property at the whim of police who can seize property based on nothing more than gossip and rumors from informants, who often get kickbacks from the proceeds.[10]

This displacement of the protective mechanisms of criminal procedure is anathema to the Anglo-Saxon legal tradition. That is why when some British law enforcement officers, covetous of U.S. asset forfeiture powers, pushed for a similar law, the British government in 1986 rejected out of hand this "draconian power" that is "out of sorts with anything we have

---

[10]*Review of Asset Forfeiture Program.* Hearing before the Legislation and National Security Subcommittee of the House Committee on Government Operations. 103d Congress, 1st session, 22 June 1993, 382–83; Congressman Hyde reports that in 1990 and 1991 the Justice Department paid out $30 million to forfeiture informants, including "65 informants more than $100,000 each, 24 of whom were paid between $100,000 and $250,000, and 8 received over $250,000." Hyde, *Forfeiting Our Property Rights,* p. 46; Columnist Jack Anderson reported in a *Washington Post* column, "Drug Informants Beating the System," on 10 September 1992, that the highest paid federal forfeiture informant got a $780,018.39 bounty in 1990.

hitherto done." A legal report for the British Police Foundation in 1989 came to the identical conclusion that Justice Bradley had reached in the *Boyd* decision in 1886: It is impermissible to pursue criminal charges in the guise of civil forfeiture, much less against the innocent.

One hundred years after *Boyd*, the British still hold to the Rights of Englishmen, the achievement of a 1,000-year struggle. In the United States these rights have disappeared with faint notice. In March 1996 the Supreme Court had an opportunity in *Bennis v. Michigan* to repair the damage. Tina Bennis lost her car because her husband had used it in an encounter with a prostitute. But by 1996 the law also had been lost. Only four Supreme Court justices (Stevens, Souter, Breyer, and Kennedy) still believed, in Justice Stevens's words, that "fundamental fairness prohibits the punishment of innocent people." Employing a sham history to hide an act of judicial activism, the Rehnquist majority placed its imprimatur on the resurrection of the ancient "deodand," by which guilt is inferred to property, giving government virtually unbridled power to confiscate the property of innocents.

In *A Man for All Seasons*, Sir Thomas More, Chancellor of England, asks his critic, who wants him to disregard the law in pursuit of wrongdoing, what will happen to the innocent when the law is cut down. When the law turns on us, More asks, where will we stand? Assistant U.S. Attorney Leslie Cayer Ohta came face to face with this question in 1992 when her eighteen-year-old son, Miki, was arrested for selling LSD out of her car and suspected of selling marijuana out of her house. Under the asset forfeiture laws that she had aggressively applied, her property was forfeit. But the even-handed administration of justice is another casualty of the forfeiture statutes. As a reward for the $20 million that she had confiscated for the government—including eighty-three-year-old Paul Derbacher's home because he had a grandson with drugs—U.S. Attorney Albert

Debrowski ruled that Ohta's property was privileged against forfeiture.[11]

Today Americans who are not members of the privileged class of law enforcement face, in the words of House Judiciary Committee chairman Henry Hyde (R-Illinois), "endless possibilities to be caught in the snare of government forfeiture." "Owners," Hyde says, "must police their property against all possible criminal activity—or lose it." And even that may not be enough. Levy reports that the majority of the 200 civil forfeiture statutes across the country lack even the feeble innocent owner's defense. In the overwhelming majority of these forfeiture cases, by which government has seized billions of dollars, no one is prosecuted. Representative Hyde reports that Florida, Texas, and other states now permit civil forfeitures for "*any* criminal activity." New Jersey allows forfeiture for any *alleged* criminal activity.

With the law cut down, none of us has anywhere to stand.

---

[11]Larry Rosenthal, "Drug Prosecutor Found to Live in Glass House," *Los Angeles Times*, 17 May 1992.

CHAPTER TEN

AMBITION
OVER JUSTICE

THE RIGHTS OF Englishmen are the best defense against tyranny and injustice that humans have been able to muster. But even these rights are impotent to defend us once prosecutors abandon the traditional ethic that their function is to find justice and serve truth. Until recent years it was legal tradition that the prosecutor works equally for the defense and for the prosecution. This prosecutorial ethic was well expressed in the quotes from Supreme Court Justices Jackson and Sutherland in chapter 1. Since the prosecutor's function is to find truth, he must not override the rights of the defendant in order to gain conviction. The prosecutor must not withhold exculpatory evidence or use his power to suborn perjury. He must try the defendant in the courtroom, not in the media. Charges should not be overdrawn in order to elicit a plea, and the full power of the government should never be brought against an individual citizen as a means of gaining conviction.

This ethic has been lost. In its place is a win-at-all-costs mentality that results in the withholding of exculpatory evidence, the manipulation of the media to convict a defendant, routine suborned perjury, and the use of coerced consent decrees to establish precedents for quotas in the civil rights arena. In March 1998, former Deputy U.S. Attorney General

Arnold I. Burns warned in the *Wall Street Journal* that "it is time for a sober reassessment of the power we have concentrated in the hands of prosecutors and the alarming absence of effective checks and balances to prevent the widespread abuse of that power." Earlier in the same month U.S. Representatives Joseph McDade (R-Pennsylvania) and John Murtha (D-Pennsylvania) introduced the Citizens Protection Act to protect U.S. citizens from being framed and abused by federal prosecutors. In a press release accompanying the introduction of the bill, Representative McDade observed, "There are Justice Department employees who engage in questionable conduct without penalty and without oversight, using the full weight and power of the U.S. government. A win-at-all-costs attitude blinds them into suppressing exculpatory evidence, falsifying evidence, misleading grand juries, and other misconduct which most of the time goes unpunished."

The ethic was lost to a variety of factors: the Benthamite emphasis that sacrifices the individual's rights for a "greater good"; police frustration with *Miranda* and other court rulings limiting the ability to collect evidence, with the result that frame-ups became the easiest way to obtain conviction; and the conservatives' war on drugs, which abruptly expanded the number of assistant U.S. attorneys from 1,200 to 7,000 and in the process overwhelmed the ability of seasoned prosecutors to inculcate the tradition of just prosecution.

The precedent of chasing after devils was set in the early 1960s by Attorney General Robert Kennedy in his vendetta against Teamster's Union president Jimmy Hoffa. Just as Herman Melville's character Captain Ahab in *Moby Dick* monomaniacally pursues the whale at the cost of dehumanizing and ultimately sacrificing himself and his crew, Kennedy broke down Justice Department ethics, tradition, and organizational structure in order to set up a twenty-lawyer "Get Hoffa Squad." As Victor S. Navasky put it, "The Hoffa drive was liberated to a significant degree from conventional Departmental procedures and at the same time from those pressures and bureaucratic restraints that sometimes conspire, almost accidentally, to preserve democratic values, to protect fundamental civil liberties and human rights." Kennedy's practice of bringing the full weight of the U.S. government against a citizen has outlasted him. The "Get Hoffa Squad" transmitted to succeeding Justice Departments the precedent of using any means to secure convictions. Kennedy picked his man and looked for the offense. Today, Justice Department prosecutors pick the offense—white-collar crimes, environmental crimes—and look for the man. As Robert Jackson warned, justice is the casualty.

Once the end justifies the means, there is no shortage of causes. Assistant Attorney General Deval Patrick effectively used the threat of litigation to cause financial institutions to "voluntarily" adopt what appear to be racial quotas, even though it is doubtful racial quotas could by required by law. To settle unfounded charges of discrimination that would disrupt business, cause bad publicity, and cost millions of dollars to defend, businesses consent to quotas in order to settle cases. The Shawmut Bank had its acquisitions blocked until it agreed to loan quotas. The Chevy Chase Bank had to not only establish quotas, but also agree to lend to black mortgagors at below-market rates of interest and to pay a portion of their down payments. Elsewhere the Justice Department has used coerced consent decrees to destroy residential zoning and covenant restrictions that prevent commercial businesses in residential neighborhoods. Prosecutorial ethics is an oxymoron when prosecutors bring cases—which cannot be won in court on the basis of existing law—for the purpose of obtaining legal precedents from coerced settlements. This is legislation through litigation.

Once the prosecutorial ethic is lost, ambition and mendacity become the driving factors, as prosecutions become a means of building careers and settling political and personal scores. A prosecutor who becomes a tool for powerful political interests can go far.

Often a case that begins in ambition ends in revenge. The Randy Weaver case, resulting in the Ruby Ridge tragedy, shows this transition. Federal agents wanted to use Weaver to infiltrate a militia group. To set him up so that he would be subject to pressure, undercover agents badgered Weaver until he finally acquiesced to their request to shorten a shotgun barrel, thus creating a firearm violation. When Weaver refused to join the militia and to spy on it, the federal agents retaliated by setting in motion the process that left two members of Weaver's family and one federal marshal dead, one FBI official imprisoned for destroying evidence, and another indicted in Idaho for wrongful killing.

Freelance operations by federal agents seeking glory took a turn for the worse in Waco, Texas, when, for publicity reasons, the Bureau of Alcohol, Tobacco, and Firearms staged an unprovoked paramilitary assault on the Branch Davidian compound. The publicity assault failed, with deaths on both sides. The FBI was called in with tanks. Attorney General Janet Reno gave her okay to an attack on the men, women, and children inside with a chemical weapon whose use in warfare is banned by international treaty. Eighty-five members of the religious sect, including twenty-four children, were killed in a fiery holocaust. Federal agents quickly bulldozed the site to destroy all evidence of the federal assault. The seven survivors were locked away by a compliant federal judge, whose wrongful sentence provoked public protests by the jury foreman and other jurors.

Such extraordinary injustices and violations of civil rights show a militarized federal law enforcement that is audacious in its contempt for the rule of law. Obviously, the federal agents who committed these massive violations of fundamental legal principles in full view of television cameras and a live audience had no concern whatsoever about being held accountable. And none has been.

Ecuadorean politician Alberto Dahik has noted the baneful influence of the bad behavior of those higher in the food chain on those lower in the food chain: "If the minister himself steals, the undersecretaries will commit assaults and the departmental directors will engage in theft, extortion, robbery, and murder. When the perception is that corruption begins at the top, everything falls into decay."[1]

Police and prison guard brutality and suspicious deaths of incarcerated persons are nothing new, but the cover-up of such murders by the FBI and high-ranking Justice Department officials *is* new. For reasons as yet unknown, Kenneth Michael Trentadue was murdered during the early hours of August 21, 1995, in his cell at the Federal Transfer Center in Oklahoma City. There is evidence that the murder was committed by an eight-man Federal Bureau of Prisons SWAT team.

Detailed autopsies from the chief medical examiner of Oklahoma state and the chief of pathology for the armed forces conclude Trentadue was beaten to death. Detailed color photographs show a brutal beating and indicate that prison authorities were aware of the true cause of his death. Multiple witnesses attest to Trentadue's cell being covered in blood and to the bloody uniforms of the guards. Despite the unambiguous and overwhelming evidence of murder, the Federal Bureau of Prisons maintains that Trentadue, who was picked up for a minor parole violation, committed suicide by hanging himself in his suicide-proof cell.

To prevent the state of Oklahoma and the U.S. Senate Judiciary Committee from investigating the murder, the

---

[1]*El Universo*, 25 January 1992. Quoted in Paul Craig Roberts and Karen LaFollette Araujo, *The Capitalist Revolution in Latin America* (New York: Oxford University Press, 1997), pp. 81, 100.

Department of Justice convened a federal grand jury. The grand jury met for only one or two hours a month, and the process dragged on for two years, thus blocking a real inquiry while evidence grew cold. The FBI threatened and cajoled witnesses to change their stories, and when they refused, the Justice Department did not permit any of the witnesses to testify before the grand jury. According to the U.S. Armed Forces' chief pathologist, Colonel William T. Gormley, the Justice Department pressured him to change his autopsy report and to testify falsely that Trentadue's death was a suicide. When Colonel Gormley refused to lie for the government, he was not permitted to testify before the grand jury as to the cause of death. Neither was Oklahoma's chief medical examiner, Fred B. Jordan. The Justice Department finally found a Texas ranger who had never seen the body and was untrained in forensic science to assure the grand jury that Trentadue had hung himself and had bumped his head in the process.

The Justice Department's cover-up of Trentadue's murder was conducted by an acting assistant attorney general for civil rights. It is hard to believe that such a cover-up could have occured without Janet Reno's approval. The cover-up ranks as one of the most transparent in history, and the message that has been sent to malefactors in law enforcement is that anything goes.[2]

Not that the bad apples did not already know. In the 1970s the *Miami News* published a series of articles exposing illegal snooping into the files of local prominent citizens by IRS agents. The agents demanded that the newspaper's general counsel, Daniel Heller, reveal to them the paper's sources in the IRS who were ratting on them. When he refused, the

---

[2]The Trentadue case received much attention, including that of Senate Judiciary Committee chairman Orrin Hatch. There are many sources for the story's details, including the *Washington Times*, 7 November 1997. Trentadue's brother, a lawyer, has brought a civil suit against the government in which he intends to prove that his brother was murdered by federal prison guards.

agents suborned the perjury of Heller's accountant and used false evidence to convict Heller of tax evasion in federal court. This blatant misuse of federal law for purposes of personal revenge was eventually exposed.[3] Taxpayers had to pay Heller $500,000 in civil damages from the IRS, but the agents who committed felonies by suborning perjury were not indicted.

Unless they are members of Congress, federal officials who misuse their power in criminal ways seldom suffer any consequence. One obvious result is that bad apples crowd out the good. IRS agents need not fear the consequences of illegal behavior and the framing of innocent people in acts of revenge. The IRS passes the buck to the taxpayers. Morale suffers, and abuses multiply. The extraordinary abuses of taxpayers by IRS agents, revealed by the Senate Finance Committee hearings in September 1997, owe much to the example set by IRS agents Doreen Kaplan, Larry Plave, and Thomas A. Lopez in the frame-up of Daniel Heller.

When law begins to collapse, the abuse of power accelerates. It soon moves from targeting small fish to large ones. Hotel proprietor Leona Helmsley was another victim of Rudolph Giuliani's ambitions. We have carefully studied her case[4] and are convinced, as are Harvard law professor Alan Dershowitz and Judge Robert Bork, that Helmsley was convicted on the basis of the suborned perjury of one of her accountants, whose own infraction in helping to defraud the Miller Brewing Company was dropped in exchange for false witness against Mrs. Helmsley. Similarly, in the case of apple juice producer Ben Lacy (see chapter 4), we believe the Justice Department suborned the

---

[3]Trevor Armbrister, "The Man Who Beat the IRS: He Endured Every Taxpayer's Nightmare Until, Finally, It Was His Turn to Pursue Justice," *Readers' Digest*, July 1996.

[4]Paul Craig Roberts, "Leona May Be Guilty, but Not as Charged," *Wall Street Journal*, 9 April 1992; Paul Craig Roberts, "Guilty of Being Rich," *National Review*, 15 November 1993.

perjury of his codefendant after the trial began in order to have a witness for the prosecution so that the judge would not dismiss the case. The prosecutors' cavalier attitude toward suborning perjury suggests that they dismiss the prohibition as an old-fashioned restraint.

When a prosecutor is intent on a frame-up or the Justice Department on a cover-up, not even money and exposure can stop the process. In high-profile cases, clever prosecutors protect themselves by first convicting their victim in the media. With the public aroused against the victim, the prosecutor has a free hand.

There is little that can be done to rein in an abusive prosecutor. An assistant attorney general, attorney general, or president can rein in a U.S. attorney, but intervention is difficult once the prosecutor has won the public relations battle in the media. Judges often dress down offending prosecutors but have no real means of holding them accountable when they commit crimes such as suborning perjury. Congress could investigate cases but lacks the fortitude. A Congress with such fortitude would soon find it had no time for any other business.

Just as Giuliani rode Michael Milken and Leona Helmsley to political office, Scot Harshbarger crushed the innocent Amiraults to become Massachusetts attorney general. Violet, Cheryl, and Gerald Amirault, a mother, daughter, and son team, operated a tony, well-established child care center until a hysterical mother began making child abuse accusations. Scot Harshbarger, an ambitious prosecutor, jumped at his chance. He inflamed public hysteria and secured the conviction of the Amiraults on what the *Wall Street Journal* has exposed as "charges so improbable as to defy belief." Subsequently state courts ordered the release of the mother (now dead from stomach cancer) and daughter, but Harshbarger succeeded in blocking the releases in order to hold on to his only claim to fame. The false accusations against the Amiraults are now widely recognized as a massive miscarriage of justice, but Harshbarger has gained name recognition and has gubernatorial ambitions.

Child abuse prosecutions are rapidly proliferating because statutes have stripped away defendants' and parents' rights. On the basis of anonymous accusation alone, Child Protective Services can seize children from parents and hold them incognito. Routinely the children are placed in the hands of child abuse specialists trained to elicit accusations against one or both parents. For example, stressed and scared children are told they can go home to Mommy once they accuse Daddy. Mommy is then told she cannot keep custody of the child or children unless she separates from Daddy. Sometimes families stay together to fight the CPS gestapo. Often fear and stress dissolves them.

That these practices are standard operating procedure is well established and not subject to dispute. The ACLU's investigation of the child sex abuse trials in Wenatchee, Washington, reports that children were locked away in mental institutions and given mind-altering drugs in order to produce testimony against innocent parents. The crimes committed against the innocent by Wenatchee public officials have been exposed in the national media, but as yet nothing has happened to a single guilty official who participated in the destruction of dozens of families. Fifty children remain in foster care, and, although courts have begun overturning the false convictions, many innocent parents remain in jail.

The difficulty of rectifying miscarriages of justice is so extreme that once the prosecutorial ethic is lost, law ceases to serve justice. The United States today is an unjust society—not because of unequal income distribution or private discrimination against minorities—but because so many prosecutors no longer see their calling as finding justice by serving truth.

The Lost Ethics of J. Edgar Hoover

AMERICA'S LAW ENFORCEMENT practices today stand in stark contrast to former FBI director J. Edgar Hoover's firm rule against practices that might taint law enforcement with unscrupulous behavior. This statement will sound odd to those who regard Hoover as the epitome of unscrupulous behavior. The FBI's wiretaps of Martin Luther King, Jr., and infiltration of the Ku Klux Klan, together with Hoover's files on politicians have certainly tainted Hoover's reputation with civil libertarians. Nevertheless, the historical record is clear that Hoover had high standards for the FBI that are not present today. Like Christians, Hoover did not always live up to his standards, but we must acknowledge that an FBI that professes high standards will be cleaner than one that pursues convictions at all costs. Moreover, the Ku Klux Klan was suspected of being capable of organizing violent acts against civil rights agitators, and Martin Luther King, Jr., was suspected of having communist ties. These suspicions may have been poorly based, but they do not appear to have been concocted in order to target anyone. The purpose of Hoover's files on politicians was to protect the bureau from political misuse. The files were a defensive weapon.

Hoover frowned on undercover operations because they risked tainting law enforcement. The importance of untainted law enforcement was foremost in the mind of Attorney General Harlan Fiske Stone when he hired Hoover in 1924.

President Calvin Coolidge had appointed Stone, dean of Columbia Law School, to clean up the Justice Department after the Harding administration's "Teapot Dome" scandal. The department's investigative operations were under fire from prominent legal scholars such as Roscoe Pound, Felix Frankfurter, and Zechariah Chaffee, Jr., who prepared a report rebuking the Department of Justice for abusive raids on communists, anarchists, and agitators (nicknamed the "Palmer's Raids" after Stone's predecessor). The report objected to the use of undercover agents: "We do not question the right of the Department of Justice to use its agents in the Bureau of Investigation to ascertain when the law is being violated. But the American people have never tolerated the use of undercover provocative agents or 'agents provocateurs' such as have been familiar in old Russia or Spain."[5]

One of the first things Stone did upon his appointment was to fire Bureau of Investigation's director William J. Burns. Stone wanted to stop the agency from being a "dumping ground for political hacks who used their patronage jobs as investigators to harass and intimidate political enemies." Stone declared, "There is always the possibility that a secret police may become a menace to free government and free institutions because it carries with it the possibility of abuses of power which are not always quickly apprehended or understood. . . . It is important . . . that its agents themselves be not above the law or beyond its reach." Stone said that henceforth, the "Bureau of Investigation is not concerned with political or other opinions of individuals. It is concerned only with their conduct and then only with such conduct as is forbidden by the laws of the United States. When a police system passes beyond these limits, it is dangerous to the proper administration of justice and to human liberty, which it should be our first concern to cherish."

Stone appointed a twenty-nine-year-old Justice Department lawyer named J. Edgar Hoover to reform the investigative bureau, which later was renamed the Federal Bureau of Investigation. In 1932, Hoover advised the attorney general

---

[5]Quoted in *Select Committee to Study Undercover Activities of Components of the Department of Justice, Final Report to the U.S. Senate*, Senate Report No. 682, 97th Congress, 2d Session, 34–42 (1982).

against using the FBI to investigate communist activities in the United States because "the Bureau would undoubtedly be subject to charges in the matters of alleged secret and undesirable methods . . . as well as to allegations involving the use of 'Agents Provocateurs.'" In the late 1960s, Hoover objected to infiltrating Vietnam war protest groups on similar grounds. William C. Sullivan, assistant director for the FBI Domestic Intelligence Division during the 1960s, noted in his memoirs, "Some agents, especially some of the younger ones, infiltrated many of the groups in spite of Hoover's insisting to me that no agent should wear long hair, dress in jeans, or wear a beard. I said 'the hell with it' and made the decision myself to go against Hoover's dogmatic ruling." Hoover's deputy Cartha D. "Deke" DeLoach wrote in his 1995 book, *Hoover's FBI: The Inside Story by Hoover's Trusted Lieutenant,* "Hoover stuck to Stone's principles throughout his career, and in many ways the bureau that Hoover remade was a product of Stone." Looking back over his career, DeLoach wrote, "Had everyone understood precisely what our mission and limitations were, as envisioned by Stone, determined by Congress, and defined by our name, many of the controversies surrounding the FBI would never have developed."

Hoover's philosophy was that the FBI should investigate crimes *after* they had been committed and reported to authorities, rather than have agents go undercover and incite people to commit crimes. Until his death in 1972, Hoover strenuously objected to the undercover practices of the Drug Enforcement Administration and other government creations of the War on Drugs. James Q. Wilson details Hoover's attitude in his 1978 book, *The Investigators: Managing FBI and Narcotics Agents:*

Hoover refused . . . to change Bureau policy when the central tasks of the agents would have to be altered. Narcotics investigation meant turning agents into investigators, working undercover in situations that required one to emulate, if not adopt, the language, style, and values of the criminal world. Not only would this expose agents to temptations involving money and valuable narcotics, it would also require them to engage in enforcement policies that, though legal, struck many citizens as unsavory. And perhaps most important, the key asset of the agent—public acceptance and confidence—might be weakened as the agent's image changed from that of a bank clerk or insurance salesman to that of a habitué of "street life."

It was not until 1976—four years after Hoover's death and sixty-eight years after the creation of the Department of Justice's investigations bureau—that the FBI requested funds for undercover operations: a mere $1,000,000. Undercover operation budgets have soared enormously ever since. FBI Director Clarence B. Kelley gutted Hoover's policy in favor of giving priority to "'proactive investigations'—investigations that create opportunities for criminals to commit crimes, as opposed to investigations of crimes previously committed." The ABSCAM sting of several congressmen during the Carter administration, in which FBI undercover agents entrapped U.S. representatives by posing as Arab sheiks offering bribes, was the first major undercover operation in the post-Hoover era. During the Reagan administration, undercover policies were formalized in federal regulations under Attorney General William French Smith. Much of the current corruption of law enforcement is traceable to this change in policy.

J. Edgar Hoover's ethic—"We can't afford merely to be right. We must give every appearance of doing right to avoid any criticism"—has been completely lost in federal law enforcement. Hoover even forbade his agents from driving government cars home for fear that neighbors might see government vehicles parked outside their homes during off-duty hours and complain, "Look at that FBI man, keeping a government car for his personal use."

Hoover's concern that undercover operations would corrupt law enforcement by absorbing the nefarious methods of the underworld was justified. On January 18, 1990, with the approval of Bush administration Attorney General Richard Thornburgh, the FBI entrapped District of Columbia Mayor Marion Barry by hiring a woman to lure the mayor with sex and cocaine while the FBI filmed. Once on this slippery slope, the bureau quickly slid to the bottom. In short order followed the Ruby Ridge cover-up; the Waco massacre of women and children; the frame-up of Archer-Daniels-Midland on price-fixing charges that were based on evidence manufactured by an FBI "witness" who was trying to avoid his own indictment; the use of FBI agents in the Filegate and Travelgate scandals as political police for the White House; the political corruption of the once-fabled crime lab; and dubious investigations of Vincent Foster's death, the Oklahoma City bombing, and the apparent prison murder of Kenneth Trentadue. From investigation to prosecution, federal law enforcement has been corrupted. Today we cannot have confidence in a Justice Department indictment or an FBI witness.

In 1960, Lord Patrick Devlin, one of England's most distinguished jurists, described English law's prosecutorial ethic at a Yale Law School lecture. He emphasized that the prosecuting counsel "is to act as a minister of justice rather than as an advocate; he is not to press for a conviction but is to lay all the facts, those that tell for the prisoner as well as those that tell against him, before the jury." No such sense of fairness characterizes prosecutions in the United States today.

According to the Senate Report, the only time Hoover accepted the use of undercover operatives in the FBI was during World War II, against Nazis in Europe at the behest of President Roosevelt, and during the Cold War, at the behest of President Eisenhower. DeLoach says that "Hoover, though by no means a plaster saint, fought just as hard to limit the powers of the FBI as he did to protect them. . . . Hoover understood, as had Stone, the dangers of a national police department. He had seen what had happened under his predecessor, Burns, and knew that if the FBI ever became such an abusive force, the American people would eventually turn on the agency."

Prosecutorial Misconduct

DURING NOVEMBER AND December 1998 the *Pittsburgh Post-Gazette* published a series of ten lengthy investigative reports drawn from its two-year investigation of prosecutorial misconduct. The reports reveal a law enforcement "culture in which the pursuit of convictions has replaced the pursuit of justice, sometimes at any price." Summing up its findings, the newspaper reported:

> Hundreds of times during the past 10 years, federal agents and prosecutors have pursued justice by breaking the law. They lied, hid evidence, distorted facts, engaged in cover-ups, paid for perjury and set up innocent people in a relentless effort to win indictments, guilty pleas and convictions. Rarely were these federal officials punished for their misconduct. . . .
>
> Perjury has become the coin of the realm in federal law enforcement. People's homes are invaded because of lies. People are arrested because of lies. People go to prison because of lies. People stay in prison because of lies, and bad guys go free because of lies.

When the limited resources of one newspaper are sufficient to expose hundreds of cases of criminal behavior by federal law enforcement officials, it casts doubts on the integrity of the entire criminal justice system in the United States.

The reader needs to understand the magnitude of the problem. The *Post-Gazette* is not talking about occasional miscarriages of justice due to overworked prosecutors and crowded court dockets. The newspaper has documented hundreds of cases of willful, purposeful, intentional frame-ups of both innocent people and criminals against whom evidence is lacking. The frame-ups protect real criminals, who pay off federal law enforcement officers and prosecutors, and advance law enforcement careers with high conviction rates. For example, the *Post-Gazette* reports that Assistant U.S. Attorney James B. Velder told several people that he was unmoved by innocence or guilt; he just wanted a high-profile indictment to further his career.

At the beginning of this chapter we noted some of the developments that have caused convictions to replace justice as the goal of prosecutors and police. With the exception of Benthamite ideology, the greatest damage to justice has been done by the unintended consequences of the conservatives' war against crime.

In 1974 Congress discarded the wisdom of J. Edgar Hoover and gave the okay to sting operations by federal agents. Today it is routine for federal agents to create criminal enterprises. Initially, these enterprises were aimed at luring known criminals into situations where they could be apprehended. Increasingly, however, stings are used to entrap unsuspecting innocents and to exaggerate the role of minor criminals so that they become "fall guys" for the kingpins.

One reason for the routine misuse of the sting is the ambition of many federal agents and prosecutors, whose careers depend on convictions. Formerly, prosecutors would only prosecute known crimes for which they had good evidence. Today, in the name of expedient justice, they create crimes by paying criminals with dropped charges, reduced sentences, and monetary payments to entrap both the guilty and the innocent in orchestrated criminal conspiracies.

The ability of prosecutors to purchase testimony was greatly enhanced by the 1987 sentencing guidelines adopted by Congress. Conservatives maintained that a rising crime rate was the result of liberal judges handing out light sentences. Lawmakers responded to these claims by taking away sentencing discretion from judges and specifying prison time according to the severity of the offense. The unintended consequence was to give prosecutors the ability to coerce pleas by manipulating charges. Now it is the prosecutor who controls the sentence by the number and severity of the charges he brings. By piling on charges, or in the case of drug infractions, exaggerating the quantity of the substance, prosecutors can elicit guilty pleas even from the innocent. A person faced with charges that mandate long sentences is likely to avoid the risk of trial and plead to a lesser charge. Moreover, the system punishes people who plead innocent. By law, a person who fights a federal charge receives a longer sentence, if found guilty, than he would receive if he pled guilty to the charge.

Plea bargaining and the ability it gives prosecutors to control sentencing has enabled prosecutors and law enforcement agents to create a vast network of informants, who finger other criminals as well as innocent people. The *Post-Gazette* reported cases in which the FBI lost control of informants and for decades protected hardened criminal operations. The FBI was used by one organized crime gang to eliminate its rivals.

It is serious enough when federal agents get into bed with criminals, but a new practice known as "jumping on the bus," which is an enormous threat to innocents, has grown up. It works as follows: Government informants sell information on open or unsolved cases to prison inmates. Sometimes prosecutors and federal agents feed the information directly. The inmate memorizes the case, which gives him the appearance of having inside knowledge. The inmate then comes forward claiming information to trade in exchange for a reduced sentence, which under the guidelines can only be granted at a prosecutor's request. The inmate then works with the prosecutor to finger someone. It might be another inmate or a person on the outside. The inmate, coached by prosecutors, weaves a story to connect the person with the crime. Sometimes the prosecutor supplies the names of the persons that he wants fingered by the fabricated testimony.

Formerly, accusations, especially self-serving accusations by criminals, were treated as leads to be investigated. If the leads panned out, evidence still had to be marshaled and presented to a grand jury and in court. Today, the accusation has become the evidence. The prisons are filled with people falsely convicted by other inmates, who use information from confidential federal law enforcement files to corroborate crimes they have not witnessed and to concoct testimony against people they do not know and have not met.

Inmates themselves, displaying more conscience than many U.S. attorneys, have repeatedly blown the whistle on this scheme. According to the *Post-Gazette*, the Department of Justice and FBI have repeatedly and intentionally turned a blind eye. The practice of buying and selling lies to obtain convictions is such an ingrained practice in law enforcement that it cannot be curtailed without acknowledging the corruption of the criminal justice system and releasing vast numbers of wrongly convicted persons. Since no attorney general is going to attempt such a clean-up, it means that in the United States today the criminal element has a big say in who goes to prison.

Often it is an innocent person. The *Post-Gazette's* investigations exposed scores of cases in which innocent people were knowingly framed by federal prosecutors with false testimony that had been purchased from criminals. Such cases demonstrate that the focus of the criminal justice system is shifting from solving crimes and convicting the guilty to setting up the innocent.

Helmut Groebe, a German criminal wanted in four countries, was hired by federal prosecutors to boost their conviction rates by entrapping victims. For his services, Groebe was paid with protection from arrest, permanent residency in the United States, and $600,000. In exchange, Groebe helped federal agents frame numerous innocent people, ranging from his naïve lovers to legitimate businessmen to a high official of a foreign government. The details of these stories reveal astonishing criminal behavior by federal prosecutors and federal agents, who had no pangs about working closely with a ruthless con artist in order to frame innocent people.

Groebe tricked his Brazilian lover into traveling to Miami to sell her condominium to a buyer he had found. He told her it would be a cash deal, because the buyer wanted to keep the transaction secret. The "buyer" was a DEA agent and Groebe's lover went to prison for money laundering. Another victim was businessman Wolfgang von Schlieffen. Groebe approached him, claiming to have buyers for his cars and condominiums. Again the buyers were DEA agents, who entrapped von Schlieffen by offering cash.

Groebe's most audacious act was to fabricate "evidence" against Faustino Rico Toro, an official of the Bolivian government in charge of anti-drug efforts. Informed that he had been indicted in the United States on the basis of charges by a person unknown to him, Toro voluntarily came to the United States to face down the charge. Unknown to Toro, federal agents had purchased testimony from four "co-conspirators" who had been coached to testify that he protected drug lords. Toro lost five years of his life to the plot fabricated against him. But he hired a savvy investigator, who managed to unearth Groebe's payments to the "co-conspirators," the federal payments to Groebe, and the exculpatory evidence that federal prosecutors had withheld. Faced with exposure in court of their criminal behavior, prosecutors offered to drop the fabricated charges against Toro in exchange for his guilty plea to a petty drug infraction. Toro accepted, "not because I am guilty but because I cannot risk fighting even false charges in a system of justice that cannot be trusted."

Groebe's freelance contract with federal prosecutors allowed him to select the victims who would be criminalized in orchestrated situations. In other cases, prosecutors identify criminals—or innocents against whom they hold a grudge— and hire criminals to help to convict them. John Pree was facing a life sentence for armed robbery. Federal agents offered to let him off in exchange for helping them convict Detroit crime boss Vito Giacalone and his accomplices. Pree described the deal to the *Post-Gazette:* Federal agents briefed Pree on several crimes to which he would plead guilty and testify that he was acting on the orders of Giacalone and his associates. In place of a life sentence for his real crime, Pree would serve less than ten years for the invented crimes. He would also receive cash and a new identity. Pree agreed to the deal. He did not know Giacalone, but federal agents fabricated his testimony to meet their needs. Pree's false testimony got seventeen suspected mobsters indicted. Pree later blew the whistle on the plot when he concluded that the federal agents were double-crossing him.

Accustomed to framing criminals, prosecutors sometimes use their unchecked powers to settle personal scores. Patrick Halliman, a member of a prominent San Francisco legal family, prevailed in contentious negotiations with Assistant U.S. Attorney Anthony White to get his client, Ciro Mancuso, a plea-bargained ten-year sentence instead of life in prison. Angry that Halliman had bested him, White struck a deal with Mancuso to link Halliman to a drug conspiracy in exchange for probation. White then piled on more charges. He attempted to get Halliman's lawyer disqualified from the case, and he seized Halliman's art collection by claiming falsely that Halliman was illegally trafficking in ancient art. Halliman eventually beat the charges. The *Post-Gazette* reports that it asked the U.S.

attorney in Las Vegas and Department of Justice officials specific questions about the case "but got no response."

Loren Pogue and his wife, Delores, have twenty-seven children, fifteen of them adopted. Pogue is serving twenty-two years in federal prison, because a paid government informant, Mitchell Henderson, lured Pogue under false pretenses into a trap. Thinking he was going to sell a land parcel to a legitimate buyer, Pogue was confronted by DEA agents posing as a hardened drug gang, who claimed they wanted the land for an airstrip. Pogue, in fear for his life, listened while the DEA agents ran up charges against him by describing the huge quantities of cocaine they planned to run through the airstrip. Unlike the agents, Pogue knew that the land was a rocky parcel on a steep hillside where no airstrip could be built. But because he listened to the agents describe their plot, he was charged with being part of a drug conspiracy.

This is what the War on Drugs has come to: setting up innocent people in order to produce "drug criminals" to justify budgets overflowing with taxpayers' money.

Dr. George Pararas-Carayannis is one of the foremost authorities on tsunami—tidal waves triggered by earthquakes. He is the grandson of Lela Carayannis, who led Greece's anti-Nazi resistance organization during World War II. He is in prison for laundering money.

Carayannis was set up by a sexy young woman who showed a romantic interest in him. He did not know that she was an illegal alien who had agreed to entrap victims in exchange for permission to remain in the United States. The woman tricked Carayannis into running through his credit card account some credit card charges that she said were from customers of her business. He was then arrested for laundering money from prostitution. Apparently, there was no prostitution, but he was convicted because the woman testified that she had told him her business was an "escort business." This allegation was the

sole "proof" that Carayannis was knowingly guilty of laundering illegal money.

FBI Director J. Edgar Hoover understood that stings
orchestrated to catch criminals would corrupt law enforcement
and be used to manufacture phony crimes with which to entrap
innocents. Hoover would not permit FBI stings, because he
did not want the FBI to become a criminal organization.

The money shoveled into the War against Crime, together
with the unfettered power of prosecutors to control sentencing, purchase testimony, operate stings, and withhold exculpatory evidence has created a situation in the United States today
not unlike that which existed in Stalinist Russia. KGB agents,
under intense pressure to arrest plotters and enemies of the
state, would periodically conduct "street sweeps" in which hap-
less passersby became fodder for the torture-confession mills
that filled the Gulag Archipelago.

The *Post-Gazette*'s investigative reporting reveals a criminal
justice system that cannot be trusted. The Justice Department
refuses to police the system and fights every effort of Congress
to impose ethical guidelines. As the *Post-Gazette* noted, the
misconduct of federal law enforcement "can touch any
American."

The *Post-Gazette* concluded that federal law enforcement
officers know that their pursuit of convictions at any cost "will
do them no harm. No matter what the misconduct, it is almost
impossible for a criminal defendant to sue a federal officer or
prosecutor for damages. No matter what the misconduct, the
Justice Department rarely disciplines agents or prosecutors
who cross the line into unethical or illegal behavior."

What, then, can we do? Jurors can stop being so gullible.
First of all, jurors need to know that a grand jury indictment is
meaningless. Former Deputy Attorney General Arnold I.
Burns recently said, "The federal grand jury is no longer a
protection of the person who is suspected of a crime. The

grand jury process is as far afield from what it was intended to be as it could possibly be."

The *Post-Gazette*'s investigations show that prosecutors have total control over the grand jury. Prosecutors alone determine the evidence jurors see and the witnesses they hear. This permits prosecutors to manipulate evidence to favor their version of events, emphasizing some testimony and ignoring contrary testimony. Even rumors are admissible as evidence. The defendant has no right to be present or to have an attorney rebut false testimony and expose the paid informants. In a 1992 split decision, the U.S. Supreme Court ruled that prosecutors can withhold exculpatory evidence from grand jurors even when it proves the innocence of the defendant. As former Deputy Attorney General Arnold Burns put it, the Court "does not have a full appreciation" of the injustice its ruling ensures.

Federal judges can do little to stop the abuses. Occasionally a judge is so offended by the prosecutor's misconduct that he dismisses all charges. The *Post-Gazette* quotes federal judges and former U.S. attorneys reprimanding identified prosecutors for egregious misconduct, but it has proven impossible to hold prosecutors accountable. In one frame-up orchestrated by Assistant U.S. Attorney Karen Cox, U.S. District Judge Steven D. Merryday threw out the indictment and prohibited the government from retrying the defendant. Judge Merryday denounced Ms. Cox for bringing a case based on lies and false witness. We must ask ourselves what kind of people would brazenly attempt to frame the innocent in a federal courtroom. The only possible answer is evil people. Evil is afoot in the criminal justice system.

According to Thomas Dillard, a high-level federal prosecutor for eighteen years, many prosecutors no longer feel restrained by law and ethics. For federal prosecutors, "the ends justify the means," Dillard says. Others agree. Robert Merkle was appointed U.S. attorney by President Ronald Reagan, and he served in that post from 1982 to 1988. Prosecution, he says, is "a result-oriented process today, fairness be damned." Prosecutors, Merkle says, are political animals pressured to justify budgets with convictions, "and that causes them to prosecute absolutely bogus cases to get those statistics." Plato Cacheris, a federal prosecutor for eight years, says that "there are unfortunately enough examples of dishonesty cropping up that it is troubling to anybody in this business."

The Justice Department, of course, denies it all. But the telltale sign of how bad the situation really is is a law school textbook, *Prosecutorial Misconduct*, now in its second edition, by Bennett Gershman, a former prosecutor turned law professor. The text schools defense attorneys in the wayward ways of prosecutors. In an honest criminal justice system, there would be no need for such a textbook.

Prosecutors are aided and abetted in their misconduct by the attitude, pervasive among the public, that crime is out of control. Jurors drawn from a population that feels insecure are unlikely to disbelieve prosecutors and police. (The exception is inner-city black jurors.) Moreover, with so many real criminals running loose, jurors are unlikely to suspect prosecutors of fabricating cases in order to obtain convictions. White jurors view prosecutors and police as allies in maintaining the fabric of civilized society, not as ambitious people pursuing careers at any cost to justice. As former U.S. Attorney Robert Merkle says, "People don't know how they're being suckered."

For years civil libertarians such as Harvey Silverglate and Alan Dershowitz have complained about abusive prosecutors. With the *Post-Gazette's* investigations, these abuses can no longer be dismissed as self-serving folklore from defense attorneys. Recently PBS *Frontline* broadcast a documentary, *Snitch*, produced by Ofra Bikel. The syndicated columnist Clarence Page described the program as follows:

"Snitch" shows self-described lying informants and their victims, male, female, young and old, white and black. It shows drug traffickers who admit to receiving money, a lighter sentence or complete freedom, simply for lying about someone else. It shows the families that have been ruined, financially and otherwise, by snitches and the get tough politicians who piously justify the laws they passed. (*Washington Times*, 1-16-99, A13)

Janet Novack, a reporter for *Forbes* magazine, periodically reports on prosecutorial misconduct. On January 25, 1999, she reported that federal prosecutors are attempting to breach the attorney-client privilege by threatening a company's lawyers with indictments for defending their clients.

Many journalists, however, are in collusion with prosecutors, serving up the prosecutorial side of the case as objective fact. As the lives of more and more innocent people are ruined, journalists and the public might catch on before false prosecution becomes a political weapon in the hands of a corrupt president or an ideologically motivated political party or faction.

The disappearance of even-handed prosecution is a taking not only of property but of the Rights of Englishmen and the majesty of law. Moreover, by creating criminal laws out of civil offenses, as in the Exxon *Valdez* and Charles Keating cases, prosecutors have become legislators like federal agencies, thus undermining the accountability of law.

CHAPTER ELEVEN

ABDICATING
LEGISLATIVE POWER

LAW IS THE set of principles that protects citizens from tyranny. When there can be no crime without intent, no retroactive liability, no self-incrimination, no invasions of the attorney-client privilege, no infringements of a vigorous and vocal defense; when a person's property is respected as an extension of himself and when prosecutors exercise sober discretion, the chances for tyranny diminish. Each of these protections, which took centuries to evolve, has taken a ferocious beating during the twentieth century in America. Today even wealthy and prominent Americans are less secure in law than unemployed English coal miners in the 1930s.

To ensure the permanence of these safeguards that make law a protector of people rather than a weapon to use against them, the Founding Fathers made law accountable to the people. In the system they devised, people would never have to suffer from the imposition of unjust rules of conduct, because the people themselves rather than governing elites would control the rules under which they agreed to live. Representatives elected through the democratic process would be the sole makers of laws. This constitutional arrangement reflects the unique precept of Anglo-Saxon law—which scholars such as Norman Cantor have traced back to Tacitus's *Germania*—that law resides in the hearts of the people rather than the mouth of the king.

The Constitution's first seventy-seven words sum up this design. Immediately following the preamble's declaration that "We the People . . . ordain and establish this Constitution for the United States of America," the first sentence of the Constitution's body states, "All legislative Powers herein granted shall be vested in a Congress of the United States which shall consist of a Senate and House of Representatives." All legislative power—the exclusive authority to make, alter, amend, and repeal laws—is reposed within the U.S. Congress. "We the People" delegated "All legislative Powers" to the U.S. Congress, period.

Legislative power must remain in the body where it is placed by the Constitution. It follows from the Constitution's preamble and Article I, Section 1, that as "We the People" have vested "All legislative Powers" in elected representatives, Congress cannot delegate the lawmaking power, which is held in trust from the people, to someone else. Otherwise, self-rule would be a farce. This corollary is expressed in the Anglo-Saxon legal maxim *Delegata potestas non potest delegari*—"A delegated power cannot itself be delegated. The purpose of this restriction on delegation is to maintain the accountability of lawmakers. Delegation allows Congress to avoid responsibility for the burdens of the law.

This principle has deep historical roots. John Locke wrote that the people cannot be bound by any laws except those that are made by their elected representatives. Elected legislators can only "make laws," Locke said; they are not permitted to "make legislators" by placing their own authority to make laws "in other hands." Montesquieu observed that when law enforcers are simultaneously lawmakers, "there can be no liberty." Alexis de Tocqueville stressed that by keeping law-making power within the legislature, rather than allowing it to be delegated to executive administrators, American authorities are forced to remember "their popular origins and the power from which they emanate." William Blackstone wrote that aristocratic regimes that lack legislative accountability are "less honest" than those in which "the right of making laws resides in the people at large."

The truth about law in the United States today is that the vast number of rules of conduct under which citizens are forced to live do not derive from accountable legislators. New York Law School professor David Schoenbrod shows in his 1993 book, *Power Without Responsibility: How Congress Abuses the People Through Delegation*, that the American people are no longer governed by statutory law enacted by legislators who are accountable to them. The requirement in Article I of the U.S. Constitution that Congress make all laws has been ignored for the greater part of the twentieth century. It is as if a Caesar had abolished the U.S. Constitution. Statutes enacted by Congress have become little more than opportunities for bureaucrats to legislate. As the twenty-first century begins, it is actually a misnomer to refer to the House of Representatives and Senate as constituting the legislative branch of the U.S. government, because the most powerful legislators, those who construct the decrees that most directly impact people's lives, are entrenched in federal bureaucracies.

This has come about because, as years passed, people secure in the law lost sight of the reasons for their safety. Other threats became more pressing. Monopolies needed to be curbed, and then the Great Depression instilled in a generation of Americans a fear of unemployment and an impecunious old age. The argument was made that government needed to do more than Congress could manage. In the 1930s a coterie of government activists loosely organized around Harvard law professor Felix Frankfurter, later to be a Supreme Court Justice, pushed the transfer of legislative power from Congress to executive branch agencies. James Burnham describes the time: Bills were written by the executive branch "at an assembly line pace. . . . There were instances when, without any member's having seen a word of the text, without anything more than the title being read . . . adoption would be at once and automatically voted."

There is tremendous paradox in this spectacle. The mistaken monetary policy of a regulatory agency—the Federal Reserve—together with mistaken fiscal policy had created the confidence-shattering Great Depression, which was then used to destroy the historic achievement of the nondelegation doctrine that was enshrined in the Constitution as a bulwark against tyranny. During Franklin D. Roosevelt's New Deal of the 1930s, Senate majority leader Joseph T. Robinson, Democrat from Arkansas, wept in humiliation as the legislative and executive powers were merged in unaccountable bureaucratic hands. This resurrection of the conditions for tyranny has been thinly veiled by the doctrine of legislative branch oversight of the regulatory agencies.

For more than a century, the nondelegation doctrine was a widely shared constitutional precept. In the 1892 *Field v. Clark* case, Justice John Marshall Harlan wrote, "That congress cannot delegate legislative power to the president is a principle universally recognized as vital to the integrity and maintenance of the system of government ordained by the Constitution." Even those who favored railroad, antitrust, and banking legislation in the late nineteenth and early twentieth centuries respected the nondelegation doctrine and attempted to draft statutes so that executive enforcement personnel could never become lawmakers.

But with the deluge of federal regulation in the New Deal, transgressing this previously "universally recognized" and "vital" constitutional precept became a hallmark of progress. The centerpiece of the New Deal was delegation of lawmaking power from Congress to administrative agencies. Although the Supreme Court initially balked at extensive New Deal legislative delegations in cases dealing with poultry sales and oil shipments, the Court's resistance to legislative delegation soon dissipated under pressure from President Franklin Delano Roosevelt's court-packing initiative. Although today the judiciary still gives lip service to the nondelegation doctrine, jurists never find delegations to be unconstitutional. Today nondelegation, the achievement of a thousand-year struggle, is a dead letter constitutional principle.

As long as administrative agencies purport to follow an undefined "intelligible principle" in a statute, such as "promoting the public interest," "fair and equitable prices," fighting "excessive profits" or "imminent hazards to public safety," unelected bureaucrats have free rein to make the law. Consequently, commentators routinely refer to the nondelegation doctrine as "moribund," "enfeebled," "lacking bite." They view legislative delegation to administrative agencies as the "legal expression" of post–New Deal government.[1]

As the administrative state was taking shape, only a learned few, such as Supreme Court Justice George Sutherland, who were not swept up in the economic hysteria of the 1930s appreciated the dangers to "personal liberty and private property" accompanying legislative delegation. Sutherland saw delegation as "obnoxious" and "unconstitutional" congressional abdication.[2] A former U.S. senator from Utah and leader of the American Bar Association, Sutherland had been trained as a

---

[1]Laurence H. Silberman, "Chevron—The Intersection of Law and Policy," *George Washington Law Review* 58 (June 1990): 821–28; Edward S. Corwin, *The Constitution: and What It Means Today*, rev. ed. By Chase, Harold W. and Ducat, Craig R. (Princeton: Princeton University Press, 1973), p. 7; Gerald Gunther and Kathleen M. Sullivan, *Constitutional Law*, 13th ed. (Westbury, New York: Foundation, 1997); Theodore J. Lowi, *The End of Liberalism: The Second Republic of the United States*, 2d ed. (New York: Norton, 1979), pp. 92–93 ("Policy without law is what a broad delegation of power is").

[2]Hadley Arkes, *The Return of George Sutherland: Restoring a Jurisprudence of Natural Rights* (Princeton: Princeton University Press, 1994); *Carter v. Carter Coal Co.*, 298 U.S. 238 (1936).

lawyer at the University of Michigan under the tutelage of the premier late-nineteenth-century constitutional scholar, Thomas Cooley. As the American frontier was being settled, Cooley's popular treatise, *Constitutional Limitations*, captured the American legal mind with an intensity similar to that which had made Blackstone's *Commentaries* a best-seller in colonial America. But to a fearful nation stricken with mass unemployment, Justice Sutherland's defense of the constitutional order appeared as an unaffordable and irrelevant luxury.

Prior to the New Deal, legislation tended to be specifically and tightly written in order to avoid delegating the law to executive branch enforcers. This minimized the opportunity for executive branch interpretation. The perils of the new delegation, Sutherland realized, came from the broad, even blanket, delegation that, in the words of his nemesis James M. Landis, "means, of course, that the operative rules will be found outside the statute book."

Landis, a New Dealer who resigned as chairman of the Securities and Exchange Commission in January 1938 to become at age thirty-seven Harvard Law School's youngest dean, used a Yale Law School Storrs Lecture to assail Justice Sutherland's defense of Article I as mindless invective against our savior, the administrative state. Had Landis acquired the religious demeanor of his Presbyterian missionary parents, he would, no doubt, have compared the coming of the administrative state with the coming of Christ. People would be saved. For Landis, the New Deal was a missionary undertaking.

Landis justified the unprecedented broad delegations of power on the grounds of bureaucratic expertise. The professionals who knew best would fill in the blanks. He excoriated Sutherland for his distrust of unaccountable bureaucratic power, the very power that expertise justified. As Morton J. Horwitz has noted in his book *The Transformation of American Law, 1870–1960: The Crisis of Legal Orthodoxy*, Landis's "joyous celebration of the virtues" of expertise became the basis for the growth of the administrative state. Landis fervently believed that wisdom lay in the bureaucrat's expertise, not in "procrustean" constitutional standards that limit administrative discretion in favor of liberty.

Justice Sutherland's warnings against encroachment on the Constitution by arbitrary power and the erosion of "the fundamental rights, privileges and immunities of the people" by a multitude of petty extensions of bureaucratic power seemed quaint to New Dealers. The Soviet state, with totally unaccountable law, was promising a New Man and a New Society. Italy had Benito Mussolini's corporative state. New Dealers were not going to let America be left behind the tide of history. As Schoenbrod has noted, the "massive delegation of power to President Roosevelt took place in the same year that the German Reichstag delegated all its powers to Adolph Hitler." Upon hearing of the National Industrial Recovery Act, Mussolini remarked of Roosevelt, "*Ecco un ditatore*" ("Behold a dictator").

Landis's faith that men bred to the facts were superior in governance to men bred to politics is still the hope of our time. Democracy and Congress are belittled across the ideological spectrum. The contending forces struggling to influence the shape of society focus on controlling the executive agencies and the federal courts. For example, four days prior to Ronald Reagan's inauguration in January 1981, the Carter administration issued two volumes of new regulations to advance agendas that the people had just voted against. Democracy has no friends. The administrative state grows irrespective of the political coloration of Congress and the White House. Landis's New Government doctrine of merged legislative, executive, and judicial functions, united through "rule-making, enforcement, and the disposition of competing claims," resonates today in Republican jurist Laurence Silberman's defense of judicial deference to regulatory authorities.[3] The separation of powers, which gave accountability to law and protections to citizens, has faded away.

The consequences, predicted by Sutherland, are showing up in our own time. We have so far avoided, as Sutherland thought we would, "the fatal consequences of a supreme autocracy." But we have experienced the invasion of personal rights and loss of control over our property that he predicted. It has become routine to read of American citizens being manhandled by regulatory bureaucrats in whose hands lawmaking has been combined with law enforcement.

An article in *Forbes* (1 December 1997) shows how the pillars of justice have crumbled. Today bureaucrats can define criminal offense on the spot by how they interpret the regulation that they write. This gives regulatory bureaucrats vast discretion in defining the law. This wide range of discretion is an example of delegation at its worst. The same court system that overturned vagrancy laws because they gave the police officer and local judge too much discretion to define the offense permits the regulatory bureaucrat not only to define the violation but also to determine whether it is a civil or criminal offense. A cooperative "offender" may get off with a civil penalty, whereas a person who sticks up for his rights may receive a criminal indictment. The ability of bureaucrats to define the law dispenses with the hallowed principle of no crime without intent and no retroactive crimes. Federal bureaucrats, interpreting East Honolulu's municipal waste discharge permit differently than the plant managers, swooped in and indicted them. A federal appeals court upheld their convictions on the grounds that it is irrelevant that the managers didn't know they had committed an illegal action.

The spontaneous creation of criminal offenses by bureaucratic interpretation has contributed to the destruction of prosecutorial restraint. Investigators raided the office of Michigan

---

[3]Silberman, *Chevron*, pp. 821–28.

osteopath Nicholas Bartz looking for evidence of billing fraud. After more than a year the investigators came up with $300 of dubious charges in a practice that billed three-quarters of a million dollars annually. Obviously, there was no basis for the investigation, but instead of apologizing for wasting the tax-payers' money and disrupting the doctor's practice, the government indicted Dr. Bartz. He spent a half-million dollars on lawyers before a judge finally dismissed the $300 charge.[4]

These kinds of outrages are so routine that some Americans today are as likely to be wrongfully prosecuted as to be victims of crimes. When the United States was founded, piracy, treason, and counterfeiting were the only federal crimes. Today there are more than 3,000 that derive from statutes and 10,000 that have been created by regulation. This vast criminalization of normal behavior, such as that of farmers who clean drainage ditches and ranchers who repair fence posts and protect their livestock from predators, means that Americans are at risk when they make routine use of their property and operate their businesses in time-honored ways.

Crime and punishment are increasingly an Alice-in-Wonderland experience. Ocie and Carey Mills, armed with a state permit, used clean dirt to level a building lot. Their action was legal under Florida law, but federal bureaucrats stepped in and claimed jurisdiction under the Clean Water Act, which regulates the discharge of pollutants into the "navigable waters of the U.S." No waters, navigable or otherwise, were affected by the property improvement. For putting clean dirt on their dry land, father and son spent twenty-one months in prison. A federal bureaucrat ruled that the Mills' dry property was a "wetland" even though the State of Florida did not recognize it as such.[5]

---

[4]Brigid McMenamin and Janet Novack, "The White-Collar Gestapo: When the Criminal Laws Are So Expansive That Everyone Is Guilty of Something," *Forbes*, 1 December 1997, 82. See also James V. Delong, "The Criminalization of Just About Everything," *The American Enterprise*, March/April 1994, 26–35.
[5]McMenamin and Novack, "The White-Collar Gestapo," 82.

Ocie Mills and his son were imprisoned for a regulatory violation that had no statutory basis. The Clean Water Act makes no reference to wetlands and conveys no powers to the executive branch to create wetlands regulations. This has been acknowledged by the Clinton Administration, which said, "Congress should amend the Clean Water Act to make it consistent with the agencies' rulemaking." Two U.S. senators, Max Baucus (D-Montana) and John Chafee (R-Rhode Island) introduced a bill to codify the wetlands regulations that are being enforced without any statutory basis.

This is the codification of tyranny. The constitutional disintegration is so pervasive that it does not occur to the president of the United States or to U.S. senators to ask bureaucrats what they are doing making law that has not even been delegated. The wetlands regulations are not even a delegated authority; they are purely a bureaucratic initiative.

Congress's power and that of "We the People" have collapsed as thoroughly as the power of medieval kings who delegated to their officers. Charlemagne's successors found themselves unable to revoke the fiefs they had delegated to their appointed officials. Independent rulers—counts and dukes—grew out of the delegated powers. Unable to stop hereditary assumption of the fiefs, kings retained for a period the right to confirm the heir in office. A ceremony would be held in which the heir would accept his fief and powers as if they were still conveyed by the king. It is the same kind of legal pretense that Senators Baucus and Chafee were engaging in when they sponsored the bill to create, after the fact, a statutory basis for wetlands regulations.

The wetlands regulations show that bureaucrats today create law without waiting for Congress to delegate the powers to them. The Equal Employment Opportunity Commission guidelines show that they use their unaccountable powers to overthrow statutory law and require in its place the very behavior that the statute prohibits.

The 1964 Civil Rights Act explicitly prohibits racial quotas.
It explicitly defines discrimination as an intentional act
committed by one person against another. It explicitly denies
the EEOC any power to interpret the Civil Rights Act.
Nonetheless, it took only one bureaucrat, Alfred W.
Blumrosen, a short time to redefine discrimination as uninten-
tional statistical group disparities and to establish a hardened
system of racial quotas throughout the government and private
sectors.[6] Blumrosen bet that the federal judiciary would defer
to his reinterpretation of the act despite the statutory prohibition against regulatory interpretation. Blumrosen won his bet.
Chief Justice Warren Burger said in an unanimous opinion,
"The administrative interpretation of the act by the enforcing
agency is entitled to great deference."

We no longer have a constitutional order, a separation of
powers, self-rule, or a rule of law when the Supreme Court
permits a federal bureaucrat to usurp powers explicitly prohibited in statutory law in order to make prohibited actions the
law of the land. Little wonder that the Federal Communication
Commission has usurped the power of the purse and imposed
a telephone tax effective January 1998.[7] Long accustomed to
legislating, it is no big step for bureaucrats to impose taxation.
We the People have vanished. Our place has been taken
by wise men and anointed elites. We still have the pretense
of congressional oversight and the scholasticism of the
Administrative Procedure Act. This facade lacks the honesty of
the Enabling Act, passed by the German Reichstag, which
drained it of power by "delegating" legislative power to Hitler's
executive branch and which reads as follows:

---

[6]Paul Craig Roberts and Lawrence M. Stratton, *The New Color Line: How Quotas
and Privilege Destroy Democracy* (Washington, D.C.: Regnery, 1995), pp. 63–101.
[7]"New Phone Tax," Review and Outlook, *Wall Street Journal*, 9 December 1997;
"Phone Tax, Continued," Review and Outlook, *Wall Street Journal*, 23 December
1997.

In addition to the procedure for the passage of legislation outlined in the Constitution, the Reich Cabinet is also authorized to enact Laws. . . . The national laws enacted by the Reich Cabinet may deviate from the Constitution. . . . The national laws enacted by the Reich Cabinet shall be prepared by the Chancellor and published in the official gazette. They come into effect, unless otherwise specified, upon the day following their publication.

CHAPTER TWELVE

WHAT IS TO BE DONE?

ONE OF THE first movies released in 2000 is the story of Rubin "Hurricane" Carter, a black boxer who, according to his supporters, was twice framed for murder by New Jersey police. Mr. Carter spent twenty years in prison before he was exonerated because of trial improprieties. This movie provided an opportunity to educate the public about corruption in the criminal justice system, but in our politically correct era most viewers will conclude that Hurricane Carter was the victim of racism. The emphasis on racist "white justice"—as if whites are any safer—blinds the public to the real problem with the criminal justice system: the erosion of the Rights of Englishmen, not only in law but in the consciousness and attitudes of police, prosecutors, lawyers, and judges. It has become more important for the police to produce a suspect than to produce the right one. It is more important for the prosecutor to obtain a conviction (usually with a plea bargain) than to obtain justice. The justice system serves careers, not truth, and when our rights get in the way of careers, it is our rights that are cast aside.

Hurricane Carter was eventually exonerated, because celebrities made him a cause célèbre. But when billionaire Michael Milken and hotel queen Leona Helmsley were framed, celebrities did not rush to their cause. Milken and

Helmsley are white and rich and obviously not victims of racist white justice. The presumption is that they must have been guilty. The supposition that only blacks and other minorities can be framed hinders any concerted effort to reform a justice system that has become tyrannical.

This tyranny spreads like cancer. What happens, for example, when corrupt prosecutors, who gained name recognition by using any means to convict a "high-profile" target, capitalize on their fame and enter politics or prestigious law firms? Their lack of ethics and their manipulative ways go with them. Politics becomes even dirtier. Law firms are shaken loose from time-honored principles as partners are pried loose from their ethics in order to compete in the new ways.

Bill Gates is the richest person in the world. His company, Microsoft, is the most valuable company. In the parlance of this era, Gates and Microsoft are at the top of the "hegemonic order." This did not stop an ambitious and previously unknown assistant attorney general, Joel I. Klein, from targeting Microsoft with an antitrust case that would capture the imagination of the country and make a name for Joel Klein.

As this book goes to press, the Microsoft case has not concluded. The presiding judge, Thomas Penfield Jackson, realized that he was over his head in a mess that he had allowed to develop. He called in Judge Richard Posner, a famed jurist and antitrust expert, to oversee a settlement between Microsoft and the Department of Justice, with the aim of ensnaring Microsoft in the plea bargaining process. As of early April, 2000, Microsoft had not capitulated. In response, Judge Jackson increased the pressure by issuing another unfavorable ruling. Despite its vast resources, Microsoft's plight is essentially no different from that of Eric Washington (see chapter 6), a nineteen-year-old black man who was forced to admit to something he did not do in order to escape the government's grasp.

How did Microsoft find itself in federal court? Most antitrust experts believe the case against Microsoft is without foundation. Prominent legal scholars, such as Yale University's George L. Priest and the University of Chicago's Richard Epstein, have criticized both the Justice Department and Judge Jackson. Consumer harm is an essential ingredient of an antitrust case. Yet the Justice Department's own outside expert witness, Franklin M. Fisher of MIT, when asked during his testimony if consumers were being victimized by Microsoft, answered, "On balance, I think the answer was No."

Realizing that he had undermined Klein's case, Fisher quickly added that the harm would come in the future when Microsoft began acting like a monopolist. In other words, Microsoft was on trial for how it was allegedly going to act in the future. Here in all its glory is Jeremy Bentham's proactive approach of punishing crimes before they are committed.

Microsoft was hauled into court because defeated competitors sought to regain through political campaign contributions and government lobbying what they had lost in the marketplace. The political agitation against Microsoft created Klein's opportunity. He recruited an outside lawyer, David Boies, who is famous for eating with his hands in Washington, D.C., restaurants and gambling in Las Vegas. Boies's legal hallmark is an ability to manipulate witnesses and lure them into indefensible positions.

Klein and Boies recognized that Microsoft was a high-profile case that could be tried in the media and that Bill Gates's childlike personality would make him a poor witness. In a brilliant piece of journalism in the *New Yorker* (16 August 1999), Ken Auletta shows that Microsoft and its legal counsel, William H. Neukom, relied on the law and factual evidence and were out-foxed by Klein and Boies, who tried Gates on his personality. Gates, believing that evidence mattered, was an easy mark for the Justice Department. Prosecutors carefully courted the media. As the trial progressed, prosecutors supplied the interpretations of events that people read in their newspapers and watched on TV.

Gates, outraged over the charges against his company, felt that he was being demonized and turned into a victim charged with vague crimes, like Joseph K. in Kafka's novel *The Trial*. Burdened with this frame of mind and hindered by his personality, Gates's deposition was wobbly. When a man who is known to be very smart comes across as a poor witness, it creates the suspicion that he is lying or hiding the truth. This is especially the case when the substantive issues are over the heads of jurors, reporters, and the judge himself.

Klein and Boies succeeded with their plan to substitute a personal attack on Bill Gates in the place of evidence of anticompetitive conduct by Microsoft. Their success, in full view of the public and the legal profession, in using law as a weapon against Microsoft is a clear indication that our legal system has degenerated into tyranny.

Prospects for Reform

AUTHORS WHO EXPOSE such a deplorable state of affairs are expected to provide proposals for reform. The plight of American democracy is beyond the reach of legal reform alone. Our constitutional system and its precepts have lost the allegiance of American elites. Legislation is no solution when bureaucrats stand statutes on their heads and the Supreme Court will not defend the Constitution, or Congress its own powers.

Without an intellectual rebirth, a revival of constitutionalism, there is no hope for American democracy. As Justice George Sutherland said, "Arbitrary power and the rule of the Constitution cannot both exist. They are antagonistic and incompatible forces; and one or the other must of necessity perish whenever they are brought into conflict." Homogenous bureaucracies staffed with ideological zealots will devour the rights of the American people in the name of their causes, just as German Nazis and Soviet communists devoured the rights of their subjects.

The fervent belief that government power is a force for good and must be more and more unrestrained is the opposite of liberalism. Historically, evil was restrained as power was restrained. The New Deal transformation of liberalism, by unrestraining power, has unleashed evil and injustice.

Today Americans increasingly feel defenseless in the face of the government that they supposedly control. What was formerly a patriotic, flag-waving element of the population has been organizing itself for the past few years into private militias. In 1995, in the Oklahoma City bombing, a terrorist act was committed by Americans against the American government. Numerous polls show a widespread distrust and alienation of "We the People" from our own government. The attitudes of militarized federal law enforcement agencies toward the people show the same distrust. In 1995, Pennsylvania Avenue was closed off around the White House, making the symbol of the American republic similar to the walled Kremlin of the Soviets.

We see one hope for an intellectual rebirth that would let us reclaim our legal tradition of restrained power. This cause for hope is the universal failure of government. The twentieth century's disasters are all based in high hopes placed on government power. German National Socialism, Soviet and Chinese communism, French "indicative planning," Italy's corporative state, Latin American and African development planning, Asian industrial policy, and American New Dealism have all failed. The Benthamite commitment to government that has colored society and thinking about law must be approaching exhaustion. The proselytizing power of the secular worship of government is on the wane.

If experience counts, the time is ripe for true liberalism to make a comeback and again secure the allegiance of men of good will. The reclamation of accountable power will be no less a fight than the long struggle that first achieved it, culminating in the Glorious Revolution in seventeenth-century England and the U.S. Constitution in eighteenth-century America. With a few exceptions, such as Theodore J. Lowi and David Schoenbrod, American legal scholars support the coercive power assumed by the courts in the aftermath of *Brown v. Board of Education* as well as the New Deal delegation of legislative power to bureaucrats. The Benthamite misinterpretation of government power as a force for good has destroyed accountable law.

Today not even lawyers know what the law is. The unpredictability of law is one reason trials are rare. The vast majority of civil suits are settled prior to trial, and the vast majority of criminal cases are resolved with plea bargains.

Even when we do know what the law is, the law becomes subservient to the expansion of liability. For example, as University of Chicago law professor Richard Epstein has noted, tobacco companies have successfully defended against every case that tries to hold them responsible for health harms from tobacco, because it has been known for forty years that smoking can injure health. The Surgeon General's warning has been printed on cigarette packages since the 1960s, and long before that it was common among people to refer to cigarettes as "coffin nails." This established immunity, however, did not stop state attorneys general from banding together and coercing the tobacco companies into a settlement totaling $368 billion for the benefit of state budgets and innumerable plaintiffs' lawyers, including the brother of First Lady Hillary Rodham Clinton and the brother-in-law of Senate Majority Leader Trent Lott (R-Mississippi). The losers are the tobacco company shareholders and the rule of law.

In the tobacco case, we see the marriage of government with the plaintiffs' bar. If Superfund's search for deep pockets could assign liability to total innocents, the tobacco settlement can impose liability where the law found none. As the retroactive impositions of liability destroy companies—asbestos (Johns Manville, Keene, and scores of others) and breast implants (Dow Corning)—and the personal finances of the shareholders, any public health claim becomes grounds for confiscating property. Ralph Nader, who is closely tied to these lawsuits, has said that the next ones are alcoholic beverage makers, sugar, fat, and cholesterol-laden food producers, beef producers, makers of fiber-deficient foods, X-ray equipment manufacturers, pharmaceutical manufacturers, refrigerator manufacturers, hospital chains, automobile manufacturers, bicycle makers, and gun manufacturers.[1]

Once under way, it is hard to know where the assault on private property in the name of public causes stops. A pizzeria got a Superfund clean-up bill because a pizza box made its way to a Superfund site, even though the box was not a pollutant. Under the liability rulings associated with Superfund, anyone who can be connected in any way to a site is liable. This means that the paper and plastic companies that package dairy products and fat-laden fast foods can be made liable once these foods come under class action attacks. In keeping with the S&L suits, so could the companies' accountants and lawyers. What we've done, and are doing, from Superfund to tobacco, is to declare open season on property through a total separation of liability from fault. We have more in common with the anarchy of the Dark Ages, when marauding bands could confiscate whatever they could get their hands on, than we do with Blackstone's England, where "so great is the regard of the law for private property, that it will not authorize the least violation of it; no, not even for the general good of the whole community."

---

[1] Walter Olson, "Better Living Through Litigation?" *Public Interest* 103 (Spring 1991): 76–87. See also Ralph Nader and Mark Green, eds., *Verdicts on Lawyers* (New York: Crowell, 1976).

Public harm, of course, isn't limited to health. There is a vast corpus of antitrust law. It is more and more nebulous what an antitrust violation is. We have reached the point where a company that outperforms its competitors has by definition violated antitrust provisions. A successful company is vulnerable, like Microsoft, to a government suit. This is another problem with regulators as legislators, because the definition of a violation is up to them. The attack on corporations that eventually separated liability from fault began with Friedrich Kessler's writings about corporate fascism. Just as it took decades of attacks on Jews in Germany to set them up for ruin by the Nazis, Kessler's emotional denunciations of corporations exposed them to plunder by the plaintiffs' bar. The attack on corporations could eventually result in the confiscation of all property in the name of a public cause. We even have the case of Federal Reserve bureaucrat Alicia Munnell, who rose to become assistant secretary of the U.S. Treasury in the Clinton Administration, proposing to confiscate 15 percent of every American's pension fund to make up for the fact that contributions and earnings of pension funds are not taxed until distributed. With proposals such as this in the air, it does not take much imagination to picture the IRS proposing to confiscate people's assets on the grounds that part of their incomes went untaxed because of personal exemptions and the standard deduction. Whatever it is, a system with such uncertain rights is not a rule of law.

Constitutional law has been trivialized. In July 1997, the authors of a leading textbook on constitutional law, Daniel A. Farber, William N. Eskridge, Jr., and Philip P. Frickey, declared that "the emerging constitutional issue of the '90s" is "the extent to which the Constitution protects gay men, lesbians, and bisexuals from discriminatory treatment." The text's authors do not explain how a Constitution, whose major articles are dead as a doornail, can protect anyone, much less behavior that was regarded as a sin and a crime when the Constitution was written. When the Constitution was last interpreted on this issue by the Supreme Court in 1986, state law against homosexual sodomy was upheld.

These legal facts are not relevant to the text's authors, because what they mean by "Constitutional protection" is the granting of protected minority status by a federal judge. The protection-granting decree has no basis other than the preference of the judge. We fully expect to see in our lifetimes a constitutional text declare the emerging issue of the decade to be "the extent to which the Constitution protects pedophiles and practitioners of bestiality from discriminatory treatment."

The Constitution has been lost in poor teaching and the legal profession's accommodation to unaccountable power. Little wonder Lowi's attempt to resurrect accountable law has, after thirty years, still produced no response worthy of the name. In 1994, New York lawyer Phillip K. Howard published *The Death of Common Sense*. His book excoriated bureaucratic regulators for "suffocating America" in rules that defy common sense and achieve results that are the opposite of what is desired. Howard's response to the extraordinary bureaucratic invasion of private life, which brought even the voluntary charitable activities of Mother Teresa to a halt, is to recommend even more discretionary power for agencies.

The problem, Howard says, is our penchant for living under law. By issuing rules, regulators are carrying on the tradition of Congress's governing through specific statutory law. The solution, says Howard, is to dispense with the rulemaking and allow the agencies complete discretion to achieve their goals as they best think fit.

Howard's naïve confidence in a bureaucracy that power does not corrupt, brimming with wisdom and public spirit, is an extraordinary thing. His confidence in good intentions and the unrestrained power of government to do good has not been shaken by the massive corpus of work analyzing bureaucratic behavior or by the twentieth century's unsavory experiences with unaccountable government power.

One hears in Howard and legal scholarship generally echoes of Lenin's doctrine of power. The dictatorship necessary for the creation of a new and better society, Lenin said, is a "scientific concept." It "means neither more nor less than unlimited power, resting directly on force, not limited by anything, not restricted by any laws, nor any absolute rules. Nothing else but that."

This is the doctrine of government that Howard recommends when he opts for bureaucrats who are unconstrained even by their own rules. Congress can be abolished altogether. The bureaucrats who know best how to achieve goals will know best which goals to pick. This is the direction taken by legal scholarship, which consists of advocacy of coercive government power on behalf of one cause or another.

Perhaps never before in history have a people lived in such a hollowed-out legal order as Americans today. The American republic established by the Founding Fathers is long gone, destroyed by the Civil War and the New Deal. The Second Republic under which we live is a republic in name only. It is governance by bureaucrats, who make law under broadly delegated powers, and judges, who legislate and tax from the bench. Lowi's proposal for a Third Republic would bring an end to the arbitrary basis of government by marrying the administrative state to the Constitution. Under the Third Republic, legislation would be far more specific, removing the blanket element from the delegation of rulemaking authority. Lowi's attempt to restore accountable law, however, is too much for legal scholars, who identify with the causes that coercive power has advanced.

The Charlemagne model of government, which leaves the fate of people in the hands of a just and benevolent ruler, works only if there is a Charlemagne. Every regulator, judge, and law school dean may, like James Landis and Alfred Blumrosen, fancy himself as Charlemagne, but history's verdict is that Charlemagnes are rare. Tyranny is the consequence of unrestrained power, a point that the Founding Fathers understood well when they separated the powers of a small and restrained government. Contrary to Messrs. Farber, Eskridge, and Frickey, the constitutional issue of our time is the emerging tyranny of unaccountable law.

BIBLIOGRAPHY

Abbott, Jacob. *King Alfred of England*. New York: St. Hubert Guild, 1906.

Abernathy, Charles F. *Law in the United States: Cases and Materials*. Washington, D.C.: International Law Institute, 1995.

Abraham, Spencer. "Litigation Tariff: The Federal Case for National Tort Reform." *Policy Review*, Summer 1995.

Abrams, Floyd. "Why Lawyers Lie." *New York Times Magazine*, 9 October 1994.

Abramson, Jeffrey. *We, the Jury: The Jury System and the Ideal of Democracy*. New York: Basic Books, 1994.

Adler, Stephen J. *The Jury: Trial and Error in the American Courtroom*. New York: Random House, 1994.

Aiken, Jane Harris. "Ex Post Facto in the Civil Context: Unbridled Punishment." *Kentucky Law Journal* 81, no. 2 (1992–1993): 323–67.

Albrecht, Virginia S., and Good, Bernard N. *Wetland Regulation in the Real World*. Washington, D.C.: Beveridge and Diamond, February 1994.

Allen, Carleton Kemp. *Law in the Making*. 7th ed. Oxford: Clarendon Press, 1964.

Allen, Charlotte. "Disabling Businesses." *Insight*, 29 March 1992.

Alschuler, Albert W. "The Defense Attorney's Role in Plea Bargaining." *Yale Law Journal* 84, no. 6 (May 1975): 1179–1314.

Alschuler, Albert W. "The Failure of Sentencing Guidelines: A Plea for Less Aggregation." *University of Chicago Law Review* 58, no. 3 (Summer 1991): 901–51.

Alschuler, Albert W. "Implementing the Criminal Defendant's Right to Trial: Alternatives to the Plea Bargaining System." *University of Chicago Law Review* 50, no. 3 (Summer 1983): 931–1050.

Alschuler, Albert W. "Plea Bargaining and Its History." *Columbia Law Review* 79, no. 1 (January 1979): 1–43.

Alschuler, Albert W. "The Prosecutor's Role in Plea Bargaining." *University of Chicago Law Review* 36 (1968): 50–112.

Alschuler, Albert W. "The Trial Judge's Role in Plea Bargaining, Part I." *Columbia Law Review* 76, no. 7 (November 1976): 1059–1154.

Amar, Akhil Reed. "The Bill of Rights as a Constitution." *Yale Law Journal* 100, no. 5 (March 1991): 1131–1210.

Amar, Akhil Reed. *The Constitution and Criminal Procedure: First Principles.* New Haven: Yale University Press, 1997.

Amar, Akhil Reed. "Double Jeopardy Law after Rodney King." *Columbia Law Review* 95, no. 1 (January 1995): 1–59.

Amar, Akhil Reed. "Fourth Amendment First Principles." *Harvard Law Review* 107, no. 4 (February 1994): 757–857.

Amar, Akhil Reed. "The Future of Constitutional Criminal Procedure." *American Criminal Law Review* 33, no. 4 (Summer 1996): 1123–40.

Amar, Akhil Reed, and Hirsch, Alan. *For the People: What the Constitution Really Says about Your Rights.* New York: Free Press, 1998.

Anderson, Jerry L. "The Hazardous Waste Land." *Virginia Environmental Law Journal* 13 (Fall 1993): 1–56.

Anderson, John. "This Land Was Your Land." *Reader's Digest,* October 1997.

Arblaster, Anthony. *The Rise and Decline of Western Liberalism.* Oxford: Basil Blackwell, 1984.

Arens, Richard. "Conspiracy Revisited." *Buffalo Law Review* 3 (1953–1954): 242–68.

Arkes, Hadley. *First Things: An Inquiry into the First Principles of Morals and Justice.* Princeton: Princeton University Press, 1986.

Arkes, Hadley. *The Return of George Sutherland: Restoring a Jurisprudence of Natural Rights.* Princeton: Princeton University Press, 1994.

Arlen, Jennifer. "The Potentially Perverse Effects of Corporate Criminal Liability." *Journal of Legal Studies* 23 (June 1994): 833–67.

Armbrister, Trevor. "The Man Who Beat the IRS." *Readers' Digest,* July 1996.

Arnold, Thurman W. "Law Enforcement—An Attempt at Social Dissection." *Yale Law Journal* 42, no. 1 (November 1932): 1–24.

Atchison, Jack D. *Legal Extortion: The War against Lincoln Savings and Charles Keating.* Salt Lake City: Northwest Publishing, 1995.

Atkinson, Charles Milner. *Jeremy Bentham: His Life and Work.* New York: Augustus M. Kelley, 1969.

"Attorney-Client Privilege: Fixed Rules, Balancing, and Constitutional Entitlement." *Harvard Law Review* 91, no. 2 (December 1977): 464–87.

Auletta, Ken. "Hard Core." *New Yorker*, 16 August 1999.

Aylmer, G. E. *A Short History of 17th Century England: 1603–1689.* London: Blandford Press, 1963.

Bailey, Fenton. *Fall from Grace: The Untold Story of Michael Milken.* New York: Birch Lane, 1992.

Baird, Douglas G. *The Elements of Bankruptcy.* Westbury, New York: Foundation Press, 1992.

Baker, George D. "Principles for a New Superfund Program, 27 April 1995." Washington, D.C.: Superfund Reform 1995, 1995.

Baker, J. H. *An Introduction to English Legal History.* 3d ed. London: Butterworths, 1990.

Baker, Nancy V. *Conflicting Loyalties: Law and Politics in the Attorney General's Office, 1789–1990.* Lawrence: University Press of Kansas, 1992.

Baker, Newman F., and DeLong, Earl H. "The Prosecuting Attorney and His Office." *Journal of the American Institute of Criminal Law and Criminology* 25 (1934–1935): 695–720.

"Ballad of Ocie Mills." *Pacific Legal Foundation: At Issue,* 30 August 1993.

Banks, Margaret A. "Drafting the American Constitution: Attitudes in the Philadelphia Convention towards the British System of Government." *American Journal of Legal History* 10, no. 1 (1966): 15–33.

Barber, Sotirios A. *The Constitution and the Delegation of Congressional Power.* Chicago: University of Chicago Press, 1975.

Barnett, Randy E. "Foreword: Guns, Militia, and Oklahoma City." *Tennessee Law Review* 62 (Spring 1995): 443–59.

Barnett, Randy E. *The Rights Retained by the People: The History and Meaning of the Ninth Amendment.* Fairfax, Virginia: George Mason University Press, 1989.

Barnett, Randy E. "Some Problems with Contract as Promise." *Cornell Law Review* 77 (July 1992): 1022–33.

Barr, Lewis M. "CERCLA Made Simple: An Analysis of the Cases under the Comprehensive Environmental Response Compensation and Liability Act of 1980." *Business Lawyer* 45, no. 3 (May 1990): 923–1001.

Barrow, Brian P. "*Buckley v. Fitzsimmons:* Tradition Pays a Price for the Reduction of Prosecutorial Misconduct." *Whittier Law Review* 16 (1995): 301–29.

Bastiat, Frederic. *The Law*. 1850. Reprint, Irvington-on-Hudson, New York: Foundation for Economic Education, 1950.

Bator, Paul M.; Meltzer, Daniel J.; Mishkin, Paul J.; and Shapiro, David L. *Hart and Wechsler's The Federal Courts and the Federal System*. 3d ed. Westbury, New York: Foundation Press, 1988.

Beaver, James E., Narodick, Kit G., and Wallin, Joseph M. "Civil Forfeiture and the Eighth Amendment after Austin." *Seattle University Law Review* 19 (Fall 1995): 1–46.

Becker, Gary S., and Stigler, George J. "Law Enforcement, Malfeasance, and Compensation of Enforcers." *Journal of Legal Studies* 3, no. 1 (January 1974): 1–18.

Berger, Raoul. "Bills of Attainder: A Study of Amendment by the Court." *Cornell Law Review* 63, no. 3 (March 1978): 355–404.

Beschloss, Michael R. "Clifford Speaks." *New Yorker*, 6 September 1993.

Bidinotto, Robert James, ed. *Criminal Justice?: The Legal System vs. Individual Responsibility*. 2d. ed. Irvington-on-Hudson, New York: Foundation for Economic Education, 1996.

Bishop, Joel Prentiss. *New Commentaries on the Criminal Law*. 8th ed. Chicago: T. H. Flood, 1892.

Blackstone, William. *Commentaries on the Laws of England*. 4 vols. 1765–1769. Reprint, Chicago: University of Chicago Press, 1979.

Blaymore, Amy. "Retroactive Application of Superfund: Can Old Dogs Be Taught New Tricks?" *Environmental Affairs* 12, no. 1 (1985): 1–50.

Blomquist, Robert F. "The EPA Science Advisory Board's Report on 'Reducing Risk': Some Overarching Observations Regarding the Public Interest." *Environmental Law* 22 (1991): 149–88.

Bloom, Allan, ed. *Confronting the Constitution: The Challenge to Locke, Montesquieu, Jefferson, and the Federalists from Utilitarianism, Historicism, Marxism, Freudianism, Pragmatism, Existentialism. . . .* Washington, D.C.: AEI Press, 1990.

Bolt, Robert. *A Man for All Seasons: A Play of Sir Thomas More*. London: Educational Books, Ltd., 1963.

Boorstin, Daniel J. *The Americans: The Colonial Experience*. New York: Vintage, 1958.

Boorstin, Daniel J. *The Mysterious Science of the Law: An Essay on Blackstone's Commentaries*. Cambridge, Massachusetts: Harvard University Press, 1941.

Boudreaux, Donald J., and Pritchard, A. C. "Civil Forfeiture and the War on Drugs: Lessons from Economics and History." *San Diego Law Review* 33 (Winter 1996): 79–135.

Boudreaux, Donald J., and Pritchard, A. C. "Innocence Lost: *Bennis v. Michigan* and the Forfeiture Tradition." *Missouri Law Review* 61 (Summer 1996): 593–632.

Boudreaux, Donald J., and Pritchard, A. C. Review of *A License to Steal: The Forfeiture of Property*. *Cato Journal* 16, no. 1 (Spring/Summer 1996): 152–54.

Bovard, James. *Freedom in Chains: The Rise of the State and the Demise of the Citizen*. New York: St. Martin's, 1999.

Bovard, James. "The IRS vs. You." *American Spectator*, November 1995.

Bovard, James. *Lost Rights: The Destruction of American Liberty*. New York: St. Martin's, 1994.

Bovard, James. "The Real Superfund Scandal." *Cato Policy Analysis*, no. 89, 14 August 1987.

Bovard, James. "Seizure Fever: The War on Property Rights." *The Freeman*, January 1996.

Bowen, Catherine Drinker. *The Lion and the Throne: The Life and Times of Sir Edward Coke 1552–1634*. London: Hamish Hamilton, 1957.

Bowen, Catherine Drinker. *Yankee from Olympus: Justice Holmes and His Family*. Boston: Little, Brown, 1944.

Bowman, Frank O., III. "A Bludgeon by Any Other Name: The Misuse of 'Ethical Rules' against Prosecutors to Control the Law of the State." *Georgetown Journal of Legal Ethics* 9 (1996): 665–780.

Bradbury, Michael D. *Report on the Death of Donald Scott*. Office of the District Attorney, Ventura County, California, 30 March 1993.

Bradford, M. E. *Original Intentions: On the Making and Ratification of the United States Constitution*. Athens: University of Georgia Press, 1993.

Bradley, Barbara. "Juries and Justice: Is the System Obsolete?" *Insight*, 24 April 1995.

Brennan, William J., Jr. "The Criminal Prosecution: Sporting Event or Quest for Truth?" *Washington University Law Quarterly* 1963, no. 3 (June 1963): 279–95.

Breyer, Stephen G. *Breaking the Vicious Cycle: Toward Effective Risk Regulation*. Cambridge, Massachusetts: Harvard University Press, 1993.

Brimelow, Peter, and Spencer, Leslie. "The Plaintiff Attorneys' Great Honey Rush." *Forbes*, 16 October 1989.

Brown, Donald A. "EPA's Resolution of the Conflict between Cleanup Costs and the Law in Setting Cleanup Standards under Superfund." *Columbia Journal of Environmental Law* 15 (1990): 241–305.

Brown, Donald A. "Superfund Cleanups, Ethics, and Environmental Risk Assessment." *Boston College Environmental Affairs Law Review* 16 (Winter 1988): 181–97.

Brownell, Herbert. *Advising Ike: The Memoirs of Attorney General Herbert Brownell*. Lawrence: University Press of Kansas, 1993.

Bruck, Connie. *The Predators' Ball*. New York: Simon and Schuster, 1988.

Bunn, Richard L. "Statement of Richard L. Bunn, President and Chief Executive Officer, UGI Utilities, Inc. on Litigation Involving Ancient Liability Sites under Superfund." Testimony before the Senate Environment and Public Works Committee, 29 March 1995.

Burnham, David. *Above the Law: Secret Deals, Political Fixes, and Other Misadventures of the U.S. Department of Justice*. New York: Scribner, 1996.

Burnham, David. "The FBI: A Special Report." *The Nation*, 11 August 1997.

Burnham, James. *Congress and the American Tradition*. 1959. Reprint, Washington, D.C.: Regnery, 1996.

Burt, Dan M. *Abuse of Trust: A Report on Ralph Nader's Network*. Chicago: Regnery Gateway, 1982.

Bury, J. B. *A History of Freedom of Thought*. London: Oxford University Press, 1952.

Bush, Graeme W. "The Impact of RICO Forfeiture on Legitimate Business." *Notre Dame Law Review* 65 (1990): 996–1008.

Butterfield, Sir Herbert. *The Englishman and His History*. Camden, Connecticut: Archon Books, 1970.

Byron, Christopher. "The RICO Squeeze: Who's a Racketeer, Anyway?" *New York*, 17 July 1989.

Cahn, Edmond. *The Sense of Injustice*. Bloomington: Indiana University Press, 1964.

Cain, C. Edward. "The Attorney's Obligation of Confidentiality—Its Effect on the Ascertainment of Truth in an Adversary System of Justice." *Glendale Law Review* 3, no. 1 (1978–1979): 81–94.

Campbell, R. H., and Skinner, A. S. *Adam Smith*. New York: St. Martin's, 1982.

Cantor, Norman F. *The Civilization of the Middle Ages*. New York: HarperCollins, 1993.

Cantor, Norman F. *The English*. New York: Simon and Schuster, 1967.

Cantor, Norman F. *Imagining the Law: Common Law and the Foundations of the American Legal System.* New York: HarperCollins, 1997.

Cantor, Norman F., ed. *William Stubbs on the English Constitution.* New York: Thomas Y. Crowell, 1966.

Cardozo, Benjamin. *The Growth of the Law.* New Haven: Yale University Press, 1924.

Carey, George W. *The Federalist: Design for a Constitutional Republic.* Urbana: University of Illinois Press, 1989.

Carey, George W. *In Defense of the Constitution.* Cumberland, Virginia: James River Press, 1989.

Carter, Jimmy. "Remarks on Signing Comprehensive Environmental Response, Compensation, and Liability Act of 1980, December 11, 1980." In *Public Papers of the Presidents of the United States: Jimmy Carter,* 1980–81. Vol. 3. Washington, D.C.: U.S. Government Printing Office, 1982.

Cassella, Stefan D. "Forfeiture Is Reasonable, and It Works." *Federalist Society Criminal Law and Procedure News,* Spring 1997.

Cataldo, Bernard F.; Kempin, Frederick G., Jr.; Stockton, John M.; and Weber, Charles M. *Introduction to Law and the Legal Process.* 3d ed. New York: John Wiley, 1980.

Catlin, George. *The Story of the Political Philosophers.* New York: Tudor Publishing, 1939.

Ceci, Stephen J., and Bruck, Maggie. *Jeopardy in the Courtroom: A Scientific Analysis of Children's Testimony.* Washington, D.C.: American Psychological Association, 1995.

Chambers, Mortimer; Grew, Raymond; Herlihy, David; Rabb, Theodore K.; and Woloch, Isser. *The Western Experience, Volume I: Antiquity to the Middle Ages.* New York: Alfred A. Knopf, 1974.

Chambers, Mortimer; Grew, Raymond; Herlihy, David; Rabb, Theodore K.; and Woloch, Isser. *The Western Experience, Volume II: The Early Modern Period.* New York: Alfred A. Knopf, 1974.

Chase, Anthony. *Law and History: The Evolution of the American Legal System.* New York: New Press, 1997.

Cheh, Mary M. "Can Something This Easy, Quick, and Profitable Also Be Fair? Runaway Civil Forfeiture Stumbles on the Constitution." *New York University Law Review* 39 (1994): 1–47.

Cheh, Mary M. "Constitutional Limits on Using Civil Remedies to Achieve Criminal Law Objectives: Understanding and Transcending the Criminal-Civil Law Distinction." *Hastings Law Journal* 42 (July 1991): 1325–67.

Choharis, Peter Charles. "A Comprehensive Market Strategy for Tort Reform." *Yale Journal on Regulation* 12 (1995): 435–525.

Christenson, Ronald. "A Political Theory of Show Trials." *Journal of Law and Criminology* 74, no. 2 (1983): 547–77.

"Cleaning Up Old Pollution." *Economist*, 26 February–6 March 1992.

Cleary, Edward W., ed. *McCormick on Evidence*. 3d ed. St. Paul: West, 1984.

Clifford, Clark. *Counsel to the President: A Memoir*. New York: Anchor Books, 1992.

Coalition on Superfund Research Report. Vol. 2. Chicago: Center for Hazardous Waste Management, 1989.

Cohen, Stephen F. *Bukharin and the Bolshevik Revolution: A Political Biography, 1888–1938*. New York: Vintage Books, 1973.

Cohen, Warren I. "The Fall of Clark Clifford: Portrait of a Fixer." *The Nation*, 5 October 1992.

Cohen, William, and Danelski, David J. *Constitutional Law: Civil Liberty and Individual Rights*. 4th ed. Westbury, New York: Foundation Press, 1997.

Cohen, William, and Varat, Jonathan D. *Constitutional Law: Cases and Materials*. 10th ed. Westbury, New York: Foundation Press, 1997.

Connery, Donald S., ed. *Convicting the Innocent*. Cambridge, Massachusetts: Brookline Books, 1996.

Conroy, Theresa. "The Devil in Bucks County." *Philadelphia*, April 1991.

Cook, Walter Wheeler. "Act, Intention, and Motive in the Criminal Law." *Yale Law Journal* 26, no. 7 (May 1917): 645–63.

Cooley, Thomas M. *A Treatise on the Constitutional Limitations Which Rest upon the Legislative Power of the States of the American Union*. Boston: Little Brown, 1871.

"The Conspiracy Dilemma: Prosecution of Group Crime or Protection of Individual Defendants." *Harvard Law Review* 62 (1948): 276–86.

Corwin, Edward S. *The Constitution: and What It Means Today*. 13th rev. ed. by Chase, Harold W, and Ducat, Craig R. Princeton: Princeton University Press, 1973.

Cotts, Cynthia. "The Pot Plot: Donald Scott Was Killed When the Cops Raided His Malibu Ranch Looking for Dope. But Were They after Pot Plants, or Profit?" *Voice*, 15 June 1993.

Cousens, Theodore W. "The Delegation of Federal Legislative Power to Executive Officials." *Michigan Law Review* 33, no. 4 (February 1935): 512–44.

"Criminal Liability of Corporations for Acts of Their Agents." Note. *Harvard Law Review* 60, no. 2 (December 1946): 283–89.

Cromartie, Alan. *Sir Matthew Hale, 1609–1676: Law, Religion and Natural Philosophy.* Cambridge: Cambridge University Press, 1995.

Cropsey, Joseph. "Adam Smith." In Strauss, Leo, and Cropsey, Joseph, ed. *History of Political Philosophy.* 3d ed. Chicago: University of Chicago, 1987.

Crosskey, William Winslow. "The True Meaning of the Constitutional Prohibition of Ex-Post-Facto Law." *University of Chicago Law Review* 14, no. 4 (June 1947): 539–66.

Crovitz, L. Gordon. "How Law Destroys Order." *National Review*, 11 February 1991.

Crovitz, L. Gordon. "Milken and His Enemies." *National Review*, 1 October 1990.

Crovitz, L. Gordon, and Rabkin, Jeremy A., eds. *The Fettered Presidency: Legal Constraints on the Executive Branch.* Washington, D.C.: American Enterprise Institute, 1989.

Cunningham, Roger A., Stoebuck, William B., Whitman, Dale A. *The Law of Property.* St. Paul: West, 1984.

Current, Richard N., Williams, T. Harry, and Freidel, Frank. *American History: A Survey.* 4th ed. New York: Alfred A. Knopf, 1975.

Currie, David P. *The Constitution in the Supreme Court: The First Hundred Years, 1789–1888.* Chicago: University of Chicago Press, 1985.

Danitz, Tiffany. "Child Sex Abuse: Caught in the Trappings of Justice." *Insight*, 24 November 1997.

Davidow, Robert P., ed. *Natural Rights and Natural Law: The Legacy of George Mason.* Fairfax, Virginia: George Mason University Press, 1986.

Davies, Joseph E. *Mission to Moscow.* New York: Simon and Schuster, 1941.

Davis, Kenneth Culp. *Discretionary Justice: A Preliminary Inquiry.* 1969. Reprint, Westport: Greenwood Press, 1980.

Dawson, John P., Harvey, William Burnett, and Henderson, Stanley D. *Cases and Comment on Contracts.* 5th ed. Mineola, New York: Foundation Press, 1987.

DeBenedictis, Don J. "RICO Guidelines: Justice Department Plays Down Clarification of RICO Policy." *ABA Journal*, February 1990.

Deitz, Robert. *Willful Injustice: Government's Ruthless Abuse of Power in the Rodney King Episode.* Washington, D.C.: Regnery, 1995.

DeLoach, Cartha D. "Deke." *Hoover's FBI: The Inside Story by Hoover's Trusted Lieutenant.* Washington, D.C.: Regnery, 1995.

DeLong, James V. "The Criminalization of Just About Everything." *The American Enterprise*, March/April 1994.

DeLong, James V. *The New 'Criminal' Classes: Legal Sanctions and Business Managers.* Washington, D.C.: National Legal Center for the Public Interest, 1997.

DeLong, James V. "Privatizing Superfund: How to Clean Up Hazardous Waste." *Cato Policy Analysis* no. 247, 18 December 1995.

DeLong, James V. *Property Matters: How Property Rights Are under Assault—And Why You Should Care.* New York: Free Press, 1997.

DeLong, James V. *Superfund XVII: The Pathology of Environmental Policy.* Washington, D.C.: Competitive Enterprise Institute, 1997.

Delderfield, Eric R. *Kings and Queens of England and Great Britain.* London: David and Charles, 1975.

Dershowitz, Alan M. *The Best Defense.* New York: Random House, 1982.

Dershowitz, Alan M. *Reasonable Doubts.* New York: Simon and Schuster, 1996.

De Tocqueville, Alexis. *Democracy in America.* Reprint, New York: Doubleday Anchor, 1969.

De Toledano, Ralph. *Hit and Run: The Rise—and Fall?—of Ralph Nader.* New Rochelle: Arlington House, 1975.

"Developments in the Law—Privileged Communications." *Harvard Law Review* 98, no. 7 (May 1985): 1450–1666.

Dicey, A. V. *Introduction to the Study of the Law of the Constitution.* 1915. Reprint, Indianapolis: Liberty Classics, 1982.

Dickens, Charles. *A Child's History of England.* Boston: Estes and Lauriat, 1890.

Dickenson, Mollie. "The Real S&L Scandal." *Worth*, September 1994.

DiDomenico, Catherine M. "Civil RICO: The Propriety of Concurrent State Court Subject Matter Jurisdiction." *Fordham Law Review* 57 (1988): 271–89.

Dinwiddy, John. *Bentham.* Oxford: Oxford University Press, 1989.

Dobbs, Dan B. *Torts and Compensation: Personal Accountability and Social Responsibility for Injury.* St. Paul: West, 1995.

Dorn, James A., and Manne, Henry G., eds. *Economic Liberties and the Judiciary.* Fairfax, Virginia: George Mason University Press, 1987.

Douglas, William O. *The Right of the People.* New York: Pyramid Books, 1962.

Drewry, Gavin. *Law, Justice and Politics.* Essex: Longman House, 1981.

Drinan, Robert F. "Lawyer-Client Confidentiality in the Campus Setting." *Journal of College and University Law* 19, no. 4 (Spring 1993): 305–14.

Dripps, Donald A. "Police, Plus Perjury, Equals Polygraphy." *Journal of Criminal Law and Criminology* 86, no. 3 (1996): 693–716.

Duckett, Eleanor Shipley. *Alfred the Great*. Chicago: University of Chicago Press, 1956.

Dunfee, Thomas W., and Gibson, Frank F. *Legal Aspects of Government Regulation of Business*. New York: John Wiley, 1984.

Dunn, James R., and Kinney, John E. *Conservative Environmentalism: Reassessing the Means, Redefining the Ends*. Westport, New York: Quorum, 1996.

Dworkin, R. M., ed. *The Philosophy of Law*. New York: Oxford University Press, 1977.

Dziech, Billie Wright, and Schudson, Charles B. *On Trial: America's Courts and Their Treatment of Sexually Abused Children*. Boston: Beacon Press, 1991.

Easterbrook, Gregg. *A Moment on the Earth: The Coming Age of Environmental Optimism*. New York: Viking, 1995.

Ekirch, Arthur A. *The Decline of American Liberalism*. New York: Longmans, Green, 1955.

Elias, Christopher. "The Man with the High-Yield Vision." *Insight*, 12 June 1989.

Ely, James W., Jr. *The Guardian of Every Other Right: A Constitutional History of Property Rights*. New York: Oxford University Press, 1992.

Epstein, Richard. "The Principles of Environmental Protection: The Case of Superfund." *Cato Journal* 2, no. 1 (Spring 1982): 9–54.

Epstein, Richard. *Takings: Private Property and the Power of Eminent Domain*. Cambridge, Massachusetts: Harvard University Press, 1985.

Epstein, Richard A. *Simple Rules for a Complex World*. Cambridge, Massachusetts: Harvard University Press, 1995.

Ernst, Morris L. *The First Freedom*. New York: Macmillan, 1946.

Evans, M. Stanton. *The Theme Is Freedom: Religion, Politics, and the American Tradition*. Washington, D.C.: Regnery, 1994.

Evans, Rowland, and Novak, Robert. *The Reagan Revolution: An Inside Look at the Transformation of the U.S. Government*. New York: E. P. Dutton, 1981.

Evans, Tim. "Statement of Tim Evans on Behalf of the National Association of Criminal Defense Lawyers, House Judiciary Committee, 12 September 1996."

Ezersky, Peter R. "Intra-Corporate Mail and Wire Fraud: Criminal Liability for Fiduciary Breach." *Yale Law Journal* 94, no. 6 (May 1985): 1427–46.

Farber, Daniel A., Eskridge, William N., Jr., and Frickey, Philip P. *Constitutional Law: Themes for the Constitution's Third Century.* St. Paul: West, 1993.

Farber, Daniel A., Eskridge, William N., Jr., and Frickey, Philip P. *1997 Supplement to Constitutional Law: Themes for the Constitution's Third Century.* St. Paul: West, 1997.

Fein, Bruce. "Landmark Property Protection." *Washington Times,* 27 February 1995.

Fein, Bruce. "Taking a Look at Civil Forfeiture." *Washington Times,* 24 August 1993.

Fein, Bruce. "Time to Rein in the Prosecution." *ABA Journal,* July 1994.

Felkenes, George T. "The Prosecutor: A Look at Realty." *Southwestern University Law Review* 7, no. 1 (Spring 1975): 98–123.

Fessier, Michael, Jr. "Trail's End: Deep in a Wild Canyon West of Malibu, a Controversial Law Brought Together a Zealous Sheriff's Deputy and an Eccentric Recluse. A Few Seconds Later, Donald Scott Was Dead." *Los Angeles Times Magazine,* 1 August 1993.

Final Report of the Select Committee to Study Undercover Activities of Components of the Department of Justice to the U.S. Senate, December 15, 1982. 97th Congress, 2d Session, Senate Report No. 97–682. Washington, D.C.: U.S. Government Printing Office, 1983.

Finkelman, Paul. "James Madison and the Bill of Rights: A Reluctant Paternity." *Supreme Court Review* (1990): 301–47.

Fischel, Daniel R. "Antitrust Liability for Attempts to Influence Government Action: The Basis and Limits of the *Noerr-Pennington* Doctrine." *University of Chicago Law Review* 45, no. 1 (Fall 1977): 80–122.

Fischel, Daniel R. *Payback: The Conspiracy to Destroy Michael Milken and His Financial Revolution.* New York: HarperBusiness, 1995.

Fisher, Michael T. "Harmless Error, Prosecutorial Misconduct, and Due Process: There's More to Due Process Than the Bottom Line." *Columbia Law Review* 88 (October 1988): 1298–1324.

Fogelson, Steven. "The Nuremberg Legacy: An Unfulfilled Promise." *Southern California Law Review* 63, no. 3 (March 1990): 833–905.

Foster, Finley M. K., and Watt, Homer A., eds. *Voices of Liberty.* New York: Macmillan, 1941.

Francis, Samuel. *Revolution from the Middle.* Raleigh: Middle American Press, 1997.

Frank, William Harris, and Atkeson, Timothy B. *Superfund: Litigation and Cleanup.* Washington, D.C.: Bureau of National Affairs, 1985.

Franklin, David. "Civil Rights v. Civil Liberties: The Legality of State Court Lawsuits under the Fair Housing Act." *University of Chicago Law Review* 63, no. 4 (Fall 1996): 1607–38.

Frantz, Douglas, and McKean, David. *Friends in High Places: The Rise and Fall of Clark Clifford*. Boston: Little, Brown, 1995.

Freedman, Monroe H. "The Professional Responsibility of the Prosecuting Attorney." *Georgetown Law Journal* 55, no. 6 (May 1967): 1030–64.

Freeman, George Clemon, Jr., "A Public Policy Essay: Superfund Retroactivity Revisited." *Business Lawyer* 50, no. 2 (February 1995): 663–85.

Freeman, George Clemon, Jr. "Inappropriate and Unconstitutional Retroactive Application of Superfund Liability." *Business Lawyer* 42, no. 1 (November 1986): 215–48.

Freeman, George Clemon, Jr., and McSlarrow, Kyle E. "RICO and the Due Process 'Void for Vagueness Test.'" *Business Lawyer* 45, no. 3 (May 1990): 1003–11.

Freeman, Kathleen. *The Paths of Justice*. New York: Roy, n.d.

Freidel, Frank. "The Sick Chicken Case." In Garraty, John A., ed. *Quarrels That Have Shaped the Constitution*. New York: Harper and Row, 1987.

Fried, Charles. "The Lawyer as Friend: The Moral Foundations of the Lawyer-Client Relation." *Yale Law Journal* 85, no. 8 (July 1976): 1060–89.

Fried, Charles. *Order and Law: Arguing the Reagan Revolution—A Firsthand Account*. New York: Simon and Schuster, 1991.

Fried, David J. "Criminal Law: Rationalizing Criminal Forfeiture." *Journal of Criminal Law and Criminology* 79 (Summer 1988): 328–405.

Friedman, Lawrence M. *American Law: An Introduction*. New York: W. W. Norton, 1998.

Friedman, Lawrence M. *Crime and Punishment in American History*. New York: Basic Books, 1993.

Friedman, Lawrence M. *A History of American Law*. 2d ed. New York: Touchstone, 1985.

Fuller, Timothy. "Jeremy Bentham and James Mill." In Strauss, Leo, and Cropsey, Joseph, eds. *History of Political Philosophy*. 3d ed. Chicago: University of Chicago, 1987.

Gairdner, William D. *The War against the Family: A Parent Speaks Out on the Political, Economic, and Social Policies That Threaten Us All*. Toronto: Stoddart, 1992.

Gardner, Richard A. *Sex Abuse Hysteria: Salem Witch Trials Revisited*. Cresskill, New Jersey: Creative Therapeutics, 1991.

Gaul, Brian X. "Prosecutorial Misconduct." *Georgetown Law Journal* 76 (February 1988): 1004–17.

Gellhorn, Walter; Byse, Clark; Strauss, Peter L.; Rakoff, Todd; and Schotland, Roy A. *Administrative Law: Cases and Comments*. 8th ed. Mineola, New York: Foundation Press, 1987.

Gergacz, John William. *Attorney-Corporate Client Privilege*. New York: Garland Law Publishing, 1987.

Gergen, Michael J. "The Failed Promise of the 'Polluter Pays' Principle: An Economic Analysis of Landowner Liability for Hazardous Waste." *New York University Law Review* 69 (June 1994): 624–91.

Gershman, Bennett L. "The New Prosecutors." *University of Pittsburgh Law Review* 53 (Winter 1992): 393–458.

Gerstein, Robert S. "The Demise of *Boyd*: Self-Incrimination and Private Papers in the Burger Court." *UCLA Law Review* 27, no. 2 (December 1979): 343–97.

Gilder, George. "Freedom and the High Tech Revolution." *Imprimis*, November 1990.

Gillman, Howard. *The Constitution Besieged: The Rise and Demise of Lochner Era Police Powers Jurisprudence*. Durham: Duke University Press, 1993.

Gilmore, Grant. *The Ages of American Law*. New Haven: Yale University Press, 1977.

Ginsburg, Douglas H. "Delegation Running Riot." Review of *Power Without Responsibility: How Congress Abuses the People through Delegation*, by David Schoenbrod. *Regulation* 1995, no. 1: 83–87.

Goldstein, Abraham S. *The Passive Judiciary: Prosecutorial Discretion and the Guilty Plea*. Baton Rouge: Louisiana State University Press, 1981.

Goldstein, Abraham S. "The State and the Accused: Balance of Advantage in Criminal Procedure." *Yale Law Journal* 69, no. 7 (June 1960): 1149–99.

Goldstein, Alvin H., Jr. "The Krulewitch Warning: Guilt by Association." *Georgetown Law Journal* 54, no. 1 (Fall 1965): 133–55.

Goldwasser, Katherine. "After ABSCAM: An Examination of Congressional Proposals to Limit Targeting Discretion in Federal Undercover Investigations." *Emory Law Journal* 36 (Winter 1987): 75–128.

Goldwin, Robert A. *From Parchment to Power: How James Madison Used the Bill of Rights to Save the Constitution*. Washington, D.C.: AEI Press, 1997.

Gordon, Jon E. "Prosecutors Who Seize Too Much and the Theories They Love: Money Laundering, Facilitation, and Forfeiture." *Duke Law Journal* 44 (February 1995): 744–76.

Gosnell, Cullen B., Lancaster, Lane W., and Rankin, Robert S. *Fundamentals of American National Government*. New York: McGraw-Hill, 1955.

Grad, Frank P. *Environmental Law: Sources and Problems*. New York: Matthew Bender, 1971.

Grad, Frank P. *Treatise on Environmental Law*. New York: Matthew Bender, 1973.

Graham, Fred P. *The Due Process Revolution: The Warren Court's Impact on Criminal Law*. New York: Hayden, 1970.

Grant, George Parkin. *English-Speaking Justice*. Notre Dame: University of Notre Dame Press, 1985.

Grant, R. W. *Bring Us the Head of Michael Milken: The Three Reasons Behind the Downfall of "Junk Bond King" Michael Milken*. Manhattan Beach, California: Quandary House, 1994.

Grantland, Brenda, Weiss, Reba, and Steinborn, Jeffrey. *Forfeiture and Double Jeopardy: How to Turn Prosecutorial Overreaching into Release of Prisoners or Return of Seized Property*. Mill Valley, California: F.E.A.R. Foundation, 1995.

Gray, John. *Hayek on Liberty*. Oxford: Basil Blackwell, 1984.

Greco, Gary J. "Standards or Safeguards: A Survey of the Delegation Doctrine in the States." *Administrative Law Journal* 8 (Fall 1994): 567–603.

Green, Bruce A. "Policing Federal Prosecutors: Do Too Many Regulators Produce Too Little Enforcement?" *St. Thomas Law Review* 8 (Fall 1995): 69–95.

Green, Richard. *Sexual Science and the Law*. Cambridge, Massachusetts: Harvard University Press, 1992.

Greene, Norman L. "A Perspective on 'Nazis in the Courtroom.'" *Brooklyn Law Review* 61 (Winter 1995): 1121–39.

Greene, Thurston. *The Language of the Constitution: A Sourcebook and Guide to the Ideas, Terms, and Vocabulary Used by the Framers of the United States Constitution* Westport: Greenwood, 1991.

Greve, Michael S. *The Demise of Environmentalism in American Law*. Washington, D.C.: AEI Press, 1996.

Greve, Michael S., and Smith, Fred L., Jr., eds. *Environmental Politics: Public Costs, Private Rewards*. New York: Praeger, 1992.

Gunther, Gerald, and Sullivan, Kathleen M. *Constitutional Law*. 13th ed. Westbury, New York: Foundation Press, 1997.

Gunst, Peter H., and Levin, Robert B. "RICO: A Runaway Anticrime Law." *Nation's Business*, January 1990.

Haar, Charles M., and Liebman, Lance. *Property and Law*. 2d ed. Boston: Little, Brown, 1985.

Halbrook, Stephen P. *That Every Man Be Armed: The Evolution of a Constitutional Right*. Albuquerque: University of New Mexico Press, 1984.

Hale, Matthew. *The History of the Common Law of England*. 1713. Reprint, Chicago: University of Chicago Press, 1971.

Hall, Kermit L. *The Oxford Companion to the Supreme Court of the United States*. Oxford: Oxford University Press, 1992.

Hall, Ridgway M., Jr. "The Problem of Unending Liability for Hazardous Waste Management." *Business Lawyer* 38, no. 2 (February 1983): 593–612.

Haller, Mark H. "Plea Bargaining: The Nineteenth Century Context." *Law and Society* 13, no. 2 (Winter 1979): 273–80.

Halliday, F. E. *A Concise History of England: From Stonehenge to the Microchip*. London: Thames and Hudson, 1991.

Hammond, J. L., and Foot, M. R. D. *Gladstone and Liberalism*. New York: Collier, 1966.

Hanson, Gayle. "Activists Attract HUD Thought Police." *Insight*, 19 September 1994.

Hanson, Gayle. "Superfund Supermess: Loaded for Bear, EPA Hits Worms Instead." *Insight*, 3 May 1993.

Harno, Albert J. "Intent in Criminal Conspiracy." *University of Pennsylvania Law Review* 89, no. 5 (March 1941): 624–47.

Harrison, Ross. *Bentham*. London: Routledge and Kegan Paul, 1983.

Harrison, Thomas F. "Look Who's Using RICO." *ABA Journal*, February 1989.

Hart, H. L. A. *Essays on Bentham*. Oxford: Oxford University Press, 1982.

Hart, H. L. A. *Law, Liberty and Morality*. Stanford: Stanford University Press, 1963.

Hart, Henry M. "The Aims of Criminal Law." *Law and Contemporary Problems* 23, no. 3 (Summer 1958): 401–41.

Hayek, Friedrich A. *The Constitution of Liberty*. Chicago: University of Chicago Press, 1960.

Hayek, Friedrich A. *The Road to Serfdom: A Classic Warning against the Dangers to Freedom Inherent to Social Planning*. Chicago: University of Chicago Press, 1976.

Hazard, Geoffrey C., Jr. "An Historical Perspective on the Attorney-Client Privilege." *California Law Review* 66, no. 5 (September 1978): 1061–91.

Heath, James. *Torture and English Law: An Administrative and Legal History from the Plantagenets to the Stuarts*. Westport: Greenwood, 1982.

Hector, Gary. "How Junk Regained Its Shine." *Fortune*, 15 July 1991.

Hector, Gary. "Junk's Bad Times Are Just Starting." *Fortune*, 4 June 1990.

Heilbroner, David. "The Law Goes on a Treasure Hunt." *New York Times Magazine*, 11 December 1994.

Henricks, Burton J. *Bulwark of the Republic*. Boston: Little, Brown, 1937.

Heumann, Milton. *Plea Bargaining: The Experiences of Prosecutors, Judges, and Defense Attorneys*. Chicago: University of Chicago Press, 1978.

Heward, Edmund. *Matthew Hale*. London: Robert Hale, 1972.

Hickok, Eugene, Jr., ed. *The Bill of Rights: Original Meaning and Current Understanding*. Charlottesville: University of Virginia Press, 1993.

Hill, B. W., ed. *Edmund Burke: On Government, Politics and Society*. New York: International Publications Service, 1976.

⌐ Hill, Frances. *A Delusion of Satan: The Full Story of the Salem Witch Trials*. New York: Doubleday, 1995.

Hilton, John. *Rich Man, Poor Man*. London: George Allen and Unwin, 1944.

Himmelfarb, Gertrude. "The Haunted House of Jeremy Bentham." In Herr, Richard, and Parker, Harold T., eds. *Ideas in History: Essays Presented to Louis Gottschalk by his Former Students*. Durham: Duke University Press, 1965.

Hirsh, Michael. "Infernal Revenue Disservice." *Newsweek*, 13 October 1997.

Hittinger, Russell. "Power to the People: States and Local Communities Battle the Feds for the Ball." *American Enterprise*, March/April 1995.

Hochman, Charles B. "The Supreme Court and the Constitutionality of Retroactive Legislation." *Harvard Law Review* 73, no. 4 (February 1960): 693–727.

Hoffman, Sharona. "Criminal Sanctions in Accidental Oil Spill Cases— Punishment without a Crime." *Nebraska Law Review* 71 (1992): 1033–48.

Hogue, Arthur R. *Origins of the Common Law*. 1966. Reprint, Indianapolis: Liberty Press, 1985.

Holden, Constance. "Love Canal: False Alarm Caused by Botched Study." *Science* 208, no. 4449 (13 June 1980): 1239–44.

Holdsworth, William. *A History of English Law*. 16 vols. 1925. Reprint, London: Methuen and Co., 1966.

Holmes, Oliver Wendell. *The Common Law*. 1881. Reprint, Boston: Little, Brown, 1963.

Hook, Sidney. *Marx and the Marxists: An Ambiguous Legacy.* New York: D. Van Nostrand, 1955.

Hopkins, Ann. *"Mens Rea* and the Right to Trial by Jury." *California Law Review* 76, no. 2 (March 1988): 391–420.

Horn, Miriam. "A Dead Child, a Troubling Defense." *U.S. News and World Report,* 14 July 1997.

Horsky, Charles A. *The Washington Lawyer.* Boston: Little, Brown, 1952.

Horwitz, Morton J. *The Transformation of American Law: 1780–1860.* Cambridge, Massachusetts: Harvard University Press, 1977.

Horwitz, Morton J. *The Transformation of American Law: 1870–1960.* Cambridge, Massachusetts: Harvard University Press, 1992.

Houtz, Peter David. "Casenote: The Innocent Owner Defense to Civil Forfeiture Proceedings." *University of Richmond Law Review* 31 (January 1997): 257–285.

Hovenkamp, Herbert. *Enterprise and American Law 1836–1937.* Cambridge, Massachusetts, Harvard University Press, 1991.

Howard, Philip K. *The Death of Common Sense: How Law Is Suffocating America.* New York: Random House, 1995.

Hoyt, Michael. "The *Chutzpah* Man v. *Den of Thieves." CJR,* January/February 1992.

Huber, Peter. "Junk Science in the Courtroom." *Forbes,* 8 July 1991.

Huber, Peter W. *Liability: The Legal Revolution and Its Consequences.* New York: Basic Books, 1988.

Huber, Peter W., and Litan, Robert E., eds. *The Liability Maze: The Impact of Liability Law on Safety and Innovation.* Washington, D.C.: Brookings Institution, 1991.

Humphreys, R. A. "The Rule of Law and the American Revolution." *Law Quarterly Review* 209 (January 1937): 1–98.

Hutt, Allen. *The Post-War History of the British Working Class.* New York: Coward-McCann, 1938.

Hyde, Henry. "Civil Asset Forfeiture Reform Act of 1993—A Briefing Paper."

Hyde, Henry. *Forfeiting Our Property Rights: Is Your Property Safe from Seizure?* Washington, D.C.: Cato Institute, 1995.

Hyneman, Charles S. *Bureaucracy in a Democracy.* New York: Harper and Brothers, 1950.

Irons, Peter H. *The New Deal Lawyers.* Princeton: Princeton University Press, 1982.

Ives, Angela. *Love Canal: How Lost Information Can Lead to Environmental Tragedy.* Clemson, South Carolina: Center for Policy and Legal Studies, 1997.

Jackson, Robert H. "The Federal Prosecutor: An Address by Robert H. Jackson, Attorney General of the United States, Delivered at the Second Annual Conference of U.S. Attorneys, Great Hall, Department of Justice, Washington, D.C." 1 April 1940.

Jacobs, Andrew M. "*Romer* Wasn't Built in a Day: The Subtle Transformation in Judicial Argument Over Gay Rights." *Wisconsin Law Review* 1996, no. 5 (1996): 893–969.

Jacobs, Paul. "Extracurricular Activities of the McClellan Committee." *California Law Review* 51 (1963): 296–310.

Janerich, Dwight T.; Burnett, William S.; Feck, Gerald; Hoff, Margaret; Nasca, Philip; Polednak, Anthony P.; Greenwalk, Peter; and Vianna, Nicholas. "Cancer Incidence in the Love Canal Area." *Science* 212 (19 June 1981): 1404–1407.

Jeffreys, Kent. *Reinventing Superfund: The Clinton Reform Proposal and an Alternative.* Washington, D.C.: Competitive Enterprise Institute, June 1994.

Jeffreys, Kent. "Whose Lands Are Wetlands?" *Journal of Regulation and Social Costs* 2, no. 1 (March 1992): 1–60.

Jenkins, Philip. "Defenders of Democracy: Covert Policing and Dirty Tricks." *Chronicles*, December 1995.

Jensen, Ronald H. "Reflections on *United States v. Leona Helmsley:* Should 'Impossibility' Be a Defense to Attempted Income Tax Evasion?" *Virginia Tax Review* 12 (Winter 1993): 335–96.

Johnson, Paul. *The Birth of the Modern: World Society 1815–1830.* New York: HarperCollins, 1991.

Johnson, Paul. *A History of the American People.* New York: HarperCollins, 1998.

Johnson, Phillip E. *Criminal Law: Cases, Materials and Text.* 5th ed. St. Paul: West, 1995.

Johnson, Phillip E. "The Unnecessary Crime of Conspiracy." *California Law Review* 61 (September 1973): 1137–88.

Johnston, J. Richard. "Paying the Witness: Why Is It OK for the Prosecution, but Not the Defense?" *Criminal Justice* 11, no. 4 (Winter 1997): 21–24.

Jolowicz, H. F. "Was Bentham a Lawyer?" In Keeton, George Williams, and Schwarzenberger, Georg. *Jeremy Bentham and the Law: A Symposium.* London: Stevens, 1948.

Joseph, Lawrence. *Lawyerland: What Lawyers Talk About When They Talk About Law.* New York: Farrar, Straus, and Giroux, 1997.

Jost, Kenneth. "Tampering with Evidence: The Liability and Competitiveness Myth." *ABA Journal*, April 1992.

"Junk Turns into Gold." *Economist*, 16 April 1994.

Kadish, Sanford H., "The Decline of Innocence." *Cambridge Law Journal* 26, no. 2 (November 1968): 273–90.

Kadish, Sanford H. and Schulhofer, Stephen J. *Criminal Law and Its Processes: Cases and Materials*. 5th ed. Boston: Little, Brown, 1989.

Kahan, Dan M. "Is *Chevron* Relevant to Federal Criminal Law?" *Harvard Law Review* 110, no. 2 (December 1996): 469–521.

Kamisar, Yale, LaFave, Wayne R., and Israel, Jerold H. *Modern Criminal Procedure: Cases, Comments, Questions*. 7th ed. St. Paul: West, 1990.

Kaplan, John, and Weisberg, Robert. *Criminal Law: Cases and Materials*. Boston: Little, Brown, 1986.

Katkov, George. *The Trial of Bukharin*. New York: Stein and Day, 1969.

Kaus, Mickey. *The End of Equality*. New York: Basic Books, 1992.

Keeton, George Williams, and Schwarzenberger, Georg. *Jeremy Bentham and the Law: A Symposium*. London: Stevens, 1948.

Keeton, W. Page. *Prosser and Keeton on Torts*. 5th ed. St. Paul: West, 1984.

Kendall, Willmoore. *John Locke and the Doctrine of Majority-Rule*. Urbana: University of Illinois Press, 1965.

Kens, Paul. *Justice Stephen Field: Shaping Liberty from the Gold Rush to the Gilded Age*. Lawrence: University Press of Kansas, 1997.

Kessler, Friedrich. "Automobile Dealer Franchises: Vertical Integration by Contract." *Yale Law Journal* 66, no. 8 (July 1957): 1135–90.

Kessler, Friedrich. "Contracts of Adhesion—Some Thoughts about Freedom of Contract." *Columbia Law Review* 43 (1943): 629–42.

Kessler, Friedrich. "Natural Law, Justice and Democracy—Some Reflections on Three Types of Thinking about Law and Justice." *Tulane Law Review* 19 (1944): 32–61.

Kessler, Freidrich. "Products Liability." *Yale Law Journal* 76, no. 5 (April 1967): 887–938.

Kessler, Friedrich. "The Protection of the Consumer under Modern Sales Law: A Comparative Study." *Yale Law Journal* 74, no. 2 (1964): 262–85.

Kessler, Friedrich, and Fine, Edith. "Culpa in Contrahendo, Bargaining in Good Faith, and Freedom of Contract: A Comparative Study." *Harvard Law Review* 77 (January 1964): 401–49.

Kessler, Friedrich, and Stern, Richard H. "Competition, Contract and Vertical Integration." *Yale Law Journal* 69, no. 1 (November 1959): 1–129.

Kim, Douglas. "Asset Forfeiture: Giving Up Your Constitutional Rights." *Campbell Law Review* 19 (Spring 1997): 527–78.

King, John J., Jr. "Prosecutorial Misconduct: The Limitations upon the Prosecutor's Role as an Advocate." *Suffolk University Law Review* 14, no. 4 (Summer 1980): 1095–1135.

Kirk, Russell. *America's British Culture.* New Brunswick: Transaction Publishers, 1993.

Kirk, Russell. *The Conservative Mind: From Burke to Eliot.* 7th ed. Chicago: Regnery, 1986.

Klein, Solomon A. "Conspiracy—The Prosecutor's Darling." *Brooklyn Law Review* 24, no. 1 (December 1957): 1–11.

Kocontes, Lonnie. "Client Confidentiality and the Crooked Client: Why Silence Is Not Golden." *Georgetown Journal of Legal Ethics* 6, no. 2 (Fall 1992): 283–318.

Koch, H. W. *In the Name of the Volk: Political Justice in Hitler's Germany.* New York: Barnes and Noble, 1997.

Kornbluth, Jesse. *Highly Confident: The Crime and Punishment of Michael Milken.* New York: William Morrow, 1992.

Kozinski, Alex. "The Ceausescu Show Trial and the Future of Romania." *ABA Journal*, January 1991.

Kris, Mary Ellen, and Vannelli, Gail L. "Today's Criminal Environmental Enforcement Program: Why You May Be Vulnerable and Why You Should Guard against Prosecution through an Environmental Audit." *Columbia Journal of Environmental Law* 16, no. 2 (1991): 227–51.

Kriz, Margaret. "Taking Issue." *National Journal*, 1 June 1996.

Kriz, Margaret. "War over Wastes." *National Journal*, 11 May 1996.

Kutler, Stanley I. *Privilege and Creative Destruction: The Charles River Bridge Case.* New York: W. W. Norton, 1971.

LaFave, Wayne R. "The Prosecutor's Discretion in the United States." *American Journal of Comparative Law* 18 (1970): 532–48.

LaFave, Wayne R., and Israel, Jerold H. *Criminal Procedure.* St. Paul: West, 1985.

LaFave, Wayne R., and Scott, Austin W., Jr. *Criminal Law.* 2d ed. St. Paul: West, 1986.

Laffer, William G., III. "The Private Property Rights Act: Forcing Federal Regulators to Obey the Bill of Rights." *Heritage Foundation Issues Bulletin*, no. 173, 3 April 1992.

Laffer, William G. III. "Protecting Ecologically Valuable Wetlands without Destroying Property Rights." *Heritage Foundation Backgrounder*, no. 840, 15 July 1991.

Landis, James M. *The Administrative Process*. New Haven: Yale University Press, 1938.

Landy, Marc K., Roberts, Marc J., and Thomas, Stephen R. *The Environmental Protection Agency: Asking the Wrong Questions from Nixon to Clinton*. Expanded ed. New York: Oxford University Press, 1994.

Lane, Barbara Miller, and Rupp, Leila J., eds. *Nazi Ideology before 1933: A Documentation*. Austin: University of Texas Press, 1978.

Langbein, John H. "The Criminal Trial before the Lawyers." *University of Chicago Law Review* 45, no. 2 (Winter 1978): 263–316.

Langbein, John H. "The Historical Origins of the Privilege against Self-Incrimination at Common Law." *Michigan Law Review* 92, no. 5 (March 1994): 1047–85.

Langbein, John H. "Land without Plea Bargaining: How the Germans Do It." *Michigan Law Review* 78, no. 2 (December 1979): 204–25.

Langbein, John H. "On the Myth of Written Constitutions: The Disappearance of Criminal Jury Trial." *Harvard Journal of Law and Public Policy* 15, no. 1 (Winter 1992): 119–27.

Langbein, John H. *Prosecuting Crime in the Renaissance: England, Germany, France*. Cambridge, Massachusetts: Harvard University Press, 1974.

Langbein, John H. *Torture and the Law of Proof: Europe and England in the Ancien Regime*. Chicago: University of Chicago Press, 1976.

Langbein, John H. "Torture and Plea Bargaining." *The Public Interest*, Winter 1980.

Langbein, John H. "Understanding the Short History of Plea Bargaining." *Law and Society* 13, no. 2 (Winter 1979): 261–72.

LaPierre, Wayne. *Guns, Crime, and Freedom*. Washington, D.C.: Regnery, 1994.

Larina, Anna. *This I Cannot Forget: The Memoirs of Nikolai Bukharin's Widow*. New York: W. W. Norton, 1993.

Laub, Paul. "The Killing of Donald Scott." *Freedom of Speech*, vol. 3, no. 7. n.d.

Lawless, Joseph F., Jr. *Prosecutorial Misconduct: Law, Procedure, Forms*. New York: Kluwer Law Book Publishers, Inc., 1985.

Lawson, Gary. "The Rise and Rise of the Administrative State." *Harvard Law Review* 107 (April 1994): 1231–54.

Lea, Henry Charles. *Torture.* 1866. Reprint, Philadelphia: University of Pennsylvania Press, 1973.

Lee, Mary Caroline. "The Conflict between 'Fair Housing' and Free Speech." *William and Mary Bill of Rights Journal* 4, no. 3 (Summer 1996): 1223–58.

Lefcourt, Gerald, and Horwitz, Erica. "Megatrials Mean Megaproblems: Costly RICO Trials Damage Our Entire Justice System." *Criminal Justice,* Fall 1988.

Lempert, Richard O., and Saltzburg, Stephen A. *A Modern Approach to Evidence: Text, Problems, Transcripts, and Cases.* 2d ed. St. Paul: West, 1982.

Leoni, Bruno. *Freedom and the Law.* Princeton: D. Van Nostrand, 1961.

"Lessons of Milkenomics." *Nation,* 21 May 1990.

Levinson, Sanford. "The Embarrassing Second Amendment." *Yale Law Journal* 99, no. 3 (December 1989): 637–59.

Levmore, Saul. "The Case for Retroactive Taxation." *Journal of Legal Studies* 22 (1993): 265–307.

Levy, Beryl Harold. *Anglo-American Philosophy of Law: An Introduction to Its Development and Outcome.* New Brunswick: Transaction, 1991.

Levy, Leonard W. *The Establishment Clause: Religion and the First Amendment.* New York: Macmillan, 1986.

Levy, Leonard W. *A License to Steal: The Forfeiture of Property.* Chapel Hill: University of North Carolina Press, 1996.

Levy, Leonard W. *Origins of the Fifth Amendment: The Right against Self-Incrimination.* 2d. ed. New York: Macmillan, 1986.

Levy, Leonard W. *Seasoned Judgments: The American Constitution, Rights, and History.* New Brunswick: Transaction, 1995.

Li, Victor H. *Law without Lawyers.* Stanford: Stanford Alumni Association, 1977.

Light, Alfred R. *CERCLA Law and Procedure.* Washington, D.C.: Bureau of National Affairs, 1991.

Lind, Michael. "Jury Dismissed." *New Republic,* 23 October 1995.

Litan, Robert E., and Winston, Clifford, eds. *Liability: Perspectives and Policy.* Washington, D.C.: Brookings Institution, 1988.

Lochmiller, David A. *Sir William Blackstone.* Chapel Hill: University of North Carolina Press, 1938.

Locke, John. *The Second Treatise on Government.* 1690. Reprint, Indianapolis: Bobbs-Merrill, 1952.

Locke, R. Christopher. "Environmental Crimes: The Absence of 'Intent' and the Complexities of Compliance." *Columbia Journal of Environmental Law* 16, no. 2 (1991): 227–51.

Long, Douglas G. *Bentham on Liberty: Jeremy Bentham's Idea of Liberty in Relation to His Utilitarianism.* Toronto: University of Toronto Press, 1977.

Lowi, Theodore J. "Delegation of Powers to Administrative Agencies: Principal Power: Two Roads to Serfdom: Liberalism, Conservatism, and Administrative Power." *American University Law Review* 36 (Winter 1987): 295–322.

Lowi, Theodore J. *The End of Liberalism: The Second Republic of the United States.* 2d ed. New York: Norton, 1979.

Luna, Erik Grant. "Fiction Trumps Innocence: The *Bennis* Court's Constitutional House of Cards." *Stanford Law Review* 49 (January 1977): 409–37.

Lynch, Timothy. "Dereliction of Duty: The Constitutional Record of President Clinton." *Cato Policy Analysis*, no. 271, 31 March 1997.

Lynch, Timothy. "Polluting Our Principles: Environmental Prosecutions and the Bill of Rights." *Temple Environmental Law and Technology Journal* 25, no. 2 (Fall 1996): 161–94.

Macedo, Stephen. *Liberal Virtues: Citizenship, Virtue, and Community in Liberal Constitutionalism.* Oxford: Clarendon Press, 1990.

Maguire, Kathleen, and Pastore, Ann L., eds. *Sourcebook of Criminal Justice Statistics, 1994.* U.S. Department of Justice, Bureau of Justice Statistics. Washington, D.C.: U.S. Government Printing Office, 1995.

Maier, Timothy W. "Suffer the Children: Horrors of the Non-Home." *Insight*, 24 November 1997.

Maine, Henry Sumner. *Ancient Law.* 1861. Reprint, New York: Dorsett Press, 1986.

Maine, Henry Sumner. *Popular Government.* 1885. Reprint, Indianapolis: Liberty Classics, 1976.

Maitland, Frederic W., and Montague, Francis C. *A Sketch of English Legal History.* New York: G. P. Putnam's Sons, 1915.

Malcolm, Joyce Lee. *To Keep and Bear Arms: The Origins of an Anglo-American Right.* Cambridge, Massachusetts: Harvard University Press, 1994.

Manne, Henry G. *Insider Trading and the Stock Market.* New York: Free Press, 1966.

Manne, Henry G., and Ribstein, Larry E. "The SEC v. the American Shareholder." *National Review*, 25 November 1988.

Marzulla, Nancie G. "What Is a Wetland?" *Your Property Matters*, March 1997.

Marzulla, Nancie G., and Roger J. Marzulla. *Property Rights: Understanding Government Takings and Environmental Regulation*. Rockville, Maryland: Government Institutes, 1997.

Maxeiner, James R. "Bane of American Forfeiture Law—Banished at Last?" *Cornell Law Review* 62, no. 4 (April 1977): 768–802.

McAllister, Breck P. "Ex Post Facto Laws in the Supreme Court of the United States." *California Law Review* 15, no. 4 (May 1927): 269–88.

McClellan, James. *Liberty, Order and Justice: An Introduction to the Constitutional Principles of American Government*. Washington, D.C.: Center for Judicial Studies, 1989.

McDonald, Forrest. *Novus Ordo Seclorum: The Intellectual Origins of the Constitution*. Lawrence: University Press of Kansas, 1985.

McDonald, William F., and Cramer, James A., eds. *Plea-Bargaining*. Lexington, Massachusetts: D. C. Heath, 1980.

McGee, Jim, and Duffy, Brian. *Main Justice: The Men and Women Who Enforce the Nation's Criminal Laws and Guard Its Liberties*. New York: Simon and Schuster, 1996.

McGee, Robert W. "Superfund: It's Time for Repeal after a Decade of Failure." *UCLA Journal of Environmental Law and Policy* 12 (1993): 165–82.

McGough, Lucy S. *Child Witnesses: Fragile Voices in the American Legal System*. New Haven: Yale University Press, 1994.

McGuigan, Patrick B., and Rader, Randall R., eds. *Criminal Justice Reform: A Blueprint*. Washington, D.C.: Free Congress, 1983.

McKenzie, Richard B. *Bound to Be Free*. Stanford: Hoover Institution Press, 1982.

McMenamin, Brigid. "It Can't Happen Here." *Forbes*, 20 May 1997.

McMenamin, Brigid. "Un-Natural Justice." *Forbes*, 5 May 1997.

McMenamin, Brigid, and Novack, Janet. "The White-Collar Gestapo." *Forbes*, 1 December 1997.

Meares, Tracey L. "Rewards for Good Behavior: Influencing Prosecutorial Discretion and Conduct with Financial Incentives." *Fordham Law Review* 64 (December 1995): 851–919.

Medvedev, Roy A. *Nikolai Bukharin: The Last Years*. New York: W. W. Norton, 1980.

Meese, Edwin III. "Big Brother on the Beat: The Expanding Federalization of Crime." *Texas Review of Law and Politics* 1, no. 1 (Spring 1997): 1–23.

Menell, Peter S., and Stewart, Richard B. *Environmental Law and Policy.* Boston: Little, Brown, 1994.

Merchant, David B. "Defense Counsel as Prosecution Witnesses: A Combined Doctrine to Govern Attorney Disclosure." *Washington Law Review* 66, no. 4 (October 1991): 1081–98.

Merryman, John Henry. *The Civil Law Tradition: An Introduction to the Legal Systems of Western Europe and Latin America.* Stanford: Stanford University Press, 1985.

Michaels, James W., and Berman, Phyllis. "My Story—Michael Milken." *Forbes,* 16 March 1992.

Mill, John Stuart. *Autobiography.* 1867. Reprint. In Charles W. Eliot, ed. *Harvard Classics,* vol. 25. New York: P. F. Collier and Son, 1909.

Mill, John Stuart. *Mill on Bentham and Coleridge.* Cambridge: Cambridge University Press, 1980.

Miller, Charles A. "The Challenges to the Attorney-Client Privilege." *Virginia Law Review* 49, no. 2 (March 1963): 262–74.

Miller, Stephen A. "The Case for Preserving the Outrageous Government Conduct Defense." *Northwestern University Law Review* 91 (Fall 1996): 305–73.

Miniter, Richard. "Ill-Gotten Gains: Police and Prosecutors Have Their Own Reasons to Oppose Forfeiture-Law Reform." *Reason,* August/September 1993.

Miniter, Richard. "Muddy Waters: The Quagmire of Wetlands Regulation." *Policy Review,* Spring 1991.

Miniter, Richard. "Wetlands Sends Man up the River." *Insight,* 29 November 1992.

Misner, Robert L. "Recasting Prosecutorial Discretion." *Journal of Criminal Law and Criminology* 86, no. 3 (1996): 717–77.

Moore, W. John. "Crime Is Paying Local Dividends." *National Journal,* 25 February 1989.

Moore, W. John. "Justice on Trial." *National Journal,* 25 June 1994.

Moorehead, Alan. *The Russian Revolution.* New York: Harper and Brothers, 1958.

Morgan, Edmund S. *Inventing the People: The Rise of Popular Sovereignty in England and America.* New York: W. W. Norton, 1988.

Morison, Samuel Eliot. *The Oxford History of the American People.* 3 vols. New York: Signet, 1972.

Morris, Edward L. "Money Matters." *National Review*, 31 December 1994.

Morris, Richard B. *Witnesses at the Creation: Hamilton, Madison, Jay and the Constitution*. New York: Mentor, 1985.

Morton, Lyn M. "Seeking the Elusive Remedy for Prosecutorial Misconduct: Suppression, Dismissal, or Discipline?" *Georgetown Journal of Legal Ethics* 7 (Spring 1994): 1083–1116.

Moses, Jonathan M. "Legal Spin Control: Ethics and Advocacy in the Court of Public Opinion." *Columbia Law Review* 95 (November 1995): 1811–56.

Mosteller, Robert P. "Child Abuse Reporting Laws and Attorney-Client Confidences: The Reality and the Specter of Lawyer as Informant." *Duke Law Journal* 42, no. 2 (November 1992): 203–78.

Moushey, Bill. "Win at All Costs: Government Misconduct in the Name of Expedient Justice." Reprint, *Pittsburgh Post-Gazette*, Pittsburgh, Pennsylvania, 1998.

Moynihan, Brian. *Comrades: 1917—Russia in Revolution*. Boston: Little, Brown, 1992.

Munk, Nina. "We're Partying Hearty!" *Forbes*, 24 October 1994.

Murphy, Walter E., Fleming, James E., and Barber, Sotirios A. *American Constitutional Interpretation*. 2d ed. Westbury, New York: Foundation Press, 1995.

NACDL Legislative Policy Statements. Washington, D.C.: National Association of Criminal Defense Lawyers, 1995.

Nader, Ralph, and Green, Mark, eds. *Verdicts on Lawyers*. New York: Crowell, 1976.

Nagareda, Richard A. "In the Aftermath of the Mass Tort Class Action." *Georgetown Law Journal* 85, no. 2 (December 1996): 295–368.

"The Nature and Consequences of Forensic Misconduct in the Prosecution of a Criminal Case." *Columbia Law Review* 54 (1954): 946–83.

Navasky, Victor S. *Kennedy Justice*. New York: Atheneum, 1971.

Needham, Helen Cohn, and Menefee, Mark, eds. *Superfund: A Legislative History*. Washington, D.C.: Environmental Law Institute, 1982.

"Negligence and the General Problem of Criminal Responsibility." Note. *Yale Law Journal* 81 (1971–1972): 949–79.

Noakes, Jeremy, and Pridham, Geoffrey, eds. *Documents on Nazism, 1919–1945*. New York: Viking, 1975.

Nocera, Joseph. "Michael Milken: The Midas of the Eighties Tells Us Where Tomorrow's Wealth Lies." *Fortune*, 30 September 1996.

Novack, Janet. "How About a Little Restructuring?: Department of Justice Needs to Curtail Expenses." *Forbes*, 15 March 1993.

Nowak, John E., and Rotunda, Ronald D. *Constitutional Law*. 5th ed. St. Paul: West, 1995.

O'Callaghan, Mike. "Commentary: War on Drugs Hitting Innocent Citizens." *Consumer Finance Law Quarterly Report* 47 (Fall 1993): 380–84.

O'Connell, Jeffrey. *The Lawsuit Lottery: Only the Lawyers Win*. New York: Free Press, 1979.

Odgers, William Blake. "Sir William Blackstone." *Yale Law Journal* 27 (1917–1918): 599–618.

Oliva, Karin. "Lender Liability under CERCLA." *Southern California Law Review* 68 (July 1995): 1417–46.

Olson, Jon. "True Confessions of a Recovering Lawyer." *American Enterprise* 7, no. 5 (September/October 1996): 56–57.

Olson, Walter K. "Better Living through Litigation?" *Public Interest*, no. 103 (Spring 1991): 76–87.

Olson, Walter K. *The Litigation Explosion: What Happened When America Unleashed the Lawsuit*. New York: Dutton, 1991.

Osward, Lynda J. "Strict Liability of Individuals under CERCLA: A Normative Analysis." *Boston College Environmental Affairs Law Review* 20 (Summer 1993): 579–637.

Packer, Herbert L. "*Mens Rea* and the Supreme Court." *Supreme Court Review* (1962): 107–52.

Padgett, Casey Scott. "Selecting Remedies at Superfund Sites: How Should 'Clean' Be Determined?" *Vermont Law Review* 18 (1994): 361–407.

Palgrave, Francis. *History of the Anglo-Saxons*. 1876. Reprint, New York: Dorset Press, 1989.

Paschal, Joel Francis. *Mr. Justice Sutherland: A Man against the State*. Princeton: Princeton University Press, 1951.

Patterson, Edwin W. *Jurisprudence: Men and Ideas of the Law*. Brooklyn: Foundation Press, 1953.

Patterson, Richard North. "Why Are We Trial-Obsessed?" *USA Weekend*, 11–13 April 1995.

Patton, Dorothy E. "The ABCs of Risk Assessment: Some Basic Principles Help People Understand Why Controversies Occur." *EPA Journal*, January 1993.

Paul, Nanette B. *The Heart of Blackstone: Principles of the Common Law*. New York: Abingdon Press, 1915.

Peirce, Neal R. "Superfund: A Luxury We Can't Afford?" *National Journal*, 7 May 1994.

Pepper, George Wharton. *Philadelphia Lawyer: An Autobiography*. Philadelphia: J. B. Lippincott, 1944.

Perkins, Rollin M. "A Rationale of *Mens Rea*." *Harvard Law Review* 52, no. 6 (April 1939): 905–28.

Picker, Ida. "The Temptations of Jim Stewart." *Institutional Investor*, April 1992.

Picone, John V., III. "We Have Met the Enemy and They Are Us: Saving HUD from Themselves and Protecting the Viability of the Fair Housing Amendments Act." *Santa Clara Law Review* 36, no. 4 (1996): 1097–1145.

Piety, Tamara R. "Scorched Earth: How the Expansion of Civil Forfeiture Doctrine Has Laid Waste to Due Process." *University of Miami Law Review* 45 (1991): 911–78.

Pilon, Roger. "Forfeiting Reason." *Federalist Society Criminal Law and Procedure News*, Spring 1997.

Pittman, R. Carter. "The Colonial and Constitutional History of the Privilege against Self-Incrimination in America." *Virginia Law Review* 21, no. 6 (April 1935): 763–89.

"Plea Bargaining and the Transformation of the Criminal Process." *Harvard Law Review* 90, no. 3 (January 1977): 564–95.

Plucknett, Theodore F. T. *A Concise History of the Common Law*. Boston: Little, Brown, 1956.

Podgor, Ellen S., and Weiner, Jeffrey S. "Prosecutorial Misconduct: Alive and Well, and Living in Indiana?" *Georgetown Journal of Legal Ethics* 3 (Spring 1990): 657–88.

Pohlman, H. L. *Justice Oliver Wendell Holmes and Utilitarian Jurisprudence*. Cambridge, Massachusetts: Harvard University Press, 1984.

"The Policies and Practices of HUD's Office of Fair Housing and Their Effect on Investigations Initiated under the Fair Housing Act Amendments against Individuals and Groups Based on Their Protected First Amendment Activity." *Hearings before the Subcommittee on HUD Oversight and Structure of the Committee on Banking, Housing, and Urban Affairs, United States Senate, One Hundred Fourth Congress, Second Session, September 10 and 18, 1996*. Washington, D.C.: U.S. Government Printing Office, 1997.

Pollock, Stacy J. "Note: Proportionality in Civil Forfeiture: Toward a Remedial Solution." *George Washington Law Review* 62 (March 1994): 456–85.

Pollot, Mark L. *Grand Theft and Petit Larceny: Property Rights in America*. San Francisco: Pacific Research Institute, 1991.

Pombo, Richard, and Farah, Joseph. *This Land Is Our Land: How to End the War on Private Property*. New York: St. Martin's, 1996.

Poole, Robert W., Jr. "The Incredible Bond Machine." *Reason*, July 1989.

Popkin, Richard H., ed. *The Philosophy of the 16th and 17th Centuries*. New York: Free Press, 1966.

Popple, James. "The Right to Protection from Retroactive Criminal Law." *Criminal Law Journal* 31, no. 4 (August 1989): 251–62.

Portraits of the American Dream. Beverly Hills: Knowledge Exchange, 1991.

Posner, Richard A. *Economic Analysis of Law*. 3d ed. Boston: Little, Brown, 1986.

Posner, Richard A. *The Economics of Justice*. Cambridge, Massachusetts: Harvard University Press, 1983.

Posner, Richard A. *The Essential Holmes: Selections from the Letters, Speeches, Judicial Opinions, and Other Writings of Oliver Wendell Holmes, Jr.* Chicago: University of Chicago Press, 1992.

Posner, Richard A. "Juries on Trial." *Commentary* 99, no. 3 (March 1995): 49–52.

Postema, Gerald J. *Bentham and the Common Law Tradition*. Oxford: Clarendon, Oxford University Press, 1986.

Poulin, Anne Bowen. "Prosecutorial Discretion and Selective Prosecution: Enforcing Protection after *United States v. Armstrong.*" *American Criminal Law Review* 34 (1997): 1071–1125.

Pound, Roscoe. *Criminal Justice in America*. 1930. Reprint, New York: Da Capo Press, 1972.

Pound, Roscoe, ed. *Law in Action: An Anthology of the Law in Literature*. New York: Bonanza Books, 1947.

Priest, George L. "The Invention of Enterprise Liability: A Critical History of the Intellectual Foundations of Modern Tort Law." *Journal of Legal Studies* 14, no 3 (December 1985): 461–527.

"Prosecutor Indiscretion: A Result of Political Influence." *Indiana Law Journal* 34 (1958–59): 477–92.

Radin, Max. "The Myth of Magna Carta" *Harvard Law Review* 60, no. 7 (1947): 1060.

Radin, Max. "The Privilege of Confidential Communication between Lawyer and Client." *California Law Review* 16 (1927–28): 487–97.

Rakove, Jack N. *Original Meanings: Politics and Ideas in the Making of the Constitution*. New York: Alfred A. Knopf, 1996.

Raphael, D. D. *Adam Smith*. Oxford: Oxford University Press, 1985.

Rauch, Jonathan. *Demosclerosis: The Silent Killer of American Government*. New York: Times Books, 1994.

Raucher, Stephen. "Raising the Stakes for Environmental Polluters: The *Exxon Valdez* Criminal Prosecution." *Ecology Law Journal* 19, no. 1 (1992): 147–85.

Reed, Terrance G. "American Forfeiture Law: Property Owners Meet the Prosecutor." *Cato Policy Analysis*, no. 179, 29 September 1992.

Rehnquist, William H. "Reforming RICO." Speech to Brookings Institution, 7 April 1989.

Reibstein, Larry. "Looking for New S&L Culprits." *Newsweek*, 26 November 1990.

Reitz, Kevin R. "Clients, Lawyers and the Fifth Amendment: The Need for a Projected Privilege." *Duke Law Journal* 41, no. 3 (December 1991): 572–660.

"The Resurrection of Junk." *Economist*, 28 March 1992.

"RICO Revisited." *Judicial Legislative Watch Report*, 17 April 1989.

Ritchie, Donald A. *James M. Landis: Dean of the Regulators*. Cambridge, Massachusetts: Harvard University Press, 1980.

Roberts, Paul Craig. *Takings, the Economy, and Legal and Property Rights*. Frank M. Engle Lecture, 1992. Bryn Mawr, Pennsylvania: American College, 1992.

Roberts, Paul Craig, and Araujo, Karen LaFollette. *The Capitalist Revolution in Latin America*. New York: Oxford University Press, 1997.

Roberts, Paul Craig, and Stratton, Lawrence M. *The New Color Line: How Quotas and Privilege Destroy Democracy*. Washington, D.C.: Regnery, 1995.

Robinson, Paul H., "A Brief History of Distinctions in Criminal Culpability." *Hastings Law Journal* 3, no. 4 (March 1980): 815–53.

Robinson, Paul H. "Moral Credibility and Crime." *Atlantic Monthly*, March 1995.

Robinson, Paul H., and Darley, John M. *Justice, Liability and Blame: Community Views and the Criminal Law*. Boulder: Westview Press, 1995.

Rodrigues, Jess A. *Power above the Law: S&L Bailout?* San Ramon, California: Presse Foreward, 1990.

Ronner, Amy D. "Prometheus Unbound: Accepting a Mythless Concept of Civil In Rem Forfeiture with Double Jeopardy Protection." *Buffalo Law Review* 44 (Fall 1996): 655–99.

Roots, Ivan. *Commonwealth and Protectorate: The English Civil War and Its Aftermath*. New York: Schocken Books, 1966.

Rosen, Richard A. "Disciplinary Sanctions against Prosecutors for Brady Violations: A Paper Tiger." *North Carolina Law Review* 65 (April 1987): 693–743.

Rosenblum, Nancy L. *Bentham's Theory of the Modern State.* Cambridge, Massachusetts: Harvard University Press, 1978.

Rosett, Arthur, and Cressey, Donald R. *Justice by Consent: Plea Bargains in the American Courthouse.* Philadelphia: J. B. Lippincott, 1976.

Rothwax, Harold J. *Guilty: The Collapse of Criminal Justice.* New York: Random House, 1996.

Rumble, Wilfred E. "The Legal Positivism of John Austin and the Realist Movement in American Jurisprudence." *Cornell Law Review* 66 (1981): 986–1031.

Salsman, Richard M. "The Jailing of Leona Helmsley." *AOB News* 2, no. 2 (Spring 1992): 1–6.

Saunders, Laura, and Novack, Janet. "Know When to Say . . ." *Forbes*, 9 October 1995.

Sayre, Francis B. "Criminal Conspiracy." *Harvard Law Review* 62 (1949): 393–427.

Sayre, Francis Bowes. "Criminal Responsibility for the Acts of Another." *Harvard Law Review* 43 (March 1930): 689–723.

Sayre, Francis Bowes. "Mens Rea." *Harvard Law Review* 45 (1931–1932): 974–1026.

Sayre, Francis Bowes. "Public Welfare Offenses." *Columbia Law Review* 33 (1933): 55–88.

Schneider, M. Bryan. "The Supreme Court's Reluctance to Enforce Constitutional Prohibitions against Retroactive Income Tax Statutes." *Wayne Law Review* 40 (Summer 1994): 1603–28.

Schoenbrod, David. *Power without Responsibility.* New Haven: Yale University Press, 1993.

Schoenbrod, David. "Separation of Powers and the Powers That Be: The Constitutional Purposes of the Delegation Doctrine." *American University Law Review* 36 (Winter 1987): 355–89.

Schuck, Peter H., ed. *Tort Law and the Public Interest: Competition, Innovation, and Consumer Welfare.* New York: W. W. Norton, 1991.

Schwartz, Bernard. "A Decade of Administrative Law: 1987–1996." *Tulsa Law Journal* 32 (Spring 1997): 493–581.

Schwartz, Bernard. *A History of the Supreme Court.* New York: Oxford University Press, 1993.

Schwartz, Bernard. "Of Administrators and Philosopher-Kings: The Republic, the Laws, and Delegations of Power." *Northwestern University Law Review* 72, no. 4 (September–October 1978): 443–60.

Scott, Brenda. *Out of Control: Who's Watching Our Child Protective Agencies?* Lafayette, Louisiana: Huntingdon House, 1994.

Scott, Robert E., and Stuntz, William J. "Plea Bargaining as Contract." *Yale Law Journal* 101 (June 1992): 1909–68.

See, Harold. "Alabama: A Jurisdiction Out of Control?: The Need for Judicial Restraint." *Cumberland Law Review* 27 (1996/1997): 983–86.

Seligman, Joel. *The Transformation of Wall Street: A History of the Securities and Exchange Commission and Modern Corporate Finance*. Rev. ed. Boston: Northeastern University Press, 1995.

Selinger, Steve. "The Case against Civil Ex Post Facto Laws," *Cato Journal* 15, nos. 2–3 (Fall/Winter 1995/1996): 191–213.

Shad, John. "Why RICO Needs Reforming." *Fortune*, 3 March 1986.

Shanahan, John. "A Guide to Wetlands Policy and Reauthorization of the Clean Water Act." *Heritage Foundation Issue Bulletin*, no. 195, 22 June 1995.

Shanahan, John. "How to Rescue Superfund: Bringing Common Sense to the Process." *Heritage Foundation Backgrounder*, no. 1047, 31 July 1995.

Shanahan, John. "Superfund Status Quo: Why the Reauthorization Bills Won't Fix Superfund's Fatal Flaws." *Heritage Foundation Issue Bulletin*, no. 204, 3 October 1994.

Sidman, Andrew. "The Outmoded Concept of Private Prosecution." *American University Law Review* 25, no. 3 (Spring 1976): 754–94.

Silberman, Laurence H. "*Chevron*—The Intersection of Law and Policy." *George Washington Law Review* 58 (June 1990): 821–28.

Silverglate, Harvey A. "Bait and Switch: Government Makes an End Run around Defendants' Rights." *Phoenix*, 19 June 1992.

Silverglate, Harvey A., and Cormier, Philip G. "Federal Enforcement 1993: The Limitations Imposed upon Effective Prosecution and Defense Strategy by Obstruction of Justice Statutes, Ethics Codes and Norms, and Other Texts and Rules Governing Attorney Conduct: Emerging Issues." Boston: Silverglate and Good, 1993.

Sloan, Allan. "A Chat with Michael Milken." *Forbes*, 13 July 1987.

Slobogin, Christopher. "Testilying: Police Perjury and What to Do about It?" *University of Colorado Law Review* 67 (Fall 1996): 1037–60.

Smead, Elmer E. "The Rule against Retroactive Legislation: A Basic Principle of Jurisprudence." *Minnesota Law Review* 20, no. 7 (June 1936): 775–97.

Smith, Adam. *An Inquiry into the Nature and Causes of the Wealth of Nations.* 1776. Reprint, Indianapolis: Liberty Classics, 1981.

Smith, Adam. *Lectures on Jurisprudence.* 1762. Reprint, Indianapolis: Liberty Classics, 1982.

Smith, Fred L., Jr. "Superfund: A Hazardous Waste of Taxpayer Money." *Human Events,* 2 August 1986.

Smith, Fred L., Jr. "What Environmental Policy?" In Boaz, David, ed. *Assessing the Reagan Years.* Washington, D.C.: Cato, 1988.

Smith, Loren A. "A Vision of the Exchange." *William and Mary Law Review* 27, no. 4 (Summer 1986): 767–82.

Smith, Nick. "Restoration of Congressional Authority and Responsibility over the Regulatory Process." *Harvard Journal on Legislation* 33 (Summer 1996): 323–37.

Smith, Sean D. "Comment: The Scope of Real Property Forfeiture for Drug-Related Crimes under the Comprehensive Forfeiture Act." *University of Pennsylvania Law Review* 103 (November 1988): 303–34.

Smith, Steven D. *The Constitution and the Pride of Reason.* New York: Oxford, 1997.

Smith, William French. *Law and Justice in the Reagan Administration: Memoirs of an Attorney General.* Stanford: Hoover Institution Press, 1991.

Smyth, Alfred P. *King Alfred the Great.* Oxford: Oxford University Press, 1995.

Sobel, Robert. "The Junk That Saved Goodyear." *Audacity,* Summer 1996.

Solomon, Lewis D., Schwartz, Donald E., and Bauman, Jeffrey D. *Corporations Law and Policy: Materials and Problems.* St. Paul: West, 1988.

Sowell, Thomas. *A Conflict of Visions: Ideological Origins of Political Struggles.* New York: William Morrow, 1987.

Sowell, Thomas. *The Vision of the Anointed: Self-Congratulation as a Basis for Social Policy.* New York: Basic Books, 1995.

Sparks, Bertel M. "Trial by Jury vs. Trial by Judge." *Freeman* 45, no. 10 (October 1995): 612–15.

Spence, Gerry. *From Freedom to Slavery: The Rebirth of Tyranny in America.* New York: St. Martin's, 1993.

Spence, Gerry. *With Justice for None.* New York: Penguin Books, 1990.

Spencer, Leslie. "Designated Inmates." *Forbes,* 26 October 1992.

Spencer, Peter. "Facts Catch Up with 'Political' Science; Environmental Protection Agency Regulations Questioned." *Consumers' Research,* May 1993.

Standen, Jeffrey. "Plea Bargaining in the Shadow of the Guidelines." *California Law Review* 81 (December 1993): 1471–1538.

Stans, Maurice H. *The Terrors of Justice: The Untold Side of Watergate.* New York: Everest House, 1978.

Starr, Kenneth W. "Judicial Review in the Post-*Chevron* Era." *Yale Journal on Regulation* 3 (Spring 1986): 283–312.

Steele, Walter W., Jr. "Unethical Prosecutors and Inadequate Discipline." *Southwestern Law Journal* 38 (November 1984): 965–88.

Stein, Benjamin J. *A License to Steal: The Untold Story of Michael Milken and the Conspiracy to Bilk the Nation.* New York: Simon and Schuster, 1992.

Stengel, Richard. "More Muscle for Crime Fighters: A New Federal Code Tilts toward the Government." *Time,* 29 October 1984.

Stephen, H. L., ed. *State Trials: Political and Social.* London: Duckworth, 1899.

Stern, Max D., and Hoffman, David A. "Limitations on the Effectiveness of Criminal Defense Counsel: Legitimate Means or 'Chilling Wedges'? Privileged Informers: The Attorney Subpoena Problem and a Proposal for Reform." *University of Pennsylvania Law Review* 136 (June 1988): 1783–1854.

Stewart, James B. *Den of Thieves.* New York: Simon and Schuster, 1991.

Stewart, James B. *The Prosecutors: Inside the Offices of the Government's Most Powerful Lawyers.* New York: Simon and Schuster, 1987.

Stoeffler, John. "Judicial Taxation: The States Respond." *Chronicles,* February 1998.

Stone, Dan G. *April Fools: An Insider's Account of the Rise and Collapse of Drexel Burnham.* New York: D. I. Fine, 1990.

Stone, Geoffrey R.; Seidman, Louis M.; Sunstein, Cass R.; and Tushnet, Mark V. *Constitutional Law.* 3d ed. Boston: Little, Brown, 1996.

Storing, Herbert J. "William Blackstone." In Strauss, Leo, and Cropsey, Joseph, eds. *History of Political Philosophy.* 3d ed. Chicago: University of Chicago Press, 1987.

Strader, J. Kelly. "Taking the Wind Out of the Government's Sails?: Forfeitures and Just Compensation." *Pepperdine Law Review* 23 (1996): 449–94.

Strauss, Leo, and Cropsey, Joseph, eds. *History of Political Philosophy.* 3d ed. Chicago: University of Chicago Press, 1987.

Strauss, Peter L. "The Place of Agencies in Government: Separation of Powers and the Fourth Branch." *Columbia Law Review* 84, no. 3 (April 1984): 573–669.

Stuebner, Stephen. "Triumph, Idaho to EPA: Don't Tread on Me." *Garbage*, Spring 1994.

Stuntz, William J. "The Substantive Origins of Criminal Procedure." *Yale Law Journal* 105, no. 2 (November 1995): 393–448.

Sunstein, Cass R. *Legal Reasoning and Political Conflict.* New York: Oxford University Press, 1996.

Superfund—An Environmental Failure. Washington, D.C.: National Environmental Trust Fund, January 1993.

Superfund in America: A Portrait of Its Impact. Washington, D.C.: PowerComm, 1995.

"'Superfund' Legislation, H.R. 85, H.R. 7020, S. 1480." *Heritage Foundation Issue Bulletin,* no. 64, 17 September 1980.

Taifa, Nkecki. "Civil Forfeiture v. Civil Liberties." *New York Law School Law Review* 39 (1994): 95–120.

Taube, David J. "Civil Forfeiture." *American Criminal Law Review* 30 (Spring 1993): 1025–47.

Taylor, Jerry. "Salting the Earth: The Case for Repealing Superfund." *Regulation,* no. 2 (1995): 53–66.

Teicholz, Tom. "Fighting a Hostile Takeover: Michael Milken." *New York Times Magazine,* 5 June 1994.

TenBroek, Jacobus. "Use by the United States Supreme Court of Extrinsic Aids in Constitutional Construction." *California Law Review* 27 (1939): 399–421.

Ten Facts about Property Rights Legislation. Washington, D.C.: Defenders of Property Rights, 1997.

Thompson, Larry D. "Supreme Court Rules That Civil Forfeiture Is Not Punishment for Double Jeopardy Purposes." *Federalist Society Criminal Law and Procedure News,* Fall 1996.

Thomson, David. *England in the Twentieth Century: 1914–1979.* London: Penguin, 1981.

Thornburgh, Dick. "America's Civil Justice Dilemma: The Prospects for Reform." *Maryland Law Review* 55 (1996): 1074–92.

Toffler, Alvin, and Toffler, Heidi. *Creating a New Civilization: The Politics of the Third Wave.* Atlanta: Turner Publishing, 1995.

Tonsor, Stephen. "Order and Degree: The Medieval Quest for Individuality within the Bounds of Community." *Intercollegiate Review* 24, no. 1 (Fall 1988): 29–38.

"Toxic Waste: Paying for the Past." *Economist,* February 26–March 6, 1992.

Treanor, William Michael. "The Original Understanding of the Takings Clause and the Political Process." *Columbia Law Review* 95, no. 4 (May 1995): 782–887.

Trevelyan, G. M. *A Shortened History of England.* London: Penguin Books, 1987.

Tribe, Laurence H. *American Constitutional Law.* 2d ed. Mineola, New York: Foundation Press, 1988.

Trotter, Andrew. "Down in the Dumps: Superfund Litigation Lays Waste to Schools." *American School Board Journal,* December 1993.

Tucker, William. "Superfund Sparks Industrial Flight." *Insight,* 29 November 1993.

Tullock, Gordon. *Autocracy.* Boston: Kluwer Academic Publishers, 1987.

Turner, J. W. C. "The Mental Element in Crimes at Common Law." *Cambridge Law Journal* 6, no. 1 (1936): 31–66.

Turner, Perry. *Unto Themselves: Recapturing Control of Our Legal System from the Self-Serving Legal Profession.* Northridge, California: Telic Publishing, 1994.

"Twelfth Survey of White Collar Crime." *American Criminal Law Review* 34, no. 2 (Winter 1997): i–1070.

"Twenty-Sixth Annual Review of Criminal Procedure." *Georgetown Law Journal* 85, no. 4 (April 1997): 775–1625.

Twining, W. L., and Twining P. E. "Bentham on Torture." In James, M. H. *Bentham and Legal Theory.* Belfast: Northern Ireland Legal Quarterly, 1973.

"The Unconstitutionality of Plea Bargaining." *Harvard Law Review* 83, no. 6 (April 1970): 1387–1411.

Ungar, Sanford J. *FBI.* Boston: Little, Brown, 1975.

U.S. Advisory Commission on Intergovernmental Relations. *For a More Perfect Union—Prosecution Reform.* Washington, D.C.: U.S. Government Printing Office, 1971.

U.S. Congress, House Judiciary Committee, Hearings on H.R. 1835 (105th Congress), 11 June 1997, Testimony of National Association of Criminal Defense Lawyers Asset Forfeiture Abuse Task Force.

U.S. Department of Justice. "Annual Report to the Attorney General: 1992, Office of Professional Responsibility." Washington, D.C., 1994.

U.S. Department of Justice. *Financial Institution Fraud: Special Report.* Washington, D.C. 1995.

U.S. Department of Justice, Criminal Division. *Forfeitures: Volume I Introduction to Civil Statutes, Asset Forfeiture Office, August 1984.* Washington, D.C. 1984.

U.S. Department of Justice, Office of the Inspector General. "The FBI Laboratory: An Investigation into Laboratory Practices and Alleged Misconduct in Explosives-Related and Other Cases, Michael R. Bromwich, Inspector General." Washington, D.C., April 1997.

U.S. Environmental Protection Agency. *Reducing Risk: Setting Priorities and Strategies for Environmental Protection.* Science Advisory Board, A-101, September 1990. Washington, D.C., 1990.

U.S. General Accounting Office. *Asset Forfeiture Programs.* Washington, D.C., 1995.

U.S. General Accounting Office. *High Yield Bonds: Issues Concerning Thrift Investments in High Yield Bonds.* No. GAO/GGD-89-48. Washington, D.C., March 1989.

U.S. General Accounting Office. *Superfund: Legal Expenses for Cleanup-Related Activities of Major U.S. Corporations.* No. GAO/RCED-95-46. Washington, D.C., December 1994.

Uviller, H. Richard. *Virtual Justice: The Flawed Prosecution of Crime in America.* New Haven: Yale University Press, 1996.

Van Caenegem, R. C. *The Birth of the English Common Law.* Cambridge: Cambridge University Press, 1973.

Van Hourven, George L., and Cropper, Maureen L. "When Is a Life Too Costly to Save? The Evidence from Environmental Regulations." *Resources,* Winter 1994.

Vetri, Dominick R. "Guilty Plea Bargaining: Compromises by Prosecutors to Secure Guilty Pleas." *University of Pennsylvania Law Review* 112 (1963–1964): 865–908.

Viscusi, W. Kip, and Hamilton, James T. "Cleaning up Superfund." *Public Interest,* Summer 1996.

Voegelin, Eric. *The Nature of Law and Related Writings. Volume 27.* In Pascal, Robert Anthony, Babin, James Lee, and Corrington, John William, eds. *The Collected Works of Eric Voegelin.* Baton Rouge: Louisiana State University Press, 1991.

Von Ihering, Rudolf. *Law as a Means to an End.* New York: Macmillan, 1924.

Wagner, David. "Child Removal Lacks Due Process." *Insight,* 24 November 1997.

Wanniski, Jude. "Insider Reporting." *National Review,* 2 December 1991.

Weiler, Andrew C. "Has Due Process Struck Out?: The Judicial Rubberstamping of Retroactive Economic Laws." *Duke Law Journal* 42 (March 1993): 1069–1139.

Wellman, Francis L. *The Art of Cross-Examination.* 1903. Reprint, New York: Dorset, 1986.

Whelan, Maura F. "Lead Us Not into (Unwarranted) Temptation: A Proposal to Replace the Entrapment Defense with a Reasonable-Suspicion Requirement." *University of Pennsylvania Law Review* 133 (June 1985): 1193– 1230.

Whitebread, Charles H., and Slobogin, Christopher. *Criminal Procedure: An Analysis of Cases and Concepts.* Mineola, New York: Foundation Press, 1986.

Wiens, Susan K., and Keyes, Lisa S., eds. *CERCLA Primer.* Chicago: American Bar Association, 1995.

Wigmore, John H. "The Privilege against Self-Crimination: Its History." *Harvard Law Review* 15, no. 8 (April 1902): 610–37.

Wigmore, John Henry. *Evidence in Trials at Common Law.* 10 vols. Rev. ed. McNaughton, John T., ed. Boston: Little, Brown, 1961.

Willcox, Breckinridge L. "*Martin Marietta* and the Erosion of the Attorney-Client Privilege and Work-Product Protection." *Maryland Law Review* 49, no. 4 (1990): 917–46.

Williams, Edward Bennett. *One Man's Freedom.* New York: Atheneum, 1962.

Williams, Nathan B. "Forfeiture Laws." *American Bar Association Journal* 16, no. 9 (September 1930): 572–73.

Wilson, James Q. "The Changing FBI—The Road to Abscam." *Public Interest* no. 59 (Spring 1980): 3–14.

Wilson, Roland Knyvet. *History of Modern English Law.* London: Rivingtons, 1875.

Wilson, Woodrow. *Congressional Government: A Study in American Politics.* 1885. Reprint, New York: Meridian Books, 1956.

Winfield, Percy Henry. *The History of Conspiracy and Abuse of Legal Procedure.* Cambridge: Cambridge University Press, 1921.

Wolfe, Bertram D. *An Ideology in Power: Reflections on the Russian Revolution.* New York: Stein and Day, 1969.

Wolfe, Bertram D. *Three Who Made a Revolution.* Boston: Beacon Press, 1948.

Woll, Peter. *Constitutional Democracy.* 2d ed. Boston: Little, Brown, 1986.

Wollstein, Jarret B. "The Government's War on Property." *The Freeman,* July 1993.

Wood, Gordon S. *The Radicalism of the American Revolution.* New York: Vintage, 1991.

Yago, Glenn. "Financial Repression and the Capital Crunch Recession: Political and Regulatory Barriers to Growth Economics." In Zycher, B., and Solmon, L. C., eds. *Economic Policy, Financial Markets, and Economic Growth.* Boulder: Westview Press, 1993.

Yago, Glenn. *Junk Bonds: How High Yield Securities Restructured Corporate America.* New York: Oxford University Press, 1991.

Yago, Glenn. "Ownership Change, Capital Access, and Economic Growth." *Critical Review* 7, no. 2–3 (Spring–Summer 1993): 205–24.

Yago, Glenn, and Siegel, Donald. "Triggering High Yield Market Decline: Regulatory Barriers in Financial Markets." *Extra Credit: Journal of Global High Yield Bond Research*, March/April 1994.

Zander, Michael. *Confiscation and Forfeiture Law: English and American Comparisons.* London: Police Foundation, 1989.

Zane, John Maxcy. *The Story of Law.* New York: Ives Washburn, 1927.

Zauzmer, Robert A. "The Misapplication of the *Noerr-Pennington* Doctrine in Non-Antitrust Right to Petition Cases." *Stanford Law Review* 36 (May 1984): 1243–72.

Zobel, Hiller B. "The Jury on Trial." *American Heritage*, July/August 1995.

Zuesse, Eric. "Love Canal: The Truth Seeps Out." *Reason*, February 1981.

Zweiben, Beverly. *How Blackstone Lost the Colonies: English Law, Colonial Lawyers, and the American Revolution.* New York: Garland Publishing, 1990.

CASES

A.L.A. Schechter Poultry Corp. v. U.S., 295 U.S. 495 (1935).

Bennis v. Michigan, 116 S. Ct. 1560 (1996).

Berger v. United States, 295 U.S. 78 (1934).

Bordenkircher v. Hayes, 434 U.S. 357 (1978).

Bowers v. Hardwick, 478 U.S. 186 (1986).

Boyd v. U.S., 116 U.S. 616 (1886).

Brady v. U.S., 397 U.S. 742 (1970).

Calder v. Bull, 3 Dall. (3 U.S.) 386 (1798).

Calero-Toledo v. Pearson Yacht Leasing Co., 416 U.S. 663 (1974).

California Motor Transport v. Trucking Unlimited, 404 U.S. 508 (1972).

Caplin and Drysdale v. U.S., 109 S. Ct. 2667 (1989).

Coffey v. U.S., 116 U.S. 427 (1886).

Coffin v. U.S., 156 U.S. 432 (1895).

Connolly v. Union Sewer Pipe Co., 184 U.S. 540 (1902).

Cummings v. Missouri, 71 U.S. 276 (1866).

Euclid v. Ambler Realty Co., 272 U.S. 365 (1926).

Field v. Clark, 143 U.S. 649 (1892).

F.T.C. v. Rubberoid Co., 343 U.S. 487 (1952).

Greenberg v. Comptroller of the Currency, 938 F. 2d 8 (2d Cir. 1991).

Hale v. Henkel, 201 U.S. 43 (1905).

Hall v. Santa Barbara, 833 F. 2d 1270 (9th Cir. 1987).

Hampton v. U.S., 276 U.S. 394 (1928).

Harrison v. United States, 7 F. 2d 259 (2d Cir. 1925).

Hoffa v. U.S., 385 U.S. 295 (1966).

Hurtado v. California, 110 U.S. 233 (1884).

Jones v. S.E.C., 298 U.S. 1 (1936).

Keating v. Hood, 922 F. Supp. 1482 (C.D. Cal. 1996).

Keating v. Hood, 133 F. 3d. 1240 (9th Cir. 1998).

Krulewitch v. United States, 336 U.S. 440 (1949).

Miller v. United States, 78 U.S. 268 (1870).

Morissette v. United States, 342 U.S. 246 (1952).

National Organization for Women v. Scheidler, 510 U.S. 249 (1994).

New Hampshire v. Burnham, 15 N.H. 396 (1844).

North Carolina v. Alford, 400 U.S. 160 (1970).

Panama Refining Co. v. Ryan, 293 U.S. 388 (1935).

People v. Keating, 19 Cal. Rptr. 2d 899 (1993).

People v. Keating, 25 Cal. Rptr. 2d 810 (1993).

Powell v. Alabama, 287 U.S. 45 (1932).

Romer v. Evans, 116 S. Ct. 1620 (1996).

Santobello v. New York, 404 U.S. 257 (1971).

Satterlee v. Matthewson, 27 U.S. (2 Pet.) 380 (1829).

S.E.C. v. Chenery Corp., 332 U.S. 194 (1947).

Sedima, S.P.R.L. v. Imrex, 473 U.S. 479 (1985).

Shapiro v. U.S., 335 U.S. 1 (1947).

Shevlin-Carpenter v. Minnesota, 218 U.S. 57 (1910).

Stanley v. Board of Governors, 940 F. 2d 267 (7th Cir. 1991).

Touby v. U.S., 111 S. Ct. 1752 (1991).

United Mine Workers of America v. Pennington, 381 U.S. 1585 (1965).

U.S. v. Bajakajian, 118 S. Ct. 2028 (1998).

U.S. v. Balint, 258 U.S. 250 (1922).

U.S. v. Behrman, 258 U.S. 280 (1922).

U.S. v. Dotterweich, 326 U.S. 134 (1943).

U.S. v. Ellen, 961 F. 2d 462 (4th Cir. 1992).

U.S. v. Garfinkel, 29 F. 3d 1253 (8th Cir. 1994).

U.S. v. Hasting, 461 U.S. 499 (1983).

U.S. v. Helmsley, 985 F. 2d 1202 (1993).

U.S. v. Hooker Chemicals and Plastics, 850 F. Supp. 993 (W.D.N.Y. 1994).

U.S. v. Jackson, 33 F. 3d 866 (7th Cir. 1994).

U.S. v. Keating, 147 F. 3d. 895 (9th Cir. 1998).

U.S. v. Kelly, 707 F. 2d 1460 (D.C. Cir. 1983).

U.S. v. Monsanto, 924 F. 2d 1186 (2d Cir. 1991).

U.S. v. Nuckols, 606 F. 2d 566 (5th Cir. 1979).

U.S. v. Olin Corporation, 107 F. 3d 1506 (11th Cir. 1997).

U.S. v. Olin Corporation, 927 F. Supp. 1502 (S.D. Ala. 1996).

U.S. v. Omni International Corp., 634 F. Supp. 1414 (D. Md 1986).

U.S. v. Park, 421 U.S. 658 (1975).

U.S. v. Regan, 858 F. 2d 115 (2nd Cir. 1988).

U.S. v. Riverside Bayview Homes, 474 U.S. 121 (1985).

U.S. v. Robertson, 15 F. 3d 862 (9th Cir. 1994).

U.S. v. Thevis, 474 F. Supp. 134 (N.D. Ga. 1979).

U.S. v. Torres, 901 F. 2d 205 (2nd Cir. 1990).

U.S. v. Trans-Missouri Freight Association, 166 U.S. 290 (1897).

U.S. v. Ursery, 116 S. Ct. 2135 (1996).

U.S. v. Wilson, 1997 U.S. App. LEXIS 35971 (4th Cir. 1997).

U.S. v. Winstar, 518 U.S. 839 (1996).

U.S. v. $448,342.85, 969 F. 2d 474 (7th Cir. 1992).

Vanhorne's Lessee v. Dorrance, 2 U.S. 304 (1795).

Watts v. Indiana, 338 U.S. 49.

The Whiskey Cases, 99 U.S. 594 (1878).

Winstar v. U.S., 64 F. 3d 1531 (Fed. Cir. 1995).

INDEX